Program
Evaluation

The Nelson-Hall Series in Social Work

Consulting Editor: Charles Zastrow

University of Wisconsin—Whitewater

SECOND EDITION

Program Evaluation

An Introduction

David Royse
University of Kentucky

Bruce A. Thyer
The University of Georgia

NELSON-HALL PUBLISHERS
Chicago

Project Editor: Dorothy Anderson
Cover Design: Corasue Nicholas
Typesetter: Precision Typographers
Printer: Capital City Press
Cover Painting: *Inquiry* by Jane Overton

Library of Congress Cataloging-in-Publication Data

Royse, David D. (David Daniel)
    Program evaluation : an introduction / David D. Royse and Bruce A.
Thyer. — 2nd ed.
        p. cm.
    Includes bibliographical references and index.
    ISBN 0-8304-1415-0
    1. Human services—United States—Evaluation.   I. Thyer, Bruce A.
II. Title.
HV91.R76   1996
361'.0068'4—dc20
                                       95-42972
                                          CIP

CONTENTS

CHAPTER THREE

Qualitative Evaluation: Formative and Process Evaluation, Program Monitoring, and Quality Assurance 51

CHAPTER FOUR

Goal Attainment Scaling and Client Satisfaction Studies 85

CHAPTER FIVE

Single System Research Designs 107

Contents

CHAPTER TEN

Pragmatic and Political Considerations   231

CHAPTER ELEVEN

Making Sense of Evaluation Data   261

CHAPTER TWELVE

Writing the Evaluation Report   291

PREFACE

In keeping with the Council on Social Work Education's Curriculum Policy Statement (1994), this text is designed to prepare students to build knowledge for the profession and to evaluate service delivery in all areas of practice. We believe that program evaluation is vital for intelligent management of human and monetary resources. Accordingly, the purpose of this book is to help students, social work practitioners, and program managers acquire the ability to evaluate social and human service programs.

You need not have mastered a certain number of research or statistics courses to find this book helpful. Our intent is to boil down and simplify, to provide all the essentials needed to develop a critical appreciation of evaluation methodologies so that you can become skillful in conceptualizing program evaluation efforts. Further, we believe that while outcome evaluation is extremely important, there are many other forms of evaluation that generate extremely useful information at different points in a program's development.

In choosing which methodologies to present and emphasize, our bias shows clearly—we favor the systematic approaches that develop from scientific (positivistic) thought. This is not to say we don't value qualitative approaches—we do. We present an array of selected evaluation designs and strategies that move by incremental steps from the qualitative end of the evaluation design spectrum to the quantitative end. The schema in figure P.1 attempts to show this.

Formative evaluations, program monitoring, and quality assurance procedures will meet the evaluation needs of some but certainly not all agencies. While program monitoring can tell you whether the program is serving those for whom the program was orginally designed, it cannot demonstrate the quality of the program. Program monitoring cannot tell you if the consumers are happy with the program, if clients tend to improve, or if the program has made a difference in the community. Quality assurance procedures can tell you if the patient's treatment was appropriate, timely, and well documented, but these procedures typically are not concerned with whether the patient actually improved after he or she was discharged. To learn more about the impact of our programs, it is necessary to think in terms of whether they have successful outcomes.

Logically, one ought to learn early on about client impressions and reactions, problems in implementing the program and targeting specific populations, and how often the staff are in compliance with expectations.

Figure P.1
Progression of Program Evaluation Methodologies Presented in This Text

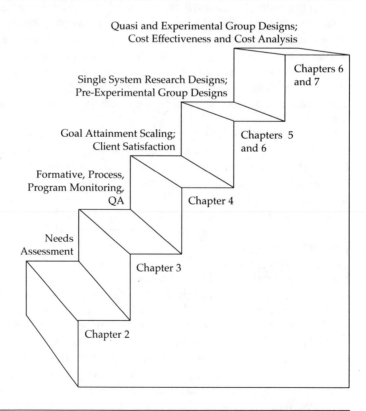

The administration and staff ought to have time to get the bugs out of the system before the program is held to hard standards of success that are best determined by group outcome studies.

While it could be argued that some things never change (e.g., inadequate compensation for foster parents and the staffs of most social service agencies), it should be apparent that we live in an age of accountability. Computers are no longer toys but useful tools that facilitate the accessing and manipulatation of prodigious amounts of client data. Not only is it easier now for most helping professionals to evaluate their efforts with clients, it is also easier for others to keep tabs on individual therapists, programs, and agencies.

There is enormous pressure to be as successful as others who are treating the same problem or client population. To practice without knowledge of current empirical studies and some form of evaluation is unethical and an invitation to litigation. Like it or not, we owe it to our clients, to society, and to our profession to provide the best possible interventions—not merely those that are convenient, fast, or "the way we have always done things." We need to have an open mind, to be innovative at times, to constantly seek to improve upon the "time-honored" ways of helping our clients.

While writing this Preface, we came across an NASW postition statement that is a powerful example of the importance of accountability and evaluation. In 1992, NASW's National Committee on Lesbian and Gay Issues prepared a position statement on so-called "reparative" or "conversion" therapies for lesbians and gay men. Reparative therapies are intended to assist homosexual individuals achieve a heterosexual orientation. The NASW position statment condemned reparative therapies as *unethical*, in part because of the following reasons:

> Proponents of reparative therapies claim—without documentation—many successess. They assert that their processes are supported by conclusive scientific data which are in fact little more than anecdotal. NCOLGI protests these efforts to "convert" people through irresponsible therapies . . . sweeping generalizations are made in the name of science, but without any of the rigor science requires. Empirical research does not demonstrate . . . that sexual orientation (heterosexual or homosexual) can be changed through these so-called reparative therapies. (NASW, 1992, p. 1)

To condemn treatment programs as unethical because they lack scientifically credible evidence of efficacy and only possess anecdotal support establishes a stringent standard by which to evaluate programs. While this may be seen as an unrealistically high standard, it is clear that the trend in human services is to require ever higher levels of evidence of effectiveness. Program evaluation efforts are not a passing fad—if anything, they will become increasingly important.

REFERENCES

National Association of Social Workers, National Committee on Lesbian and Gay Issues. (1992). *Position statement: "Reparative" or "Conversion" therapies for lesbians and gay men.* Washington, DC: NASW.

ONE

Introduction

Program evaluation is a practical endeavor, not an academic exercise and not an attempt to build theory or necessarily to develop social science knowledge (although it's wonderful when that happens). Tripodi (1987) has noted, in the *Encyclopedia of Social Work*, that "the mission of program evaluation in social work is to provide information that can be used to improve social programs" (p. 366).

Why is it necessary to tinker with established services? Because there are always alternative, and sometimes *better*, ways to solve problems. For instance, consider an article entitled "Time-Limited Therapy in University Counseling Centers: Do Time-Limited and Time-Unlimited Centers Differ?" (Gyorky, Royalty, and Johnson, 1994). The authors found that counseling centers with time limits had longer waiting lists and served a smaller percentage of the student body than did centers with no limits on counseling duration. Now, if you were in charge of a university counseling center, would you want to read this article? Would it be important to understand the authors' methodology and sample?

When we improve our programs and interventions by making them more effective and efficient, all those involved with or touched by the social service delivery system are affected. Consumers and their families may recover faster when we discover that one approach works better than another. Armed with information from the program evaluation, workers and managers can better treat and advocate for their clients—

1

possibly making their own jobs more enjoyable and less frustrating. Ultimately, even taxpayers benefit. But let's back up a bit and discuss what constitutes a program.

WHAT IS A PROGRAM?

A program is an organized collection of activities designed to reach certain objectives. Let's consider the two main elements of this definition in depth. Organized activities—programs—are not a random set of actions but a series of planned actions that are designed to solve some problem. If there is no problem, then there is no need for programmatic intervention.

So, programs are interventions or services that are expected to have some kind of an impact upon the program participants. Could a bereavement support group for school-aged children be considered a program? What about a telephone hot-line for parents? Would it be stretching things too much to describe the efforts of a residential drug treatment facility to increase client retention as a program?

Programs tend to have certain characteristics that help us to identify them. First of all, programs tend to require **staffing**. A residential drug treatment facility, for instance, is going to need lots of staff. It may even have a separate staff who run an after-care or outpatient drug treatment program. The personnel of both programs may occasionally be asked to speak to high school students and groups in the community as part of the facility's drug education program. Staff may have their time allocated among several programs or dedicated to only one.

Second, programs usually have their own **budgets**. Because employing staff requires financial resources, programs can sometimes be identified by their budgets. However, there are some fine programs that have minimal budgets because of heavy reliance upon volunteers.

Stable funding is important to the success of most programs. Morale and performance fall when employees don't get paid on a regular basis, or when they are asked to put aside normal duties and engage in last minute fund-raising or grant-writing to get the program through several more months. Programs started with "soft money" (grants or nonrecurring funds) will often experience high rates of staff turnover until the programs secure some continuity in funding.

Another characteristic of programs is that they have their own **identity**. In short, they are visible or recognizable by the public. Big Brothers/Big Sisters is an example of an organization with a national reputation for a single program. In some communities, a program may be recognized by the location where it has been housed for a number of years, or by its unique slogan, sign, letterhead, spokesperson, or public service announcements.

When an organization has multiple programs, differences are sometimes found in philosophy, policies or procedures, and mission, and perhaps even in the way their corresponding staffs dress and how they account for their time. Such contrasts make it easy to differentiate one program from another.

Within an agency, one outpatient counseling program may have the **service philosophy** that "no one is turned away," while another outpatient counseling program may have a different philosophy—providing the service only for those who meet certain eligibility guidelines, such as having private insurance or being able to afford to pay. A service philosophy may also clearly communicate how the clientele is to be treated—for example, "We respect the dignity and worth of all those we serve in caring for their physical, spiritual, psychological and social well-being" or "The customer is always right."

Unfortunately for program evaluators, programs can be vague and hard to distinguish and define. A former governor once made a public announcement that he was unveiling "a new program" to put state social workers in public schools. The program, he said, should help prevent dropouts and poor achievement among students who faced serious personal and family problems. However, the newspaper account said the program would require no additional staff or funding. In essence, some social services employees would be placed in schools that could supply them with office space and phones.

Did the governor's announcement create a program? Not in this instance. It never got off the ground. Why not? It had no name, no staff, no funding, no slogan, no visibility. Most schools did not have surplus office space. Further, there was no suggestion of any new activities or way of tackling the problems faced by children and their families.

On the other hand, starting a bereavement support group in an elementary school, even if the leadership is contributed by volunteers and the group has no budget to speak of, could be considered a program if it has an ongoing presence and a presumed impact that could be measured. For evaluation purposes, speaking to an assembly of high school students once or twice a year about drugs and alcoholism might also be considered a program.

In the best of all possible worlds, every program would be based on a sound **theoretical model**. That is, before the "helpers" jumped into a social problem and started helping, there would be some serious thinking about the problem—how and why it originated and what would work best to remedy the situation.

The theoretical model is an organizing principle for each program that provides a consistency of effort by suggesting a standard approach. It serves as a guide in recommending certain activities or procedures from all those available to be used for the intervention.

Hyperactivity in children, for instance, may be addressed with behavior therapy. Drug treatment may be used alone or in combination with behavior therapy. Are these the only approaches for dealing with hyperactivity? Not too long ago, a student brought to class an article describing the use of chiropractic manipulation to treat the problem. Can you see how the choice of a conceptual model has major implications for what is dispensed as intervention?

Consider a different problem. Suppose you are hired to run a treatment program for men who batter. Do these men fit a single profile? Is one interventive strategy all that is needed? Saunders (1992) argues that there are three theoretically distinct types of men who batter: those who were severely abused as children; emotionally volatile men with rigid sex-role attitudes, who fear losing their partners and are depressed, suicidal, and angry; and family-only aggressors who tend to have relatively liberal attitudes about sex roles, the lowest rate of abuse in childhood, and the most marital satisfaction, and who are generally nonassertive. Is there a possibility that some interventions may work better with one type of abuser than with another?

Theoretical models are important to understanding how a program should work and where one should look for indications that a program is successful. But all too often what passes for theory in many social service agencies is a blend of past experience and tradition. Evaluators would have no problem with that if the program was often successful in rehabilitating, helping, fixing, or curing clients. But when a program is not successful much of the time, the possibility exists that even though the program was implemented as designed, the underlying theory is flawed. Such a situation calls for new thinking and a new approach to the problem. Theories should tell us how to accomplish our goals (Conrad and Miller, 1987).

Program evaluation helps us to know when theories work and when they don't. Our conceptual models do, after all, sometimes turn out to be wrong. We no longer believe, for instance, that autistic children are produced by cold, aloof mothers—as the renowned child expert Bruno Bettelheim once argued.

To a certain extent, program designers and implementers are protected from many of the problems that accompany misguided and

---

BOX 1.1
Characteristics of Good
Social Service Programs

- Staffing

- Budgets

- Stable Funding

- Recognized Identity

- Conceptual or Theoretical Foundation

- A Service Philosophy

- Systematic Efforts at Empirical Evaluation of Services

---

erroneous theories when they base programs not on theories alone but also on methods of practice that have been **empirically supported** by research and evaluation. The best programs, those on the "cutting edge," will be built on a firm foundation of the latest empirical research. These programs can provide a level of confidence and knowledge about what to expect in terms of success rates. These would be the programs we would choose for ourselves if we or our families needed intervention.

Theory and programs are linked in complex ways that we will discuss at various times throughout the book. In this chapter, we will consider the ways theory and empirical research can influence and shape a program.

If you want to see how evaluators and researchers present an intervention in terms of a theoretical model, review the study by Telch et al. (1990) that examines the use of group cognitive-behavioral treatment for nonpurging bulimia. Similarly, Jemmott and Jemmott (1991) have applied the theory of reasoned action in order to increase the use of condoms and prevent the spread of AIDS. Zambelli and Derosa (1992) have looked at specific group intervention techniques for bereaved school-aged children that were theoretically based and derived from four protective mechanisms identified by Rutter (1987).

Programs vary greatly. Some are sophisticated and others simplistic—even composed of a single activity. In scale they range from a small cooperative baby-sitting program for young mothers to the federal food stamp program that touches millions of lives. It is not always easy to determine if certain activities should be considered a program or part of the collection of activities that comprise a larger single program. Either way, program evaluation can be undertaken as long as a desired objective or outcome can be stated. Although in some agencies programs are referred to as "services," in this text the terms will be used interchangeably.

PROGRAM EVALUATION DEFINED

Program evaluation is applied research used as part of the managerial process. Evaluations are conducted to aid those who must make administrative decisions about human service programs. Unlike theoretical research, where scientists engage in science for its own sake, program evaluation systematically examines human service programs for pragmatic reasons. Decision makers may need to know if a program accomplished its objectives, if it is worth funding again next year, or if a less expensive program can accomplish the same results.

Program evaluation is like basic research in that both follow a logical, orderly sequence of investigation. Both begin with a problem, a question, or a hypothesis. Normally, there is some review of what is known about the problem, including prior efforts and theoretical approaches (this is known as reviewing the literature). A research or evaluation design (a blueprint to guide the data collection efforts) is developed, and data are gathered and then analyzed. When thought of this way, both research and evaluation are similar to the task-centered or problem-solving process known to most social workers.

Research and evaluation differ with regard to the expected use or utility of the data. There may be no anticipated need or demand for "pure" research, whereas an assemblage of individuals may anxiously await the results of a program evaluation. Also, the goal of research is to produce generalizable knowledge, while information from a program evaluation may be applicable to only a specific program. However, both are approached with some degree of rigor. Think of program evaluation as a tool—a management tool that you can use to make (and to help others make) better decisions about social and human service programs. Program evaluation helps us to make the best use of our resources as we labor to improve the quality of life of our clients.

Program evaluation involves making comparisons. In fact, Schalock and Thornton (1988) have defined program evaluation as "structured comparison." Few programs can be evaluated without comparing them to something. Programs in one agency may be compared to similar programs in other agencies, to past or prior efforts, or against a stated objective, but without some form of comparison, there can be no evaluation. A major thrust of this text is to help you find or create (to conceptualize) bases for comparison for your own program evaluation efforts.

REASONS WHY PROGRAMS ARE EVALUATED

There are numerous reasons why program evaluations are conducted. Chelimsky (1989) has observed three broad purposes for evaluation:

1. Policy formulation (to assess the need for a new program and to design it to meet those needs);
2. Policy execution (to insure that a program is implemented in the most technically competent way possible); and
3. Accountability in public decision making (to help decide whether a program should be continued, modified, or terminated).

Quite often, social and human service programs are evaluated because of a need to be accountable to a sponsoring or funding agency, or because competition for scarce funds requires that only one program (normally, the most effective or efficient program) can be funded. Program evaluation is needed whenever new interventions are being tried and it is not known whether they will be as successful as former methods, or when there is a perception that a program could be improved—that it could become more productive or better in some way. We evaluate on those occasions when it is important to have some objective assessment or feedback about the worth of our social and human service programs.

The following scenarios illustrate some of the occasions when program evaluations are encountered:

Scenario 1—The Required Evaluation
Your agency is applying for funding from the United Way in your community to begin a new program designed to provide counseling to men who have been prosecuted for domestic violence. You have been asked to prepare the program proposal. As you read the instructions for preparing the proposal, you notice that besides describing the project, listing its objectives, pointing out its uniqueness, and stating the amount of funding that will be required, the proposal also requires a project evaluation. At the end of the project

7

year, data must be presented to show that the project had a successful outcome and an impact upon the problem of domestic violence.

Scenario 2—Competition for Scarce Funds

Your innovative program for men who batter has been operating for a year. You have been able to obtain some data that you hope will favorably influence the committee that will make decisions on the continuation of funding for your program. As you prepare your presentation, you discover that a second domestic violence project from another agency will also be making a request to be funded. You further learn that there is only enough money to fund one program.

Scenario 3—Evaluation of New Interventions

Many more clients desire the services of your outpatient counseling agency than you have staff to serve. At a planning session, one of the newer staff members suggests that the agency move from a one-on-one counseling model to a group services model. The benefits are clear—instead of the limitation on each practitioner of seven or eight scheduled clients a day, each therapist could conduct three or four group sessions a day and have contact with twenty-five to thirty clients. In spite of being able to serve more clients, the staff is not very supportive of this proposal, because they believe that individual counseling is much more effective than group counseling.

Scenario 4—Evaluation for Accountability

You work in a large residential agency serving young children. Unfortunately, a child care aide was recently discovered molesting one of the children. The public is in an uproar. Community leaders are calling for the agency director and all key staff to resign. You feel that the agency is a good one—better than other residential programs within the community. Since the agency director knows that you are enrolled in a program evaluation course at the nearby university, she calls you into her office and asks you to find some way of objectively documenting the strengths of the agency. "Can you show," she asks, "that the great majority of our young people have a favorable experience here, a good impression of the agency, and that they go on to do well in school and in life after they leave the agency?"

Why do we evaluate human service programs? Programs are evaluated basically because administrative decisions have to be made, and it is important to know (or to show) that our programs are "good" programs.

Individual policy or decision makers may have a hypothesis about a program (e.g., the Free Clinic's counseling program is highly effective). At other times, questions may be raised (e.g., is the Free Clinic's counseling program effective?), and hypotheses or questions provide the motivation for a program evaluation. It makes no real difference whether a question or a hypothesis serves as the catalyst for an evaluation. This can be seen in Box 1.2.

This list could easily be made much longer. An interest in exploring one question may lead to other areas where information is desired. The evaluator may start off wanting to know if clients were being helped, but in the process of designing a methodology the initial question or problem becomes modified somewhat. The evaluator may want to know not only if clients were helped but also if one approach was cheaper (more cost-effective) than another. Other questions may concern

---

BOX 1.2
Motivations for Program Evaluation

We want to show:	*We want to know:*
1. That clients are being helped.	Are clients being helped?
2. That clients are satisfied with our services.	Are clients satisfied with the services received?
3. That the program has an impact on some social problem.	Has the program made any real difference?
4. That a program has worth.	Does the program deserve the amount of money spent on it?
5. That one program or approach is better than another.	Is the new intervention better than the old?
6. That the program needs additional staff or resources.	How do we improve this program?
7. That staff are well utilized.	Do staff make efficient use of their time?

whether improvement has been made in a certain staff's productivity since last year or whether the program has reached its intended target population. On some occasions, administrators may want to use evaluation data to help garner public support for human service programs. (The public is much more likely to support tax increases for those programs perceived to be "good" than those thought to be ineffective or poorly run.) Program evaluation can also be used in terms of marketing programs to the public. (As a program manager or agency director, couldn't you use data showing that 92 percent of your clientele say that they would refer their friends or family members to your agency?)

Social and human service programs have evolved to combat such social problems as drug abuse. Think for a moment of other social problems in this country. We could begin listing such problems as:

Poverty	Substance abuse
Homelessness	Adolescent pregnancies
Unemployment	Mental illness
Child abuse	Illiteracy
Domestic violence	High infant mortality rates
Crime	Hunger
AIDS	

For each social problem, there are hundreds if not thousands of programs. Some of these programs work and need to be continued; others are ineffective. If it cannot be demonstrated that certain programs have any impact on these problems, then further evaluative research should be undertaken to discover why the programs were not successful. There may be very logical reasons: the programs could be poorly managed (e.g., the scandal at the Housing and Urban Development Corporation that occurred during the Reagan administration), underfunded, or poorly conceptualized or designed, and there are many other reasons. As social workers and human service professionals, we need to be just as interested in the outcomes of national programs as we are in our local programs. Program evaluation is not to be understood as having application only to the agency that employs us.

While the examples used thus far have helped us to understand the need for program evaluation primarily at the local level, there remains an immense need for program evaluation of national expenditures and programs. For instance, an article in *Newsweek* (June 5, 1989), entitled "Teaching Kids to Say No: How Effective Are Drug-Awareness Classes?" noted that funding for drug prevention programs by the U.S. Department of Education had risen from $3 million in 1986 to $350 million in 1989.

However, in exploring the question of whether drug education in the schools worked, the article stated, "The few studies that have tracked the effects of these programs show no dramatic or long-term reductions in drug use. That finding cuts across race and socioeconomic classes." From the viewpoint of a taxpayer, does it make sense to spend $350 million a year on drug education programs that have no evaluative research to show that they work?

According to an article in the *New York Times,* in the 1960s and 1970s, the federal government invested billions of dollars on job training "without a clue about what worked and what did not" (Passell, 1993). As a society we need to test new ideas to combat old problems. For example, do monetary incentives to mothers on welfaree for using Norplant contraceptives significantly affect the number of children they have? Is offering full college scholarships to low-income students who remain in school, pass their courses, remain drug free, and do not become pregnant or get in trouble with the law a realistic way to combat poverty?

Evaluators, through carefully controlled studies, can determine if spending money "up front"—for example, paying low-income, pregnant women to attend prenatal education and care classes—saves money in the long run. There is some indication that giving pregnant Medicaid recipients a $10 bill for each appointment they keep results in a considerable reduction in the amount of time newborn infants stay in intensive care units (Kolata, 1994).

Whether at the local, state, or national level, program evaluation often begins with the identification of a problem. Decision makers want to distinguish programs that work from those that do not and to know if their money is well spent. They may have developed questions about a program because of some incident or problems brought to their attention. These can be visible, well-recognized problems or those known only to a handful of staff, administrators, or trustees.

A problem is any undesirable situation or condition. Sometimes program evaluations are undertaken in order to determine the extent or magnitude of a problem or to confirm a suspected problem. As you think about the agency where you are working or interning, what problems come to mind? (If you do not initially think of any problems, have you seen any recent data suggesting that the program is effective or efficient?)

There are probably as many reasons for conducting program evaluation as there are different programs. In addition to the reasons already given, those in the helping professions also conduct program evaluations because they have a responsibility to improve programs. For instance, the National Association of Social Workers' Code of Ethics (1979) states:

11

"The social worker should work to improve the employing agency's policies and procedures, and *the efficiency and effectiveness of its services*" (emphasis added). The Specialty Guidelines for the Delivery of Services by Counseling Psychologists (APA, 1981) is even more specific:

> Evaluation of the counseling psychological service delivery system is conducted internally, and when possible, under independent auspices as well. This evaluation includes an assessment of effectiveness (to determine what the service unit accomplished), efficiency (to determine the total costs of providing services), availability (to determine appropriate levels and distribution of services and personnel), accessibility (to ensure that the services are barrier free to users), and adequacy (to determine whether the services meet the identified needs for such services).

We have an ethical obligation to evaluate our practice. All too often it's possible to get caught up in service delivery as measured by billable hours, home visits, numbers of phone calls, and internal audits of agency and accreditation forms without systematically appraising whether all this effort produces beneficial outcomes for clients. We have an ethical mandate to determine if our clients are being helped, if they are any better off as a result of our interventions. Program evaluation is a major means by which we can fulfill this ethical responsibility.

OVERCOMING THE SUBJECTIVE PERSPECTIVE

Anytime we have a choice, we find ourselves in a position where a decision must be made between two or more alternatives. Oftentimes, informal (and perhaps even unconscious) criteria guide us in making choices. While these criteria may be more the product of visceral reactions than of contemplation, they aid us in the making of choices. They help us to determine such things as "good" restaurants and "good" movies, and to rate the services of care providers (e.g., a "good" physician). In each of these instances, "good" is defined subjectively and somewhat arbitrarily. For example, my notion of the best restaurant in town may be one that specializes in Italian food. You, on the other hand, may intensely dislike Italian cooking. My notion of a good movie may be *Texas Chainsaw Massacres*, whereas your taste may run to less violence. My notion of a good physician may be one who, although known for a disheveled appearance, answers my every question, while your opinion of a good physician requires that the physician dress appropriately and look distinguished. Because appearance is important to you, you may have no confidence in a physician who does not look the role (whether or not your questions get answered).

What does this have to do with program evaluation? Just this: every day (sometimes many times a day) human service professionals must direct people to their programs or refer them to other programs based upon their subjective impressions. When we make referrals, we want clients to go, not to programs that aren't effective, but to the "good" programs. We want them to have the best possible chance of succeeding or doing well in that program. We have a professional responsibility to avoid making referrals to ineffective or deficient programs. We also want the programs we direct or that employ us to benefit our clients. But, how do we recognize a "good" program? A poor program?

How do we know when our programs are effective? We like to believe that we help our clients, but what actual evidence do we have that the majority of our clients are helped by our programs? Most helping professionals have had clients who have made giant strides as a result of skilled intervention. We feel rewarded by these successful clients. They help us feel that we are competent and that we have chosen the right career. Unfortunately, there are also those clients with whom we are unsuccessful. These clients, despite our best efforts, drop out of programs, make a mess of their lives, or seem to have gained nothing from our interventions. Think of all the clients who have made their exits from your programs. What is the proportion of "successful" clients to "unsuccessful" clients? Are you more successful than unsuccessful with your clients? What evidence could you present of your success?

We have raised these questions to help you understand that program evaluation involves a different perspective than you may normally employ when thinking about your clients. Clinicians and practitioners tend to evaluate their practice subjectively and in terms of selected individual cases. They think of Mrs. Smith (with whom they were successful), Mr. Arthur (who was a model client and who now comes back to volunteer his services), or perhaps Kathy M., with whom they were not a success. However, this "case focus" does not facilitate the aggregation of data at a program level so that an overall determination can be made about the effectiveness of the program as a whole. While "one bad apple" may spoil an entire bushel, one client who doesn't succeed doesn't mean that a whole program needs to be overhauled.

The problems with attempting evaluation using a "case focus" with a single client can be demonstrated easily. Consider Mrs. Smith. While you felt that you were successful in helping Mrs. Smith to quit drinking, others may not be so quick to shower accolades upon you. Those who are skeptical of your abilities as a clinician may point out that while Mrs. Smith may no longer drink, the rest of her family is in turmoil. Her husband left home; a teen-age daughter ran away. Mrs. Smith is now living with another recovering alcoholic and working for minimum wage as a waitress, although she was previously employed as a registered nurse. You reply to these critics, "She's not drinking. She feels good about herself. I think she's shown great improvement." While it may be possible to argue that any given case was or was not a success, a manager needs to look at the program as a whole. Are the clients (as an aggregate) better or worse off as a result of participating in the program?

Consider the case of Mr. Arthur. Everyone in the agency agrees that he has made significant changes in his life since becoming a client of your program. However, upon closer inspection, it is revealed that you spent twice as much time with Mr. Arthur as you did with the average client. Was he a success because he got twice as much attention? Would he have been a success if he had received only as much time as the "average client" receives? (Did he get so much time because he was an "easy" client to work with?)

We've already admitted that the program was not successful with Kathy M. However, is Kathy the typical client or the unusual client? Perhaps Kathy was the most severely disturbed client that your program has ever admitted. Given her previous history of multiple hospitalizations, perhaps no one really expected her to make any significant gains.

We can see from these examples that our perspective as practitioners often involves subjective evaluations. That is, we believe that a client has improved or not improved. The problem with subjective evaluations is that they may not be shared by others. While you think of Mrs. Smith as an example of a successful client, perhaps your best friend and co-worker thinks of Mrs. Smith as something less than a success. While you are quite pleased that Mr. Arthur has overcome a great many of his problems, perhaps your program director has sent you a strongly worded memorandum suggesting that the program's waiting list is such that you are not to spend as much time with the rest of your clients. Although Kathy M. made no progress in treatment, the same program director is not disappointed. "We learned something," she says. "We learned what won't work with clients like this. Next time, we'll try something a little different."

In conversation we can get away with saying things like, "I did a good job with that family"; "She's a good therapist"; or, "It's a good program, you'll like it there." However, my thesaurus lists nine different meanings for the word *good* as an adjective (Box 1.3). Seldom does anyone ask how we define *good*. What we are allowed to do as conversationalists we cannot do as program evaluators.

Evaluators are concerned with specificity and measurements. We want verifiable evidence, not someone's opinion. It matters to us whether

---

BOX 1.3
Denotations of the Word *"Good"*

Usage	*Example*
1. pleasant, fine	I had a *good* meal.
2. moral, virtuous	Mother Theresa is a *good* person.
3. competent, skilled	She is a *good* social worker.
4. useful, adequate	It was *good* that I read the book before the quiz.
5. reliable	Pat is a *good* source of information.
6. kind, giving	My grandmother is so *good*.
7. authentic, real	He makes a *good* point.
8. well-behaved	Rachel is such a *good* child.
9. considerable	There's a *good* deal more poverty now than five years ago.

---

a program produces changes in behavior, attitudes, or knowledge. Further, we might want to know how much change was experienced by the average client, how long it was sustained, and at what cost.

Subjective evaluations about the success of individual clients are very much like the initial examples of a "good" movie and a "good" restaurant. We can expect differences in opinion. Within most groups, if someone says, "That is not a good restaurant!" there are sure to be others within the crowd who will disagree. Someone else may say, "Well, it is my favorite restaurant!" or, "That's interesting. We were just there on Wednesday and had a wonderful meal." The problem with subjective evaluations is that everyone is usually right. The person who had a bad experience with a restaurant probably got poor service or an improperly prepared meal. The person who ate there on Wednesday could have just as easily had a wonderful meal. The individual who boldly proclaimed the restaurant to be his favorite restaurant might be quite willing to forget an occasional bad meal because he goes there for the atmosphere, he is personal friends with the proprietor, or his girlfriend works there. Another possibility is that he just does not have that discriminating a palate.

To become evaluators, we need to adjust our perspectives so that we are able to see beyond a single meal or a single client. We need to see the larger picture. We need to go from a micro focus to a macro focus. What are the experiences that most of the restaurant patrons or clients have? In a sense, we need to forget the individual and broaden our perspective to focus on the most common or frequent experience. What percent of the patrons would not return? With what percent of our caseload are we successful? We need to look for corroborative evidence that might convince neutral observers. (For instance, counting the number of patrons leaving meals unfinished or leaving in the middle of a movie might substantiate rather powerfully one's own subjective experience.)

As evaluators, we want to be able to objectively conclude that this program is a good one and that another is not—based not on our own personal opinion but on factual evidence. When we go beyond our own personal experience or opinions and collect information about the experiences that others have had, we have begun to develop an evaluative stance—we have moved from subjectivity to objectivity.

An objective stance tends to place faith in numbers and counting. As a rough rule of thumb, the more individuals we are able to interview, survey, or contact, the more confidence we can place in our evaluative findings. Numbers constitute objective data. When, for instance, ninety-seven out of a hundred clients indicate that they would recommend our services to their friends, this constitutes objective data. Anyone examining the responses of the hundred clients and sorting them into piles of "would recommend" and "would not recommend" services ought to arrive at the same conclusion.

Evaluators are, in some respects, applied scientists. Scientists seek to understand and explain the world around them. However, it is not just explanations that scientists seek, but *correct* explanations. Whether we think of ourselves as program evaluators or as applied scientists, our findings must stand independently, apart from our claims or persuasive oratory. Our findings must be replicable (reproducible); others must be able to independently arrive at the same conclusions. If someone did not like or agree with the findings from a particular program evaluation, then this person could repeat the evaluation using the same methodology. Assuming that no major changes occurred within the agency in the interim and that the original evaluation methodology was sound, findings from the second study should be the same or very similar to those of the first study.

Objectivity demands precision. Evaluators must be precise about the program they are evaluating, what they will be measuring, how they will collect and analyze their data, and who they will be interviewing or observing during a given time period. Such matters require specificity. Vagueness is rarely tolerated in research or evaluation. Note the lack of specificity in the following: "This evaluation will determine if specialized in-service training on the use of empathy helps social workers perform their jobs better." Do you find it too vague? The statement is unclear because we are left wondering: What social workers are being discussed? Has it been established that empathy is necessary to perform their jobs? What jobs are under consideration? What does it mean to perform better? How is empathy to be measured?

One way that evaluators become more specific and precise is by using **operational definitions**. An operational definition is the way a variable or concept (such as empathy) is to be defined and measured for the purposes of the evaluation. The evaluator may use a standardized scale to measure level of empathy. Or, the evaluator may use some sort of behavioral measures, such as the number of times during a session the social worker nods affirmatively or makes supportive statements such as "I understand." Social workers may be operationally defined as those holding BSW or MSW degrees or as all persons who work in a certain program regardless of their educational background (e.g., a child protection investigation unit or foster care program).

As one begins to operationally define the key concepts for a proposed evaluation or study, often the vagueness disappears. In the case of the vague statement, "This evaluation will determine if specialized in-service training on the use of empathy helps social workers perform their jobs better," operationally defining important concepts might change it to: "Do social workers with higher levels of empathy place more children in adoptive homes per year than social workers with lower levels of empathy?"

The effort to become more precise does not rule out the subjective experience in program evaluation. While a single "bad" subjective experience cannot constitute a program evaluation, it may lead to a formal evaluation as a program manager, agency director, or members of the board of directors become concerned about whether an incident or experience reflects what is "really going on" with the program. The program evaluator seeks to understand the "reality" or "truth" about a program. In the process, the evaluator may collect a large number of subjective opinions about the program. Objective evaluations seek not to rely upon the opinions of any one person (no matter how influential), but instead to gain a comprehensive view from the opinions of the aggregate or group.

Because the reality about a program's performance can sometimes be painful and have far-reaching implications (e.g., loss of funds and the corresponding laying off of a number of an agency's employees), program evaluators often seek the best possible objective evidence that they can obtain (given such pragmatic constraints as budget, time, access to clients or their records, and cooperation of the staff). Having objective or "hard data" to guide decisions about programs is superior to decision making without program evaluation data. By way of analogy, if you were on trial for an offense that you did not commit, you would want your lawyer to present as much objective evidence on your behalf as possible to assist the jury in realizing your innocence. You probably would not feel comfortable in allowing your attorney to hinge the entire case upon the subjective testimony of a single character witness who would testify that you were a "good" student or a "good" friend.

CHAPTER RECAP

Whether you are a direct service worker, program director, or an agency administrator, you want the agency that employs you to be well managed and responsive to the needs of clients and community. How does an agency become a well-managed agency? One essential way is the evaluation of its efforts, where problems are identified and corrective action taken (Sugarman, 1988).

What is essential to learn about program evaluation? Besides understanding the purpose of program evaluations and some of the various reasons why they are conducted, you need to know the difference between a subjectively held opinion and one that is derived from objective data. This text will help you develop ways of identifying, collecting, and using data that will allow you to be as objective as possible when evaluating programs in the social and human services. Objective data are seen as having greater credibility and as providing better information for the decisions that face program managers. Operational definitions are used by evaluators to obtain objective data that can be replicated if necessary. Theoretical models suggest not only what interventions may work, but also where to find the changes that have resulted.

QUESTIONS FOR CLASS DISCUSSION

1. Make a list of five or six human service programs with which you or members of the class are familiar. In another column list what is known about how well each program does its job. For example, what is its success rate? Other than subjective feelings about these

programs, what is known about how "good" these programs are? In a third column, make a list of questions that you would like to have answered about each program.

2. Evaluators must operationally define what will be recognized as "success" or a "successful outcome." Try your hand at operationally defining "success" for several of the programs you listed in question 1.

3. For the human service programs you listed in question 1, discuss your ideas about theoretical orientations on which the interventions might be based.

4. Discuss your experiences with program evaluation in your job or field practicum.

5. What are the characteristics of a "good" television program? Make a list of all the subjective opinions held by the class members about a "good" television program. How could you objectively determine if a television program is "good"?

6. Why is it necessary to develop operational definitions about such things as what constitutes recidivism or a successful client outcome? Use specific examples.

MINI-PROJECTS: EXPERIENCING EVALUATION FIRSTHAND

1. Choose a product (e.g., coffee-makers, tape recorders, VCRs, televisions, microwave ovens) and develop a set of objective standards that could help consumers select a model of superior performance and avoid the inferior models. Once you have finished, consult back issues of *Consumer Reports* to see how the standards you used compare with those used by the Consumer Products Testing Union.

2. What would you request in the way of an evaluation if you were in a position to require evaluation of a national program? Select a national program and identify what information would be needed in order for an unbiased panel of experts to conclude that the program was successful.

3. Find an example of a program evaluation in a professional journal. Briefly describe how key variables were operationally defined, how the program's success was measured, and the theoretical model for the intervention. *Evaluation Review, Evaluation and Program Planning,* and *Research on Social Work Practice* are three journals that publish program evaluations.

REFERENCES AND RESOURCES

American Psychological Association. (1981). *Specialty guidelines for counseling psychologists.* Washington, DC: APA.

Chelimsky, E. (1989). Evaluating public programs. In James L. Perry (ed.), *Handbook of public administration.* San Francisco, CA.: Jossey-Bass.

Conrad, K.J., and Miller, T.Q. (1987). Measuring and testing program philosophy. *New Directions for Program Evaluation,* no. 33, 19-42.

Evaluation and Program Planning, 12 (4) (1989). Special Issue: The theory-driven perspective.

Gyorky, Z., Royalty, G.M., and Johnson, D.H. (1994). Time-limited therapy in university counseling centers: Do time-limited and time-unlimited centers differ? *Professional Psychology: Research and Practice,* 25 (1), 50-54.

Jemmott, L.S., and Jemmott, J.B. (1991). Applying the theory of reasoned action to AIDS risk behavior: Condom use among black women. *Nursing Research,* 40 (4), 228-234.

Kolata, G. (1994). Clinic entices patients by paying them $10 a visit. *New York Times,* May 4, B8.

National Association of Social Workers. (1979). Code of Ethics. Silver Spring, MD: NASW.

Passell, P. (1993). Like a new drug, social programs are put to the test. *New York Times,* March 9, B5.

Polansky, N.A. (1986). There is nothing so practical as a good theory. *Child Welfare,* 65 (1), 3-15.

Rutter, M. (1987). Psychosocial resilience and protective mechanisms. *American Journal of Orthopsychiatry,* 57, 316-331.

Saunders, D.G. (1992). A typology of men who batter: Three types derived from cluster analysis. *American Journal of Orthopsychiatry,* 62, 264-275.

Schalock, R.L., and Thornton, C.V.D. (1988). *Program evaluation: A field guide for administrators.* New York: Plenum Press.

Sugarman, B. (1988). The well-managed human service organization: Criteria for a management audit. *Administration in Social Work,* 12 (4), 12-27.

Telch, C.F., Agras, W.S., Rossiter, E.M., Wilfley, D., and Kenardy, J. (1990). Group cognitive-behavioral treatment for the nonpurging bulimic: An initial evaluation. *Journal of Consulting and Clinical Psychology,* 58, 629-635.

Thyer, B.A. (1994). Are theories for practice necessary? No! *Journal of Social Work Education,* 30, 147-151.

Tripodi, T. (1987). Program evaluation. In Anne Minahan (ed.), *Encyclopedia of Social Work.* Silver Spring, MD: National Association of Social Workers.

Zambelli, G.C., and Derosa, A.P. (1992). Bereavement support groups for school-aged children: Theory, intervention, and case example. *American Journal of Orthopsychiatry,* 62 (4), 484-493.

TWO

The Evaluation of Need:
Needs Assessment

Ideally, planning should precede the development of programs. Long before programs begin serving clients, **needs assessments** ought to have been conducted to determine whether there is sufficient need to justify the funding of a new human service program. In fact, Hornick and Burrows (1988) define needs assessment as the first type of program evaluation—using the logic that one needs to *evaluate* whether the proposed program is needed before it is begun. Needs assessments are also known as feasibility studies or even "front-end analyses." Despite the various names that they may be called, needs assessments not only provide information about whether a program is needed but also provide guidance once a program has started.

Needs assessment is the cornerstone of responsible planning for human service programs. It is the measure against which program implementation and outcome will be compared. Lewis and Lewis (1991) have described needs assessment as the first step of a generic planning process for program development.

After needs assessment has been conducted, subsequent steps in the program development process include: development of goals and objectives for the proposed program, consideration of alternative methods for meeting these goals, and planning for the implementation of the

21

program. The cycle of program development would be complete once the program has been implemented and evaluated. In identifying the gap between a community's needs and its services, needs assessment begins the process where resources can be mobilized toward meeting those needs.

Another way to think about needs assessment is in terms of external and environmental monitoring systems. While program evaluation is an "internal monitoring system," needs assessment "data provide a fundamental navigational system for program planning and modification based on continuous assessment of changing community needs" (Nguyen, Attkisson, and Bottino, 1983, p. 107). While we, as social workers, may feel that we know the needs of our clients (or of certain neighborhoods and communities), this presumed knowledge is only subjective opinion until we can provide some documentation or hard evidence of the extent of unmet needs in our communities.

We conduct needs assessments for many reasons—not only to estimate the numbers of persons who could benefit from a specific program or service but also to learn about the geographic distribution and sociodemographic characteristics of potential clients. Where do clients live relative to the location of the agency?

Further, even though an agency or community runs a certain program, a large segment of the population may not know of its existence or may erroneously assume that they do not qualify for the program. Sometimes a service does exist, but the waiting list is so great that for all practical purposes the program is not viewed as a real source of help by those in need.

Because programs are not always located convenient to bus lines or do not have evening or weekend hours, some potential clients may have difficulty using them. What other barriers may prevent clients from getting the help they need?

In a perfect world, needs assessments would be conducted on a regular, ongoing basis to provide information to service providers and program planners. With this information, adjustments could be made as programs mature and evolve and target populations change.

Depending upon the field or specialization, needs assessment literature might be commonplace or somewhat rare. For instance, because the Older Americans Act requires that Area Agencies on Aging assess services needed by older persons and the effectiveness of resources in meeting those needs (Cheung, 1993), professionals in the field of gerontology tend to have a keen interest in needs assessment and frequently write on the topic. However, numerous needs assessments appear in the human services literature. A few examples of these illustrate their usage

---

BOX 2.1
Reasons for Conducting a Needs Assessment

1. To determine if an intervention exists in a community.

2. To determine if there are enough clients with a particular problem to justify creating a new program.

3. To determine if existing interventions are known to or recognized by potential clients.

4. To determine what barriers prevent clients from accessing existing services.

5. To document the existence of an ongoing/exacerbating social problem.

---

in quite diverse areas. Needs assessments have frequently been directed at discovering the training needs of various professionals. Pecora (1989) surveyed frontline and supervisory public child welfare staff members to assess staff training needs. Smith, Paskewicz, Evans, and Milan (1986) discussed an effort to identify the training needs of professionals in the field of corrections. Shayne and Kinney (1986) designed a needs assessment to identify the instructional needs of directors and coordinators of employee assistance programs.

Other examples of needs assessment include examining community support and residential needs of one thousand four hundred clients with severe mental illness (Ford et al., 1992), ascertaining the percentage of low-income women at risk of unwanted pregnancy but not practicing contraception (Radecki and Bernstein, 1990), and determining employee interest in attending a smoking cessation program (Fitzhugh et al., 1993). Toomey, First, Greenlee, and Cummins (1993) have discussed the methodological dilemmas of counting the rural homeless.

It is vital that accurate information be available in order for social service funding decisions to be made on a rational basis. Among the types of information necessary to determine the allocation of social welfare resources is an appraisal of the extent of **unmet needs** in a given community. An example of how these needs were assessed for the elderly in one locality is shown in Box 2.2.

23

BOX 2.2
Assessing the Health and Welfare Needs of the Elderly

Undergraduate social workers were given the names and addresses of householders randomly selected from the Tallahassee, Florida, telephone book. The students had been well trained in conducting semistructured needs assessment interviews. Each student went to the location of the randomly selected home (single-family dwelling *or* apartment, duplex, and the like) and knocked on the door of every third residence to the left of the selected home. The householders were requested to be interviewed about the health and social service needs they required. After the interview, the student then moved on three more houses, and so forth. If a householder declined to participate, or no one was at home, the students continued the process of sampling every third household until a successful interview was obtained.

Eventually a sizeable sample ($N = 70+$) of local residents was recruited, and their responses to a standardized set of questions about their present and projected health and social service needs were ascertained. Eighteen potential needs/services were asked about. The most frequently reported present needs were *periodic health screening, emergency response services, transportation services,* and *home health aides.* Projected future needs paralleled present needs, except that greater numbers of respondents anticipated requiring such services. Generally, health needs were more in demand than concrete needs (chore assistance, legal aid), which were in greater demand than counseling-type services. This information was shared with local citizens' groups and government agencies.

Like most field-type studies, this research was not "perfect." For example, the sampling procedure probably resulted in greater numbers of retired and unemployed persons being interviewed, since the interviews were mostly conducted during the day, when such persons were more likely to be at home. The frequent occurrence of people not being home or not being able to devote the time to the interview compromised our efforts at obtaining a "random" or representative sample of area residents. Even basing the initial selection of starting households on telephone book addresses means that not every household in the city had a genuinely equal opportunity to be included among the interviewees. Nevertheless, a broad-based survey of residents' needs conducted along these lines is likely to have produced more truly "representative" information than some alternative forms of gathering data, such as interviewing so-called "community-leaders" and "key-informants," or by holding community-meetings and soliciting suggestions.

Source: Wright, Thyer, and DiNitto (1985).

PLANNING NEEDS ASSESSMENTS

How do we go about evaluating whether there is sufficient need to justify the start of a new program? Let's quickly work through one example.

Suppose you feel that there is a need for a latchkey program in your community. You are particularly concerned about elementary school aged children who, because of working parents, are at home for several hours in the afternoon without adult supervision. You learn that a local foundation has expressed interest in funding a pilot latchkey program in your community the next school year.

Before beginning a needs assessment, ask yourself, "What information sources are available?" As you think about the information sources that would be helpful and obtainable, it occurs to you that among your friends are three elementary school principals. You contact them and find that two are convinced that a latchkey program is needed, while the third is undecided. You don't feel that this is sufficient information to take to the foundation. What more could you do? You could ask all of your friends and neighbors if they thought that this program was needed. Unfortunately, as another friend indicates to you, these opinions do not constitute objective information. Asking only people you know about their opinions will give you *biased information*—even if the number of people you have talked to is now up to twenty-five.

What else could you do? If there is a "true" need for the latchkey program, it would be evidenced by parents who are interested in having their children participate in the program. Their interest could be documented (with the principals' support) by sending home a brief questionnaire to every parent with elementary aged children explaining that a planning effort is being conducted to determine if there is sufficient interest in a latchkey program. When parents and guardians return the questionnaire, you will have objective information regarding the perceived need for a latchkey program. However, there is at least one other information source that could provide useful data. With the cooperation of the child protection agency, you could survey the child protection staff in your community in order to learn if they, too, perceive the need for a local latchkey program.

As this example shows, much of what constitutes needs assessment revolves around thinking about what sources of useful information you could obtain. The emphasis is on *useful*. In this day and age, information from hundreds of sources is available to us in libraries and may be as close as our computer screens. But before we start gathering information, we should focus for a few moments on the necessary steps in conducting a needs assessment (Box 2.3).

25

BOX 2.3

Steps in Needs Assessment

Step 1. Clearly understand:
   a. purpose of needs assessment.
   b. your budget; resources available to you.
   c. time allotted for the project.

Step 2. Identify the specific information you need to acquire.

Step 3. Determine if the information already exists or can be obtained with your resources.

Step 4. Collect and review data.

Step 5. Prepare report.

Step one sets the parameters for the needs assessment. The more resources at your disposal, the larger your budget, the more time you have, the more comprehensive and sophisticated your needs assessment can be. Keeping the purpose of the needs assessment constantly in mind will help you keep your efforts focused.

Step two requires that you identify information needed for decision making. Many times requests from planning committees add items to the needs assessment that could provide interesting information. However, the "test" of whether these items should be included is if they will provide information useful to program managers. If no direct use can be made of proposed information items, then they should not be added.

Step three requires that you do a little exploratory work so that you're not "reinventing the wheel" or "spinning your wheels." You might want to check with other social service agencies, look through past reports, talk with staff about the information they collect, perhaps conduct some literature searches in the library. Ultimately, you need to decide upon a methodology for providing the best information given the constraints in your particular situation.

SELECTING A NEEDS ASSESSMENT APPROACH

There are a variety of ways to go about estimating the need for a human service program. And numerous questions and issues will affect the particular needs assessment strategy you select. Besides your budget, the resources available to you, and the amount of time you have to finish the project, you need to consider whether this assessment will be a one-time phenomenon or an effort that will be built upon—perhaps even repeated each year. Is the purpose of the needs assessment to satisfy some bureaucrat in the state capital, or will the data really be used by the agency? Is it seen as "busy work" or a useful activity? Is your supervisor or agency director anxious to see the needs assessment, or are your instructions to just put "something" on paper? Is it likely the needs assessment will be used by others in the community, or will it simply be typed, submitted to some government office, and promptly forgotten?

How much can be spent on the needs assessment? Can you afford consultants and paid interviewers for your community survey? What kind of technical expertise or staff resources will be available from your agency or cooperating agencies? If one is creative, low-budget approaches to needs assessment can be found. Stefl (1984), for instance, reported on a community survey that was conducted by volunteers. The way some of these volunteers were recruited is interesting. One of the agency's board members was a probation officer. He was able to offer community service to a select group of offenders as an alternative to incarceration. These persons were screened very closely, trained as interviewers, and were said to have performed very well. Eight hundred and twenty-two telephone interviews were obtained in twenty-one days. The overall refusal rate was comparable to those reported by professional survey organizations.

Staff are also resources. Besides yourself, who else can be asked to assist with the needs assessment? What skills can they contribute?

Planning a community survey obviously takes more time than contacting a handful of key informants. If you are working against a rapidly approaching deadline, your choice of a needs assessment approach may be justifiably influenced by what can be accomplished in a short period of time.

Another issue is the amount of detail or information desired—whether the assessment has to be objective and data-oriented or whether it can be more perception-oriented. How "hard" does the data need to be? Will your audience be skeptical or supportive of your efforts? If you can't directly assess need, what surrogate measures are available to you—what programs are most similar to the one you must assess? How was need for those programs determined? Deadlines for grants and sponsors sometimes have a way of boiling down the selection issues about what data can be obtained within a certain time period. Even then, you'll have certain choices. The next section discusses different approaches available to you.

Secondary Data Approaches

Secondary data is existing information that comes from census data, public documents, and reports. Even data generated by other researchers or surveys can be re-examined for relevance to the new program. Census data, for instance, contains a wealth of information, and since it is readily available in most public libraries, it should be reviewed before collecting any other data. At a minimum, census data can provide you with estimates of the population likely to need or to benefit from the program you are proposing.

You could, for example, consult census data to learn the number of children five to nine years of age or the number of poverty level families with children in your community. Census data are available for geographical units known as census tracts and census blocks. (Note that the block data are available only for large metropolitan areas.) By referring to census data, it is possible to learn how many school aged children reside in a defined geographical area. You could learn the race and sex of these children and the number living in poverty. There is even a category that provides information on the number of females in the labor force with children under six and between six and seventeen years of age.

To switch examples for a moment, if we were planning a program for senior citizens, census data could be used to provide reliable estimates (providing the data were not too dated) of the number of persons fifty-five, sixty, or older, areas within the community where these older adults tend to reside, and the number of older adults living in poverty. Census data can also be used to provide such information as the general level of affluence in a community, the average level of educational attainment, the number of substandard dwellings, and the number of persons with work disabilities.

In order to protect the confidentiality of information supplied to it, the Census Bureau suppresses data which could be used to identify specific individuals or families. Census data *cannot* be used to gain personal information on a specific family or families. It *cannot* supply you with the addresses, names, or phone numbers of families having school-aged children or living in poverty. You can, however, use census data to plot a map of those areas in the community that have the highest concentrations of older adults or children or families living in poverty.

In addition to census data, every state maintains a wealth of useful data for planners and evaluators. It is possible to learn from the state health department such information as the number of births, marriages, deaths, and suicides that occurred in a county in a given year. If you were developing a prenatal program for teen-age mothers, it would be possible to find both the number of babies born to teen-age mothers and the number of infant deaths in the years prior to the start of the program. Persons interested in starting an alcoholism prevention or treatment program may want to document the number of persons who have died as a result of cirrhosis of the liver. These and many other categories of information are available from the state health department. (These variables and others that help us to gauge the extent of social problems are known as **social indicators.**)

From the state department of education you can find such information as the number of school dropouts, the number of ninth graders reading at grade level, and school enrollments. Other state departments keep records of such social indicators as the number of children receiving food stamps, medically indigent children, free or reduced-cost school breakfast recipients, child abuse allegations, substantiated abuse allegations, delinquency cases, unemployment, psychiatric admissions to public hospitals, and so on.

In addition to state produced reports, a little library work may uncover a national report that provides detailed information on a state-by-state basis. For example, the Annie E. Casey foundation (1994) produced *Kids Count Data Book*, which compares states on a number of variables, such as infant mortality rate, percent of births to single teens, juvenile violent crime arrest rate, percent graduating from high school, and percent of children not living with a parent.

Administrative records, reports, and files within your own agency are a source of already existing data that should not be overlooked for needs assessment purposes. Information such as this, which comes directly from the agency itself, is called **patterns of use** or **client utilization data.** It may also be known as a **rates-under-treatment approach.**

Most human services agencies report annually on the characteristics of those who have been clients in the past year. These data can be reviewed to see what groups within the community are being served (and underserved). Table 2.1 shows how the data from one counseling agency could be used for needs assessment purposes.

From this table, we can identify potentially underserved segments of the community based upon the numbers of clients who have received service. We can see that there has been greater demand for the adult program than the children's program and more usage of it than the older-adult program. These figures could be used to understand **expressed**

Table 2.1
Client Utilization Data, Public Counseling Services, Inc.

	1995	1996	1997
Children served	363	383	407
Number on waiting list	16	19	21
Adults served	785	791	818
Number on waiting list	14	12	15
Older adults served	63	72	84
Number on waiting list	0	3	9
Drug abusers served	302	414	545
Number on waiting list	75	124	183
Total clients served	1513	1660	1854
Clients on waiting list	105	158	228

need—that is, official requests for service. We can also see that the drug abuse treatment program appears to need additional staff. In 1995, almost 25 percent of their current caseload was awaiting service. Clearly, this program is in need of additional staff or resources in order to reduce the number of clients waiting for service to an acceptable level. None of the other programs had so many clients awaiting service.

Client data can also be used for such purposes as locating neighborhoods or streets with the highest prevalence rates of certain problems (e.g., drug abuse). Sundel (1983) has described placing multicolored pins in maps to help staff focus their outreach and education activities.

Secondary data sources are generally convenient to access (if they are not in your public library, a phone call to the appropriate state department will often get you what you need free or at a very nominal cost) and are easy to understand and use. (Anyone can rank counties or census tracts in terms of those having the most or least of some characteristic. Anyone can identify the county with the highest unemployment rate or determine what the unemployment rate has been in a selected county for the past five years. In metropolitan areas, census tracts or blocks may be ranked in terms of percentage of families living in poverty or number of older adults.)

However, some conspicuous problems arise when secondary data are used for needs assessment. The data may be dated, incomplete, or from an agency that isn't really similar (because it's in a different geographical region, serves a different population, or has different eligibility guidelines). Even with the best agency data, there is always the problem of counting those potential clients who qualify for services but who have never been referred and who don't self-refer. Anytime you rely solely on client utilization data, you are likely to be underestimating the problem to some extent.

Impressionistic Approaches

After you have consulted the census data or other secondary data and have a firm grasp on the extent of the problem (or of the population to be served), additional information can come from consulting with service providers and other **key informants.** Key informants are those persons who are informed about a given problem because of training or work experience—usually because they are involved in some sort of service with that population. In our latchkey example, key informants could be the principal, guidance counselor, social worker, and teachers in a school. One person conducting a key informant needs assessment for the latch-key program could easily contact all of these personnel in a single elementary school. Key informants could also include child protection workers and their supervisors, or area ministers.

Impressionistic approaches have a subjective quality to them. That is, these approaches are not as accurate or scientific as large scale community surveys. Why? For one thing, sample sizes are often too small to be representative of the larger population. Think about a situation wherein a needs assessment involved talking with three principals. Even if the needs assessment had been expanded to include three teachers, three area ministers, and three parents, we still would not have a sample necessarily representative of the opinions of all the principals, teachers, ministers, and parents in the community. Our data would not be scientific—especially if we chose these individuals because we knew them. (We'll discuss sample size and representativeness more fully in subsequent sections.) While their opinions may be well founded and based on a superb knowledge of the problem, they may also be based on nothing other than personal bias, beliefs, or values. Suppose, for example, that two of the principals you selected strongly believed that women should not be employed outside of the home. These principals may be less likely to acknowledge the need for a latchkey program than a principal with more egalitarian values. The problem of dealing with subjective opinions is also present (and perhaps more visible) in another type of impressionistic needs assessment.

Public hearings and community forums are a type of needs assessment that are "grass-roots" oriented. What is more democratic than acquiring a public meeting room and posting a notice or advertising that anyone concerned with the problem of (fill in the blank) is invited to attend and share their concerns? This approach has the advantage of

31

being reasonably inexpensive, not requiring a lot of preplanning, and again, needing little research expertise to interpret or summarize the results.

But there are some serious drawbacks to public hearings. For one, the "public" seldom seems to attend. Unless the issue is a controversial one, rarely would potential clients attend the public hearings that are supposed to generate planning data. Often, the only attendees are the planning staff and a few service providers from other agencies who have an interest in working with that specific population.

A second problem with community forums and public hearings is that even when citizens from the community attend, there is no guarantee that they represent the larger community. Sometimes certain interest groups can "pack" the meeting so that the opinions of others are not represented. Numerically small but vocal groups can dominate meetings. And persons most in need of the proposed service (e.g., families in poverty, juvenile delinquents, teen-age parents) probably will not be in attendance at all.

Several other impressionistic techniques provide good information from small groups. The nominal group technique (Delbecq, Van de Ven, and Gustafson, 1975) involves a small group of persons who, in response to a common problem or question, work independently at first, and then share their ideas. The group leader asks each person to offer one idea in round-robin fashion. These ideas are recorded in front of the group on a chalk board or large sheet of paper. This process continues until all new ideas are exhausted. This is followed by a discussion period when participants can elaborate, eliminate, combine ideas, and add new ones to the list. This phase is followed by each participant privately ranking the five most important ideas from the remaining ideas on the list. Individual rankings are compiled for the group in order to arrive at the most popular ideas or solutions to the question posed. The group then discusses the anonymous rankings to resolve any misunderstandings. After the discussion, group members are asked to give a final independent rating.

The Delphi technique (Delbecq, Van de Ven, and Gustafson, 1975) involves the use of a questionnaire that is distributed to a panel of key informants or experts. (They do not meet together in person, and may remain anonymous.) Their ideas are solicited, and their replies are compiled. If there are areas of disagreement, a second questionnaire is developed based on the responses. This new questionnaire is sent to the panel, and their opinions solicited once again. This process continues until consensus is reached in all areas.

In an interesting application of the Delphi method, Raskin (1994) sent a questionnaire to 450 directors of field instruction in accredited undergraduate and graduate social work programs and asked them to list national experts in field instruction. From this list Raskin constructed a smaller list of those who received five or more votes. The resulting twelve experts were asked to participate in a three-round Delphi study that sought to learn the critical problems in the field and whether consensus could be reached on these problems.

Focus groups represent another perception-oriented approach to assessing needs. Although focus groups originally evolved from market research, their use is increasing at a rapid rate, because they afford program designers greater knowledge and understanding of clients' problems.

Focus groups usually involve six to eight individuals who participate in structured discussion (Krueger, 1993). For needs assessment, a moderator facilitates a dialogue with constituent members of a client or target group. The goal is not to have these persons arrive at consensus, but to identify and delineate their particular needs—some of which will be common to all group members and others unique to one individual. The moderator obtains in-depth information by probing and asking clarifying questions.

Buttram (1990), for instance, has reported on the use of focus groups by a regional educational laboratory as part of its program planning cycle. She found that the needs expressed by participants were more dynamic and process-oriented than previous lists and that there was moderate overlap in the needs reported in five different cities across the region. Buttram concluded that this approach was useful in helping the laboratory management to think more broadly and ambitiously about its future work.

While impressionistic approaches have much to recommend them (they can "involve" the community, are inexpensive, are relatively quick to implement, and no special knowledge of needs assessment is required), it is difficult to know the accuracy of the obtained data. Those who are invited or chosen, or who elect themselves to participate may not be truly representative of the larger community. Their views may be atypical or not reflect those of the majority. If this is a major concern, a community survey would provide less biased and more accurate information. Perhaps the best use of impressionistic approaches is to add the "personal angle" to those approaches that have relied heavily upon "hard data."

Community Household Surveys

Surveys are familiar to most of us. Businesses use surveys to learn why we choose the brand of toothpaste that we buy; politicians use them to identify for whom we are likely to vote in the next election. Social scientists use surveys to determine our attitudes about such topics as abortion, capital punishment, and race relations and to determine the prevalence of such social problems as elder abuse (Pillemer and Finkelhor, 1988). Surveys are also used for program development purposes. For example, Rutz and Shemberg (1985) surveyed fifth and sixth graders' beliefs, feelings, and behavioral intentions toward mental health issues prior to the development of mental health education programs.

Surveys are exceptionally valuable tools to use for needs assessment. Although they require more planning and resources than the impressionistic approaches, they provide information that is much more objective and scientific. When a probability sampling design has been used, it is possible to talk very precisely and confidently about the extent of a problem in a community. You could find, for instance, that only 42 percent of the respondents had heard or read anything about a mental health center in their community (Royse, 1986). Similarly, only 44 percent knew that counseling could be obtained in the community for children who were not doing well in school or getting along with their families. Because the sample of adults was derived from a probability sampling design, the researcher was 95 percent confident that the results were accurate within plus or minus 5.5 percent. That is the type of accuracy that the other needs assessment approaches cannot provide.

In another example, Stefl (1984) reported that in a needs assessment of a five county region in south central Ohio, of those who were judged to have *no need* of mental health services, 11.8 percent did not know about the availability of mental health services. However, 21 percent of those judged to be *in need* of outpatient or inpatient mental health services did not know about the availability of services. The precise estimate of the community's needs, beliefs, values, or behavior can come about only when the survey methodology has been sound. This type of needs assessment requires knowledge of both research methodology and sampling procedure.

While it is possible to conduct surveys with persons who are near at hand and easy to access, those who are chosen merely because it is convenient may not adequately represent the community. For instance, one could choose to survey those in attendance at a meeting of the parents' organization regarding the need for a latchkey program in a specific elementary school. If the parents who attend this meeting are representative of all the parents in the community, they would be a good source of information. If, however, the parents' organization meeting was attended only by parents from upper-middle-class and two-parent households, then the organization may not represent the opinions of all the parents with children attending the school.

Why might we assume that the parents who attend the parents' organization meetings may not be representative of the larger community? First of all, parents from impoverished households may lack transportation to get to these meetings—they may not own cars. In rural areas and smaller cities, public transportation may not always be available (especially for evening meetings); even if they do have transportation, impoverished households often have multiple problems associated with day-to-day existence. Attendance at a school meeting (which is not required) often has very low priority. Additionally, single parents have the inconvenience of having to arrange for babysitters—still another financial burden upon impoverished households.

So, even if you were successful in surveying those in attendance at the monthly parents' organization meeting, your findings may be representative only of middle- or upper-middle-class households. The majority of these relatively affluent parents may have sufficient resources so that they may have no need, or perceive no need, for a latchkey program. This would be especially true in those affluent households where only one parent was employed outside the home.

In order to be representative of the whole community, every person in the population must have an opportunity to provide input. With small populations it may be necessary to contact everyone, or at least a majority, to have a representative sample of the population. With large populations, random sampling can be employed so that perhaps less than 10 percent of the population is contacted (but every person in the population still had an equal chance of being selected to provide their opinions). While the method used to select the sample is important, the size of the sample chosen to represent the population is just as important.

Although we are going to spend more time discussing sampling in chapter 10, you can understand the importance of sample size if you think about a large metropolitan community of about one million persons. Suppose a friend of yours from another country is interested in the quality of life as perceived by persons in this country who live in large cities. Your friend (who knows nothing about sampling) asks you to send her the address of one person from your metropolitan community so that she can mail this person a questionnaire. Can any one person adequately reflect the diversity of opinions, experiences, and life-styles that are found in large cities? "Do you think it would be possible," your friend later asks, "for you to send me the addresses of two more people?" Could a large metropolitan area be represented by the opinions of three persons? What if you sent thirty addresses? How many addresses would you have to send in order for this sample to be representative of the opinions held by the majority of persons living in your metropolitan area? The return or response rate is also important. A low response rate is the equivalent of inviting a large number of people to a party and only one or two show up.

The purpose of the previous illustration is to show that one needs to have a good grasp of sampling before beginning a community survey. There is nothing wrong with conducting small convenience surveys of twenty, forty, or even fifty respondents as pilot studies to provide for some beginning estimates of need. However, remember that unless all the members of the population are contacted or have an opportunity to be selected, the results will not have scientific accuracy. Even if you go to a fair amount of trouble to obtain a random sample, you still may end up with biased results. You may be particulary susceptible to this problem with a mailed survey.

For instance, Thompson, Ruma, Authier, and Bouska (1994) mailed a community needs assessment questionnaire to every household in an Iowa county ($n = 1,850$) and got a response rate of only 23 percent. They found that of those who returned completed surveys, college-educated people and those who were middle aged and upper income were overrepresented. Young adults and lower income groups were the most clearly underrepresented.

Epidemiologic surveys seek to learn the extent of problems (usually diseases and injuries) in a community and typically express these as rates within the population. Epidemiologic surveys must, by definition, be based on scientific, representative samples and for this reason tend to be much more expensive than smaller scale, more informal surveys.

Ciarlo, Shern, Tweed, and Kirkpatrick (1992), for instance, have reported that a comprehensive psychiatric survey in Colorado generating need estimates for just 6.4 percent of 751 geographic subareas cost over $700,000, or approximately $150 per respondent. This did not include questionnaire design, computer editing, and data analysis costs. At this rate, it would have cost $11 million to survey the whole state.

Done properly, large-scale community surveys are more expensive, more time consuming, and tend to require more research expertise than secondary data analysis or impressionistic approaches. But they are more scientific and offer a level of precision and confidence not found with the other two approaches.

Convergent Analysis

In our initial example of assessing the need for a latchkey program, several sources of information could be tapped. We talked first about going to the school principals, key informants, and parents. Then we discussed the use of census or secondary data, the use of public hearings, contacting the parents' organization, and doing a community survey. Since any one approach may provide a somewhat incomplete picture of the "true" need for a latchkey program, convergent analysis should be the focus of the needs assessment effort (Siegel, Attkisson, and Carson, 1978; Warheit, Bell, and Schwab, 1977).

Convergent analysis involves using multiple sources of information and attempting to confirm the need for the program by means of different assessment strategies and perspectives. For instance, Sung (1989) has reported a needs assessment that converged the views of two hundred American residents living on a military base overseas and thirty professional officers and civilians engaged in the human services. Sung initially found noticeable differences in the way the two groups ranked problems and needed services. However, Sung was able to converge the needs data by computing an average for the two groups in terms of the seriousness of problems and desired services.

When needs assessment data is obtained from more than one source, areas of agreement may not always be immediately identifiable. However, averaging is an acceptable technique to use in attempting to converge the data. Convergence of data can be thought of as similar to a process in navigation and surveying called triangulation, where multiple reference points are used to locate an exact position. Information from various sources is integrated or synthesized to provide a "reasonably viable portrait" of the community's perceptions (Nguyen, Attkisson, and Bottino, 1983, p. 104). What would this look like in our latchkey example?

NEEDS ASSESSMENT ILLUSTRATION 1

Let's imagine that as a school social worker you first became convinced of the need for a latchkey program when you learned of an eight-year-old child who started a fire in his bedroom and barely escaped without serious injury. Because both parents were at work and the child had been regularly without adult supervision from 3:20 P.M. until 5:30 P.M., legal and child protection authorities had become involved.

As you talk about your idea of a latchkey program with several elementary school teachers during lunch hour, they become excited and each names about four children who could benefit from such a program. The school principal agrees that a latchkey program is needed and suggests that you talk with the parents' organization scheduled to meet the next evening. The parents' organization wholeheartedly endorses the concept and asks the principal if a questionnaire can be sent to every child's home. The principal agrees. A small planning committee meets with you and designs a questionnaire that looks something like the one in Box 2.4.

BOX 2.4
Glenover Parents' Organization
After-School Care Questionnaire

Dear Parent:

Because of the recent fire in our Glenover community and the narrowly averted tragedy, we believe that there is a need for an after-school program. Our children would be supervised at school by teachers. Tutoring, games, and special "fun" classes could be arranged—if there is sufficient interest from the parents. The school board may agree to pay several teachers for two hours each day after school if sufficient need can be documented. Please take five minutes to complete the following survey and have your child return it tomorrow to his or her homeroom teacher.

1. If an after-school program were available January 15 and there were no charge for enrolling your child, would you enroll one or more of your children (kindergarten through sixth grade)?
   _____ YES, I WOULD ENROLL _____ (number of children)
   _____ NO, I WOULD NOT ENROLL ANY OF MY CHILDREN
   _____ UNDECIDED, I NEED MORE INFORMATION ABOUT THE PROGRAM

2. If the school board does not have sufficient funds and there is a charge of $25.00 per week for each child, would you still make use of an after-school program?
   _____ YES, I WOULD ENROLL _____ (number of children)
   _____ NO, I WOULD NOT ENROLL ANY OF MY CHILDREN
   _____ UNDECIDED, I NEED MORE INFORMATION ABOUT THE PROGRAM

3. If you want to make sure that we reserve a place for your children, please write your name and address below. However, please return the questionnaire whether or not you want us to reserve a place at this time.
   _____ (Name)_____ (Phone)
   _____ (Address)

Figure 2.1
Convergence of Data

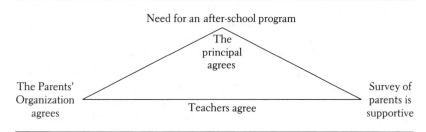

Need for an after-school program

The principal agrees

The Parents' Organization agrees

Teachers agree

Survey of parents is supportive

The needs assessment questionnaires are prepared and given to each child in the elementary school to take home. About 60 percent of the questionnaires are returned. The results are as follows:

Q1: Twelve percent of the parents would enroll their children in an after-school program if there were no charge. A total of 105 children would be expected to participate if there were no charge for the after-school program.

Q2: Five percent of the parents would enroll their children in an after-school program if there were a $25 a week charge per child. Approximately 40 children could be expected to participate if there were a $25 a week charge per child.

Q1 and 2:
8 percent of the parents were undecided about enrolling their children and wanted additional information.

Each of the informational sources explored in this fictitious example leads us to believe that there is a definite need for an after-school program. Visually, we might demonstrate this "convergence" of the data as shown in figure 2.1. The need for a latchkey program could be further supported by including secondary data such as the number of calls to police or rescue squads by unsupervised children. Such a needs assessment would make a strong and compelling argument for the proposed latchkey program. However, not every needs assessment could be expected to find such a high degree of convergence.

For instance, it is entirely possible that the Parents' Organization may not feel that a latchkey program is needed. Or, perhaps the principal, cognizant of the increased costs in utilities, janitorial services, and staff for the program, is not supportive because of an inadequate school budget.

There are no easy solutions as to what you should do if your sources of information don't converge. Sometimes you can explain away the lack of support from one sector (for example, the Parents' Organization is not representative of those parents who might make use of the latchkey program). On the other hand, the principal's concern must be addressed even if *everyone* else you contacted thought the project was viable.

Convergence of data represents a model for needs assessment planning that strives to include as many sources of data as possible. Such an effort tends to be more comprehensive and exhaustive than other forms of needs assessment—which gives it more credibility. At the same time, it is a more complex and difficult task for the individual or individuals conducting the needs assessment.

Harlow and Turner (1993), for example, in a survey of state units on aging found that forty-seven of the states had been involved in some type of needs assessment in the past seven years. However, only six states had the major components of Harlow and Turner's convergence model in place. This model included establishing goals, expected outcomes, and fiscal and human resources; identifying data bases (that is, client surveys, providers, secondary) and new data needed; evaluating the costs; and establishing lines of responsibility. It also required a data analysis plan and interpretation workshop for staff and legislators.

THINKING CREATIVELY ABOUT NEEDS ASSESSMENTS

Needs assessments do not have to be terribly complex. Sometimes the simplest of documentation procedures provides useful data for establishing that there is a need for a new program or facility. Once, after lecturing to a class about needs assessment, a student who believed that she didn't know enough about needs assessment to do an assignment came to my office to talk to me. As she told me about where she worked (a diversion program for juveniles who had been arrested) and the kinds of problems she experienced in her work, she mentioned a desperate need that she encountered every day. There simply was not enough temporary shelter for status offenders (young people who were picked up by the police for running away, being out too late, or being in possession of alcohol). Because of the lack of suitable shelter, young people were placed in jail until beds became available elsewhere.

I asked her how many times a month the jail was used inappropriately. She said about eighteen to twenty times. I asked if she could document this, and she indicated that it would be easy to do since a special form had to be completed each time. In a few minutes, we outlined an approach she could use to show county and state officials that there was an on-going need for additional shelter care for juveniles. She not only met the requirements for a class project but also used a methodology that could produce documentation for local officials and the community to help them understand the need for additional temporary shelter for status offenders.

In another example, a community mental health agency was required by a state agency to conduct a needs assessment. However, there were practically no funds available during the fiscal year. The agency improvised using data that was available from other counties. This is demonstrated in the second illustration.

NEEDS ASSESSMENT ILLUSTRATION 2

Warbler County (population 99,570) hired a consultant to conduct a community survey using a standardized instrument derived from earlier studies. This instrument contained scales from which could be inferred the extent of the population having either a possible or a probable need for mental health services. Various scales made up the instrument, but for the purposes of illustration, the relevant data from the needs assessment effort have been simplified in table 2.2.

A short time later, Thrush County (population 90,831) also retained the consultant to conduct a needs assessment of their county. Once again, a probability sample was obtained, and the same instrument used. The agency executive in adjoining Franklin County wanted very much to have a needs assessment conducted in his county, but a severely

Table 2.2
Warbler County Needs Assessment Data

Scale	Need for Counseling	Percent
Anxiety	Possible	6.2
	Probable	5.3
	Total	11.5
Depression	Possible	8.5
	Probable	4.5
	Total	13.0
Psychosocial	Possible	3.6
dysfunctioning	Probable	5.5
	Total	9.1

limited budget could not be stretched to encompass a community survey. However, he contacted the agency directors in the neighboring counties, and both were cooperative and shared the data produced from their needs assessments. With this information, it was possible to estimate needs that a similar study might have found in Franklin County (table 2.3).

Note how similar the percentages are between Warbler and Thrush counties. While there are some minor variations, the percentages of persons in need of mental health services in both counties are almost equal. We can arrive at the estimated number of persons in Franklin County in need of services by averaging the Warbler and Thrush County data. Thus, Franklin County would expect a slightly larger proportion of depressed persons than Warbler County, but less than Thrush County.

This approach uses survey data, but in its methodology it is most akin to the use of secondary data. Of course, the problem with this approach is that the data did not come from Franklin County. In actuality, 17 percent of the population of Franklin County might be depressed and 20 percent might score above normal levels of anxiety. We would not know the "true" level of these dimensions without conducting a probability survey in Franklin County. However, if a convincing case of the similarities among these three counties can be built, then this type of estimation is as good as any of the other indirect approaches. How would we know if the counties were similar? We would begin by making comparisons on such variables as the average age of the population, average income per capita, the percentage of families in poverty, and the percentage of divorced and separated persons, and by looking at the

Table 2.3
Estimated Needs in Franklin County

Scale	Need	Warbler Co.	Thrush Co.	Franklin Co.
Population		99,570	90,831	85,422
Anxiety	Possible	6.2%	6.9%	6.5%
	Probable	5.3%	5.1%	5.2%
	Total	11.5%	12.0%	11.7%
Depression	Possible	8.5%	9.6%	9.0%
	Probable	4.5%	5.1%	4.8%
	Total	13.0%	14.7%	13.8%
Psychosocial	Possible	3.6%	4.5%	4.0%
dysfunction	Probable	5.5%	6.0%	5.8%
	Total	9.1%	10.5%	9.8%

racial and religious mix of the counties. Sometimes it is relatively easy to know if two counties are similar or dissimilar. If one county borders on a large metropolitan area and the other is rural and remote from any large city, then they probably should not be compared. If two counties are primarily rural, in close proximity to each other, and compare well on demographic variables, then it is reasonable to use them to estimate needs in a third, similar county.

Even if you do not have access to needs assessment data from other counties, it may be possible to use social indicators or uniform rates as developed by others. Ciarlo, Tweed, et al. (1992) recommend that other states consider using percentage of persons in poverty and percentage of divorced males as indirect measures for estimating total need for alcohol, drug, and mental health services. However, it should be remembered that such methods are only estimates and that substantial variations across different geographical areas can be expected. See the articles by Tweed and Ciarlo (1992), Tweed, Ciarlo, Kirkpatrick, and Shern (1992), and Ciarlo and Tweed (1992) for more complete descriptions.

Needs assessments do not have to be financially burdensome to a human service agency. Some surveys (for example, key informant studies) can be conducted without major expenditures of monetary or personnel resources. On occasions when a needs assessment will cost several thousand dollars, cooperative efforts among social service providers or funders (for example, United Way) should be explored. Partial funding may also be possible with creative planning. For instance, in order to learn what was known about mental health services in one community (Royse, 1986), additional questions were incorporated that asked respondents about their favorite radio stations (during day, evening, and "drive" time). Because advertising is based on the number of listeners, radio stations were interested in purchasing this data (percentage of area listeners by age, education, and township). Several radio stations purchased that portion of the results dealing with their listening audiences and thus underwrote part of the total cost for the community awareness study.

If you are given the assignment of designing a needs assessment, think creatively. Shifman, Scott, and Fawcett (1986), for example, reported on the use of a game called "Family Few," modeled after the television program "Family Feud," to assess attitudes, beliefs, and knowledge about sexuality among female adolescents. In the process of obtaining a needs assessment profile on these adolescents, they were also able to provide didactic instruction!

Given the assignment of conducting a needs assessment, spend some time brainstorming all of the various ways one *could* go about examining the needs of the clientele. Make a list of these—whether they are feasible or not. When you run out of ideas, then review the list and choose the best approach. Following is a list of several different types of needs assessments that one mental health agency conducted during a six year period. This will give you some idea of the variety of ways in which needs assessment information can be obtained.

- **Community survey.** Over three hundred questionnaires were mailed to elected officials, school principals, attorneys, and other "key informants." In addition, over five hundred questionnaires were mailed to randomly selected community respondents.
- **Clergy survey.** Over one hundred questionnaires were mailed to clergy in two counties to ascertain their knowledge and perceptions of the community mental health system.
- **Client utilization study.** The characteristics of present and past clients of the mental health system were examined. Potential groups who were not being served (for example, minorities, low-income families) were of special interest. This client utilization data was felt to be so useful that it was subsequently prepared in an annual report for several successive years.
- **Key informant study.** Representatives from thirty-five human service organizations were contacted by phone and letter about their perceptions of the community mental health system.
- **Community awareness survey.** Over three hundred respondents were contacted by telephone to discover the extent of their knowledge about the availability of local mental health services.

FINAL THOUGHTS

This chapter only scratches the surface of needs assessment. Should you expect to have to conduct a needs assessment in the near future, you may want to skip ahead and read the chapter on measurement tools and the discussion of sampling and sample sizes. Much of the information provided later in this book (such as data analysis) will also be relevant.

If you are going to use some type of survey or structured interview to obtain your data, more than likely you will need to design an instrument to standardize your questions and structure the types of responses you expect. Sometimes, however, it is possible to use an instrument that you find either in the literature or in an agency.

Usually, a committee or group contributes questions for needs assessments so that one person does not have to do all the conceptualizing. But often these committee members do not clearly articulate what they want to know. And, assembling questions from many individuals may give the final questionnaire a disjointed, uneven feel. Worse yet, it may be difficult or impossible to determine if your instrument is reliable. However, other than conducting a pilot test with a small sample to see how well the questionnaire works, most needs assessors do not concern themselves with reliability and validity issues.

If you conduct a needs assessment by using social indicators or rates developed by others, keep in mind that obtaining rough estimates of a population in need of service doesn't mean the needs assessment process is finished. How might the problem present itself? How might it be attacked? What additional information should be obtained? What else should the agency consider before making decisions about staffing and resource allocation?

How do you learn more about needs assessment? Start by reading some of the books and articles in the "References and Resources" section at the end of this chapter. Then try to find what else has been written on the topic since this book was published. Finally, brainstorm the project with as many different people as you can. Good ideas are bound to emerge.

QUESTIONS FOR CLASS DISCUSSION

1. On the hypothetical questionnaire designed by the parents' organization, would better information have been obtained if either of the following questions were substituted? Why or why not?
   a. Do you ever leave your elementary school age children alone after school without adult supervision? If yes, how often?
   b. In an average week, how many days per week do you leave your children alone after school without adult supervision?
2. List on the board several social agencies familiar to most of those in the class. What information are these agencies likely to collect on a routine basis, and how could this information be used for needs assessment purposes?
3. Bring in census data for your community. Choose a social service program that has recently been in the news, and brainstorm ways the census data could be used to assess the need for that program.
4. Have the class identify some social service need in the community, and then discuss various ways in which this need could be documented.
5. Discuss why surveying only people you know is likely to generate biased information. Discuss what shared events or characteristics people who know each other are likely to have in common.
6. Discuss how opinions may not reflect "true" need. For instance,

is the social problem of homelessness best attacked by constructing more overnight shelters? Would there be a difference in what the homeless say their needs are and what the average citizen might say are their needs? Which is the most important need of the homeless: vocational training, job opportunities, medical care, or shelter?

7. The management staff of a public housing project comes to you for assistance. They have been given a grant to train and empower resident leaders in an effort to build a sense of community and eliminate drug abuse problems. The Resident Councils are new, and their meetings are not well attended. The management staff is convinced that the housing project should have a new playground. They ask you to help them design a needs assessment process that will show this. What would you do in this situation?

MINI-PROJECTS:
EXPERIENCING EVALUATION FIRSTHAND

1. Choose an article on needs assessment from the references list. Write a brief paper identifying:
   a. useful information that you acquired.
   b. problems, bias, or limitations of the reported needs assessment.
   c. things you might have done differently if the needs assessment had been your responsibility.
2. For some human service program with which you are familiar, design a needs assessment using exclusively secondary data. Be sure to describe:
   a. the program.
   b. the purpose of the needs assessment.
   c. the data collection procedure.
   d. estimates of the amount of time and money that will be required.
   e. the advantages and disadvantages of the approach you will be using.
3. For some human service program with which you are familiar, design a needs assessment using some impressionistic approach. Be sure to describe:
   a. the program.
   b. the purpose of the needs assessment.
   c. the data collection procedure.
   d. estimates of the amount of time and money that will be required.
   e. the advantages and disadvantages of the approach you will be using.

4. For some human service program with which you are familiar, design a needs assessment using community surveys. Be sure to describe:
   a. the program.
   b. the purpose of the needs assessment.
   c. the data collection procedure.
   d. estimates of the amount of time and money that will be required.
   e. the advantages and disadvantages of the approach you will be using.
5. For some human service program with which you are familiar, design a needs assessment that combines secondary data, impressionistic, and community survey approaches. Be sure to describe:
   a. the program.
   b. the purpose of the needs assessment.
   c. the data collection procedure.
   d. estimates of the amount of time and money that will be required.
   e. the advantages and disadvantages of the approach you will be using.

REFERENCES AND RESOURCES

American Psychological Association. (1981). *Specialty guidelines for the delivery of services by counseling psychologists.* Washington, DC: APA.

Brazil, K., Cummings, R., and Vallance, D. (1993). Mental health needs of children and youth with learning disabilities: Overview of a community needs assessment. *Evaluation and Program Planning,* 16, 193–198.

Buttram, J.L. (1990). Focus groups: A starting point for needs assessment. *Evaluation Practice,* 11(3), 207–212.

Cherry, K.E., Keller, M.J., and Dudley, W.N. (1991). A needs assessment of persons with visual impairments: Implications for older adults and service providers. *Journal of Gerontological Social Work,* 17 (3/4), 99–123.

Cheung, K.M. (1993). Needs assessment experience among area agencies on aging. *Journal of Gerontological Social Work,* 19 (3/4), 77–93.

Ciarlo, J.A., and Tweed, D.L. (1992). Implementing indirect needs-assessment models for planning state mental health and substance abuse services. *Evaluation and Program Planning* 15(2), 195–210.

Ciarlo, J.A., Tweed, D.L., Shern, D.L., and Kirkpatrick, L.A. (1992). The Colorado social health survey of mental health service needs: Sampling, instrumentation, and major findings. *Evaluation and Program Planning,* 15 (2), 133–147.

Delbecq, A.L., Van de Ven, A.H., and Gustafson, H. (1975). *Group techniques for program planning: A guide to nominal group and delphi processes.* Glenview, IL: Scott, Foresman.

DeVillaer, M. (1990). Client-centered community needs assessment. *Evaluation and Program Planning*, 13, 211–219.

Fitzhugh, E.C., Wang, M.Q., Eddy, J.M., and Westerfield, C. (1993). A risk-rated approach to a worksite health promotion needs assessment. *Health Values*, 17 (5), 57.

Ford, J., Young, D., Perez, B.C., Obermeyer, R.L., and Rohner, D.G. (1992). Needs assessment for persons with severe mental illness: What services are needed for successful community living? *Community Mental Health Journal*, 28 (6), 491–503.

Hakim, S., and Weinblatt, J. (1993). The Delphi process as a tool for decision-making: The case of vocational training of people with handicaps. *Evaluation and Program Planning*, 16, 25–38.

Hall, O., and Royse, D. (1987). Mental health needs assessment with social indicators: An empirical case study. *Journal of Mental Health Administration*, 15 (1), 36–46.

Harlow, K.S., and Turner, M.J. (1993). State units and convergence models: Needs assessment revisited. *Gerontologist*, 33 (2), 190–199.

Hoalt, P.N. (1992). A needs assessment evaluation as a basis for training of hospice volunteers. *Dissertation Abstracts International*, 53 (2-A), 414.

Hornick, J.P., and Burrows, B. (1988). Program evaluation. In R.M. Grinnell, Jr. (ed.), *Social work research and evaluation*. Itasca, IL: Peacock.

Humm-Delgado, D., and Delgado, M. (1986). Gaining community entree to assess service needs of Hispanics. *Social Casework*, 67 (2), 80–89.

Kids Count Data Book. (1994). Baltimore, MD: Annie E. Casey Foundation.

Krueger, R.A. (1993). *Focus groups: A practical guide for applied research*. Newbury Park, CA: Sage.

Lewis, J.A., and Lewis, M.D. (1991). *Management of human service programs*. Montery, CA: Brooks/Cole.

McKillip, J. (1987). *Need analysis: Tools for the human services and education*. Beverly Hills, CA: Sage.

Meissen, G.J., Gleason, D.F., and Embree, M.G. (1991) An assessment of the needs of mutual-help groups. *American Journal of Community Psychology*, 19 (3). 427–442.

Nguyen, T.D., Attkisson, C.C., and Bottino, M.J. (1983). The definition and identification of human service needs in a community. In Roger A. Bell, Martin Sundel, Joseph F. Aponte, Stanley A. Murrell, and Elizabeth Lin (eds.), *Assessing health and human service needs: Concepts, methods, and applications*. New York: Human Sciences Press.

Pecora, P. J. (1989). Improving the quality of child welfare services: Needs assessment for staff training. *Child Welfare*, 68 (4), 403–420.

Pillemer, K., and Finkelhor, D. (1988). The prevalence of elder abuse: A random sample survey. *Gerontologist*, 28 (1), 51–57.

Radecki, S.E., Berstein, G.S. (1990). An assessment of contraceptive need in the inner city. *Family Planning Perspectives*, 22 (3), 122–127, 144.

Raskin, M.S. (1994). The Delphi study in field instruction revisited: Expert consensus on issues and research priorities. *Journal of Social Work Education*, 30 (1), 75–89.

Royse, D. (1986). Community perceptions of quality of care and knowledge of specific CMHC services. *Journal of Marketing for Mental Health*, 1 (1), 151–166.

Royse, D., and Drude, K. (1982). Mental health needs assessment: Beware of false promises. *Community Mental Health Journal*, 18 (2), 97–106.

Rutz, M., and Shemberg, K.M. (1985). Fifth and sixth graders' attitudes toward mental health issues. *Journal of Community Psychology*, 13, 393–401.

Shayne, V.T., and Kinney, T.J. (1986). An employee assistance program needs assessment. *Journal of Continuing Social Work Education*, 3 (4), 40–51.

Shifman, L., Scott, C.S., and Fawcett, N. (1986). Utilizing a game for both needs assessment and learning in adolescent sexuality education. *Social Work with Groups*, 9(2), 41–56.

Siegel, L.M., Attkisson, C.C., and Carson, L.G. (1978). Need identification and program planning in the community context. In C.C. Attkisson, W.A. Hargreaves, and M.J. Horowitz (eds.), *Evaluation of human service programs*. New York: Academic Press.

Simeone, R.S., Frank, B., and Aryan, Z. (1993). Needs assessment in substance misuse: A comparison of approaches and case study. *International Journal of the Addictions*, 28 (8), 767–792.

Smith, R.R., Paskewicz, C.W., Evans, J.H., and Milan, M.A. (1986). Development, implementation, and results of a correctional mental health professional training needs assessment. *Journal of Offender Counseling, Services, and Rehabilitation*, 11 (1), 95–106.

Stafford, B., and Stafford, L.J. (1991). The building blocks of a quality day treatment program: The needs assessment. *International Journal of Partial Hospitalization*, 7 (2), 161–169.

Stefl, M.E. (1984). Community surveys in local needs assessment projects: Lessons from a case study. *Administration in Mental Health*, 12 (2), 110–122.

Stefl, M.E., and Prosperi, D. C. (1985). Barriers to mental health services. *Community Mental Health Journal*, 21 (3), 167–177.

Sullivan, C.M., Basta, J., Tan, C., and Davidson, W.S. (1992). After the crisis: A needs assessment of women leaving a domestic violence shelter. *Violence and Victims*, 7 (3), 267–275.

Sundel, M. (1983). Conducting needs assessment in a community mental health center. In Roger A. Bell, Martin Sundel, Joseph F. Aponte, Stanley A. Murrell, and Elizabeth Lin (eds.), *Assessing health and human service needs: Concepts, methods, and applications*. New York: Human Sciences Press.

Sung, Kyu-taik. (1989). Converging perspectives of consumers and providers in assessing needs of families. *Journal of Social Service Research*, 12 (3/4), 1–29.

Thompson, R.W., Ruma, P.R., Authier, K.J., and Bouska, T.C. (1994). Application of a community needs assessment survey to decategorization of child welfare services. *Journal of Community Psychology*, 22, 33–42.

Toomey, B.G., First, R.J., Greenlee, R., and Cummins, L.K. (1993). Counting the rural homeless population: Methodological dilemmas. *Social Work Research and Abstracts*, 29 (4), 23-27.

Tweed, D.L., and Ciarlo, J.A. (1992). Social-indicator models for indirectly assessing mental health service needs: Epidemiological and statistical properties. *Evaluation and Program Planning*, 15 (2), 165-179.

Tweed, D.L., Ciarlo, J.A., Kirkpatrick, L.A., and Shern, D.L. (1992). Empirical validity of indirect mental health needs assessment models in Colorado. *Evaluation and Program Planning*, 15 (2), 181-194.

Warheit, G.J., Bell, R.A., and Schwab, J.J. (1977). *Planning for change: Needs assessment approaches*. Rockville, MD: National Institute of Mental Health.

Weiner, H.R. (1993). Multi-function needs assessment: The development of a functional assessment instrument. *Psychosocial Rehabilitation Journal*, 16 (4), 51-61.

Wright, B., Thyer, B.A., and DiNitto, D. (1985). Health and social welfare needs of the elderly: A preliminary study. *Journal of Sociology and Social Welfare*, 12, 431-439.

THREE

Qualitative Evaluation: Formative and Process Evaluation, Program Monitoring, and Quality Assurance

Let's assume that the needs assessment and planning for the new program you wanted to start have been completed. The program has been implemented and has now been in operation about three months. If we were to talk to the staff, they probably would acknowledge that there are still some "rough edges" to the program due to its newness. Perhaps a few disgruntled clients have made complaints, and the agency director wants to initiate some sort of program review or evaluation. You are called into the director's office to design a process for obtaining some constructive feedback on the program. The agency director is committed to making the program successful and wants a program that the community will be proud of. Since the concern is not whether to continue or discontinue the program, but how to improve the program, what type of evaluation will you recommend to the agency director? How would you go about designing an evaluation that is concerned solely with program improvement?

FORMATIVE EVALUATION

Formative evaluation ought to be your recommendation to the agency director. Formative evaluations are employed to adjust and enhance interventions. They are not used to prove whether a program is worth

51

the funding it receives but serve more to guide and direct programs—particularly new programs. For this reason, formative evaluations are not as threatening and are often better received by agency staff than other forms of evaluation.

A good analogy for formative evaluation would be an experienced driving instructor sitting beside a beginning driver. If you have taught anyone to drive recently (or can objectively remember your own initial experiences), you may recall the beginning driver's jerky steering movements and sudden accelerations and decelerations. The driving instructor helps the beginner become a more skillful driver by observing the process of driving and making constructive suggestions. The instructor is more concerned with the process than with any particular destination. Once driving skills have been acquired, it is assumed that the driver will be more likely to reach his or her destination.

Formative evaluations, however, are not limited to new programs. Managers of well-established programs may request formative evaluations in an effort to "fine-tune" their programs. For instance, Velasquez, Kuechler, and White (1986) described a formative program evaluation system that operated for a number of years for 180 mental health and social service programs provided directly or purchased by a county Community Human Services Department in Minnesota. Among the purposes of the evaluation system were these:

—to improve program performance by providing information on strengths and weaknesses to those who manage these programs;

—to inform the planning and funding decisions which had been delegated to the local level. (P. 69)

The purpose of the formative evaluation is to provide feedback and influence a program's ongoing development. It stands to reason that formative evaluation is conducted during the running of a program and not at its conclusion (Chambers, 1994).

In fact, Dehar, Casswell, and Duignan (1993) discuss activities for the formative evaluator that should take place before the program begins: helping to develop and refine the program model, objectives, and strategies; reviewing the research literature; conducting needs assessments; pretesting program materials; and piloting of interventions. Once the program is implemented, the formative evaluator obtains feedback from participants in order to assess initial program effects.

The formative evaluator looks at interactions between clients and practitioners, management strategies and philosophies, and the costs

52

associated with a program (Chelimsky, 1985). This type of evaluation can be used to determine if a new or pilot program has been implemented as planned. Formative evaluations reveal "what services were provided, to whom, when, how often, and in what settings (Moskowitz, 1989). Such evaluations are often considered "internal" agency business. Both strengths and weaknesses of a program may be identified.

Formative evaluation does not rely upon a specific methodology or set of procedures. Instead, its focus is on acquiring information that would be useful for program improvement—whatever that would be. This information may come from interviewing staff or clients, reviewing records and progress notes, or participant observation. One could expect formative evaluators to look for glitches, breakdowns, lengthy delays, and departures from program design. They may find such problems as communication difficulties among staff or between the administration and staff, poor client participation in a program, or a need for additional in-service training to standardize what is provided as an intervention.

There is no single recipe for formative evaluation. How you would go about conducting one is somewhat dependent upon the program, your preferences, the agency, and the context of the request for a formative evaluation. Let's see what options are available in the following example.

Assume that you are the manager of a new residential program that is funded to teach independent living skills to adults with chronic mental health problems. The house has been open about six months and accommodates fourteen people—seven men and seven women. The halfway house's board of directors has discussed conducting an evaluation of the residential program. However, no definite plans ever developed because of disagreement over what kind of "success" they should expect. While one goal could be to have 100 percent of the residents learn the necessary skills to enable them to live independently, this is unrealistic given the residents' chronic mental illness. Most residents can be expected to be rehospitalized several times within any thirty-six month period.

Last month there was a tragedy. One of the male residents was killed in an accident with a freight train. The engineer said that when the train came around a bend he saw the resident sitting on the track. The engineer blew a warning whistle and braked the train but was unable to stop in time. He also indicated that the resident seemed to make no effort to get up. Later it was found that the resident had been drinking. It is not clear whether the resident was drunk and disoriented or whether this was a suicide.

The community's perception was that the resident had not been supervised closely enough and that the program was at fault. However, the staff were not aware of any suicidal tendencies the resident may have had. Prior communications between the residential program staff and the local community mental health center seem to have been rather limited. The board of directors now wants to examine this program in-depth in order to improve it and to prevent any other unfortunate occurrences.

Knowing that the goal of formative evaluation is not to provide any sort of "final" or summative evaluation but to organize information needed for program improvement, where would you start a formative evaluation of this program?

CONDUCTING A FORMATIVE EVALUATION

At least three different ways to approach this formative evaluation come to mind. Faced with such a scenario, an evaluator could recommend any one or a combination of approaches.

Approach 1: Locate Model Standards

If standards for similar programs have been developed or proposed by national accrediting or advocacy groups, then the local program could be compared against these standards and any discrepancies identified. This approach is frequently used by governmental units that fund, license, or oversee human services. When there are written standards, these are often put into the form of a checklist, and evaluators can monitor compliance with the standards and identify any areas of deficiency. This approach appears to work best when the expectations are easily defined (a window in each bedroom, a fire-escape from the second floor, and fire extinguishers every fifty feet). Standards are not so helpful when they are vague or difficult to operationalize (as when they state that a program should provide "adequate recreational opportunities").

We wish we could tell you that standards exist for every type of human service program that you might need to evaluate. Unfortunately, it is more likely that you will find the situation is somewhat "hit or miss." In some human service fields there are well-developed and substantive standards. In other areas, there are no or only minimal standards. However, you may find that standards developed for one human service program can be utilized for a similar but different program. For instance, the Child Welfare League of America has prepared standards for various programs. In the example of a residential program for the severely mentally ill, one set of standards that might prove useful to review (in the absence of more applicable standards) is entitled *Standards for Residential*

Care Centers for Children. Every residential program faces some of the same issues. For instance, facilities must have safe and effective heating systems, and they must safely store flammable and potentially dangerous materials. Residents must have their own beds and storage space, nutritional meals need to be provided, and so on. With a little bit of luck, an evaluator may be able to find a set of standards that can be adopted or slightly modified to fit the local program of interest.

If several phone calls to state or national organizations fail to produce worthwhile standards, try university libraries as resources of information. You might come upon a program evaluation in a review of professional journals that would provide useful "standards" that you can use to gauge a local program. For instance, an article reviewing the literature on inpatient alcoholism treatment may have found that the average relapse rate in five separate programs across the country was 48 percent during the first six months after discharge. If your local inpatient program was experiencing a 78 percent relapse rate within the first six months, this may be a strong indication of the need for a more in-depth formative evaluation.

Professional literature is always a source of potentially useful standards or benchmarks. Even if no "standards" are directly mentioned, a journal article might discuss how one agency dealt with the problem of suicide among halfway house residents. Even marginally relevant articles may contain the name of an agency or an "expert" who could be contacted to provide consultation for your program.

Approach 2: Get Expert Consultation

With this approach you might seek out consultation from a recognized expert or from a program with a solid reputation. A person of some authority—the director or program director—from the program could be asked to conduct a site visit of your program. The consultant could review operating policies and procedures, interview residents, staff, and board members, and make suggestions for improvement by making comparisons with his or her own program or some other "model" program. (The standards in this instance may be more informal than formal if they are drawn from the consultant's experience.) If money to pay the consultant is problematic, a low-cost alternative would be free consultation from the appropriate state officials who have an interest in the success of your program (e.g., the state department for mental health). It is not unusual for small agencies to have virtually no money for expert consultation. Since the perceived quality of the free consultation may be expected to vary considerably from community to community, and with no funds for consultation, some evaluators may be interested in still a third approach.

Approach 3: Form an Ad Hoc Evaluation Committee

This committee could be composed of halfway house staff, board members, professionals from the community, and other concerned persons. The committee might begin by interviewing staff and then move to residents and their family members, staff at the community mental health center, and other professionals in the community. Some or all of the committee members could visit other residential programs. If this is not economically feasible, the committee could write to other programs asking for copies of their policies and operating procedures. From reviewing these, new policies or procedures may be developed as the evaluation committee devise their own set of standards for the residential program. The committee may identify a number of areas or discrepancies that, in their opinion, need to be addressed so that the program can conform to local expectations.

It is impossible to predict what might come from a formative evaluation using one of these three approaches. The ad hoc evaluation committee may find that the program needs additional staff on weekends and recommend procedures for more closely monitoring residents. The same committee might find that the program lacks vocational and recreational activities and recommend increased activities in these areas. Some formative evaluation recommendations may come from examining the operation of different programs, while others may be based upon the opinions of a single "expert."

Even a not very astute consultant may be able to diagnose poor communication between the residential program and the community mental health center. Such perceptions may be admittedly subjective, but accurate. Because the staff who work day-to-day on a program are so close to it, it is not unusual for staff to be blind to certain areas where their programs could benefit from improvement. (This may be particularly true in those environments where staff are tremendously overworked.) Formative evaluations often bring in experts or outsiders in order to obtain fresh perspectives so that the existing program can be seen in a new or different light.

It is not always necessary to bring in expensive experts to provide formative evaluation. Sometimes, other concerned professionals in the community can provide useful insights. Occasionally, students have told me "horror stories" about program administration. Two instances where common sense should have prevailed come readily to mind. One former student was interning at a shelter for battered women. The shelter had a telephone, but because of concern that expensive long-distance phone calls would be charged to it, the phone was programmed to make only local calls. Whenever a long-distance call had to be placed, these victims of domestic violence had to go to a pay phone at a gas station down the block. This procedure placed in jeopardy those women who were attempting to avoid men who had assaulted them. It does not take a nationally prominent domestic violence expert to recognize procedures that place sheltered women in jeopardy and need revision.

In a second example, another graduate student told me of a residential program for children that had such an intricate and detailed admissions process that three to four weeks were often required to complete it. This certainly worked to the agency's disadvantage when, one summer, the agency had about 20 percent of its beds vacant at one time. Meanwhile, children in need of admission remained at risk in dangerous settings and without treatment because of the bottleneck in the admissions process. Again, it doesn't take a very high-powered expert to realize that the admissions process needed to be streamlined. Where cost is a major concern, it may be possible to ask friends who are social workers or other human service professionals to spend a day or two with your program in order to get some inexpensive, but potentially sound, common sense feedback that could be called a formative evaluation.

PROCESS EVALUATION

Formative evaluations are sometimes referred to as process evaluations when the focus is not the final product but the intervention. One major difference is that while a formative evaluation seeks to influence the ongoing development of a program, a process evaluation can be conducted anytime during a project—even at its end.

Why would anyone want to conduct a process evaluation at the end of a project? Process evaluations are typically required for research and demonstration projects because sponsors want to know what was learned during the implementation of the project. Such information could be valuable to other communities considering whether to start such a program.

In my community, an agency developed a proposal to recruit African-American men to serve as mentors for minority teenagers. In the original proposal, the agency specified that eighty mentors would be developed, and each would be matched with an adolescent. This proved to be a lot tougher than the agency expected. By the project's end, less than half the desired number of mentors had been obtained.

57

In this instance, process evaluators would look at the activities used to recruit mentors (for example, public service announcements, speaking with ministers of black churches)—what the project staff found that had worked and what was a waste of time. Process evaluation might also look at other problems encountered, such as difficulties in presenting the project to teenagers or their parents or in securing referrals from school counselors and other human service professionals in the community. Process evaluation informs others about what they might expect if they were to launch a similar program.

Another purpose of process evaluation is to assist in explaining why a program did or did not achieve expected outcomes. For example, a large statewide agency wanted to test whether the use of peer volunteers was more effective in reducing subsequent hospitalizations than a new procedure where clients with severe mental illness were assisted in developing a crisis support plan.

Three different sites were selected from across the state, and staff received all necessary training. Four years later, at the project's end, a process evaluation revealed that (1) some staff did not complete crisis plans with their clients—evidently because they were not aware of the necessity to do so; (2) there had been no additional training of staff after the first year; (3) monitoring of clinical records for clients without crisis support plans also was lacking.

Further, while most clients reported good experiences with their volunteers, the use of volunteers was not a standardized intervention. That is, there was tremendous variation in the volunteers' activities, responsibilities, and the amount of contact they had with assigned clients. Clients may have had daily, weekly, monthly, or only twice a year contact with a volunteer.

Obviously, even these brief observations would be important to other agencies contemplating similar projects with volunteers and crisis support plans. They surely would want to ensure greater use of crisis support plans by providing ongoing training and closer monitoring of staff's completion of these plans. Additionally, to make the interventions of volunteers more uniform, they would need to specify minimum requirements—for example, each volunteer meeting thirty minutes each week face-to-face with his or her assigned client. And, like the other recommendation, the amount of time volunteers spend with their clients should be carefully recorded and monitored.

Because process evaluations document the operations of a program, they are essential to those who want to replicate the program. Process evaluations provide the data necessary to judge the intensity and reliability with which services were delivered; they rely heavily upon data normally captured by agencies. For further detail, examples of the types of information a process evaluator might want to examine are suggested in *Evaluation Guidebook*, prepared by the U.S. Department of Health and Human Services, Office of Community Services (1992).

While the list in Box 3.1 will give you some idea of where to start your information gathering, it will by no means suggest *every* type of material that will be useful. In the project involving peer volunteers and crisis plans mentioned earlier, we interviewed consumers, staff, and volunteers. We asked open-ended questions such as:

1. If the program could be started all over again, what changes would you make?
2. How could the proactive crisis plans be made more useful?
3. What difficulties or obstacles did you encounter as a volunteer?
4. Were you better off or worse off as a result of having a volunteer?

With a mentoring project it would make sense to obtain feedback from mentors as well as students and their parents. Because we wanted

---

BOX 3.1
Types of Data Useful in Process Evaluation

1. Client socio-demographic characteristics
2. Client service usage (type and amount of services received)
3. Referral sources
4. Staff characteristics
   professional degrees
   length of experience
   socio-demographics
5. Program activities
   special events and meetings
   staff meetings
   training provided
6. Minutes of board, staff, and committee meetings
7. Correspondence and internal memos concerning the project
8. Client outcome data
9. Client satisfaction data
10. Financial data; program costs and expenditures

---

to capture anecdotal accounts from mentors about their good and bad experiences, we supplied them with notebooks that they could use like diaries. Unfortunately, few of the mentors recorded anything. We also attempted to get information from mentors about the number of hours a week they met with their charges and the kinds of activities in which they engaged. However, this effort was also not successful. Because an evaluator's struggles to acquire information about a project are not always productive, don't be opposed to trying innovative ways of getting information. An assistant once recommended that we photocopy pages from a calendar each month and mail them to the mentors to jog their memories regarding the amount of time they spent with their students. Realistically, though, better data seems to result whenever it is routinely generated by an agency or program.

When using surveys, evaluators can be limited by a low response rate, too small a sample, or a poorly designed questionnaire. But every agency collects data on its clients. From this data, process evaluators can learn if a program is reaching its intended target and the extent to which staff and clients are participating in a program.

Program monitoring can be valuable to the process evaluator who is trying to understand what happened in a program and to whom. The novice evaluator should not develop the opinion that program monitoring is conducted *only* when a process evaluation has been requested. Ongoing program monitoring is essential to the sound management of all programs.

PROGRAM MONITORING

Like formative and process evaluation, program monitoring is a basic form of program evaluation. Why is it so elemental? Because a program that is not reaching its intended population is misdirected—perhaps duplicating services to a population already well served. Further, it makes no sense to conduct a more sophisticated evaluation to determine if the intervention worked when it was not applied to the population in need.

Program monitoring does not require elaborate research designs nor does it usually require an advanced understanding of statistics. Often program monitoring starts with examining a program's specific goals and objectives and compares these with the kind of data that most human service agencies routinely collect—what we previously discussed as patterns of use and client utilization data (chapter 2). This data is "monitored" to ensure that the program is serving those for whom it was designed. It is entirely possible that with the passage of time a program may somehow get diverted and not serve the population originally targeted.

Changes occur in practically all programs. Once the initial excitement of starting a new program has worn away, staff and agency resources may be siphoned off or redirected as newer, more urgent problems come along. As the original staff take other jobs, retire, become promoted, or move to other programs, incoming staff may have different notions as to what the program should accomplish or to whom it should be directed. Subtle, almost imperceptible changes in staff, the program philosophy, the composition of the clientele, or the orientation of new employees can result in programs departing significantly from what was first proposed.

It is crucial that conscientious program managers, administrators, and agency boards of directors continuously monitor the progress of programs. Only poor management would benevolently ignore a new program for ten or eleven months, and then at the end of the funding period attempt to hold the program staff and its manager accountable. To insure that a program serves the target population in the manner expected by the funding source, regular program monitoring is required. Unlike formative evaluations which tend to be single-episode evaluations and others that we'll discuss later, program monitoring ought to be ongoing. Program monitoring should be thought of as a routine activity where a program director reviews patterns of use data on a regular basis (more often than once a year). Routine monitoring can reveal problems before they become overwhelming and track progress toward meeting the sponsor's or agency's expectations.

Becoming a Program Monitor

Human service programs exist to provide either goods or services to clientele. Some programs provide tangible goods: food (soup kitchens), beds (emergency shelter), or clothing. Other programs provide services where the products are more intangible (counseling, mental health education or prevention services, self-esteem groups).

Regardless of whether the client/consumer receives a tangible or intangible product, there is always something that can be counted. For instance, a child protection agency may provide homemaker services to 189 families during the course of a year. This same agency may complete forty-two adoptions, approve sixty-four foster homes, and provide 1,195 hours of individual or group therapy. Each of these program products can be used to provide some measure of accountability. The agency director may be unhappy with the provision of homemaker services to only 189 families, because she had hoped that two hundred families would receive homemaker services. On the other hand, the director may be pleased (since there had been major staff turnover in the program) that sixty-four foster homes were approved. (At one point it looked as if only fifty foster homes might be inspected and approved.)

The first step in program monitoring consists of deciding what program products, events, or activities are important enough to count. Not every activity associated with a program is important enough to monitor. For example, we've never seen an annual report that listed the number of times that the stapler was used. It may not be important to count the number of times that calls are placed. However, if you are the manager of a telephone crisis hotline or a telephone information and referral service, it may be important to keep records on the number of telephone contacts categorized by problem (for example, suicidal ideation, drug use, or unexpected pregnancies).

Just because something can be counted does not mean that it *ought* to be counted. Once we came across a report of a telephone counseling service that recorded daily (by shift) the number of telephone calls received by problem area. Even though they used twenty or so categories to log the type of call, about 15 percent of the calls fell into the miscellaneous category. We found this strange since, in our opinion, they already had too many categories. As we investigated a little more, we learned that they were counting incoming phone calls that might be best described as "personal." A mechanic might call to report that a staff member's car had been repaired, or a child would call a parent at work upon arriving home from school. While these calls may have been important to the person receiving them, counting them in the monthly service report gave the appearance that the telephone hotline was actually a lot busier than it was. Counting these calls could not tell us anything important about whether the program was providing the type of service originally planned. So, while there was accountability, counting for the sake of counting led to some inane results.

Mission Statements, Goals, and Objectives

In deciding what is important to count or monitor, it is helpful to become familiar with the agency's mission statement. **Mission statements** are statements of purpose—they explain what the agency is all about. Mission statements provide a common vision for the organization, a point of reference for all major planning decisions; they answer the question, "Why do we exist?" Mission statements not only provide clarity of purpose to persons within an organization, but also help gain understanding and support from those people outside the organization who are important to its success (Below, Morrisey, and Acomb, 1987). If you are in an agency that does not have a formal mission statement, or if you find it necessary to draft one, start by looking at the agency's charter, constitution, or by-laws. These documents describe the purpose behind the creation of an agency. Four examples of agency mission statements follow.

> The mission of the Northern County Victims' Assistance Program is to provide assistance to individuals who have been victims of felony crimes in Northern County. This assistance will be directed at the devastating emotional and psychological consequences that victims of crime and their families experience.

> [Excerpt from the Mission Statement of a Catholic Social Service Bureau] Our mission calls us to live out the interdependent values of love and justice, to lift oppression, and heal brokenness of individuals and families, of groups, and of society itself.

> The mission of the Western County Mental Health Board is to improve the quality of life in our community by promoting mental health, by preventing and reducing mental and emotional problems, substance abuse problems, and by minimizing their residual effects.

> It is the purpose of KET, a unique communications resource linking all Kentuckians by television, to be an institution of learning for children and adults of every age and need, a statewide town hall through which interested citizens can together explore issues of mutual significance, a performance stage for the outstanding talent of Kentucky and the great artists of the world, and a catalyst for uniting the citizens of the Commonwealth in common purpose to solve common problems and to stimulate growth and progress for all.

As can be seen from these examples, mission statements are not going to tell you exactly how they will go about their business or when they expect to complete their missions. But, they do inform as to the nature of the organization. One can readily deduce the religious orientation of the agency in the second example. Mission statements are useful in that they communicate the agency's purpose and they express values, suggesting what is important for the agency to address with its resources. Mission statements are usually stated in somewhat vague terms. They are not specific as to what types of services will be provided or how the client will get those services. How important are mission statements? Sugarman (1988), in listing six major criteria that define a well-managed human service organization, noted that the first characteristic is "a clearly defined mission or purpose, well-understood by its members, and it has goals and plans based thereon" (p. 19).

Occasionally it becomes necessary for an agency to change its mission. Perhaps the best example of this is the March of Dimes. This agency was created because of the problem of polio (an infantile paralysis caused by a virus). With advances in research, vaccines were discovered and the disease has now been virtually eliminated. The March of Dimes continues to exist, however, but its mission is now to fight birth defects. Whenever there is a change of mission, there must be a corresponding change of program goals and objectives.

Goals follow from mission statements and also tend to be general and global with regard to activities and products. Patton (1982) noted that a goal statement should specify a program direction based on values, ideals, political mandates, and program purpose. Goals are not specific as to when or how something will be accomplished but speak instead to aspirations.

Goals provide the focus, orientation, and direction needed to harness the combined energy and activities of a staff so that chaos and confusion are minimized and clients' needs are served by the program. Imagine a team of horses hitched to a wagon. Then picture that same wagon with a team of horses attached to each of the four sides. Which wagon is likely to move, and which will go nowhere?

Many people make the mistake of thinking that goals have to be accomplished within a short period of time (perhaps even within one's lifetime). However, there is no such requirement. Many human service agencies have goals that will likely never be accomplished because they involve continuing needs. How many of the following goals do you feel it will be possible to attain?

1. The agency will eliminate *all* poverty.
2. The program will *prevent* child abuse and neglect.
3. The hospital will *rehabilitate* persons who have problems with alcohol.
4. The university will *strengthen* its commitment to scholarship and academic excellence.

It is perfectly acceptable for an agency or institution to have broad goals that they may never reach. An agency (or a program for that matter) has not failed when a goal is not achieved; the reason is that the goals that human service agencies typically set are not easy to achieve.

Unlike mission statements and goals, **objectives** are specific and precise. Objectives allow us to measure progress being made toward the achievement of a goal. They declare what will be accomplished by a certain date. Objectives should have a single aim and an end-product or result that is easily verifiable. Drucker (1980) notes that program objectives such as "to aid the disadvantaged" or "to provide health care" are sentiments (and vague ones at that) explaining why a program was initiated rather than what it was meant to accomplish. He continues:

> To have a chance at performance, a program needs clear targets, the attainment of which can be measured, appraised, or at least judged. . . . Even "the best medical care for the sick," the objective of many hospitals in the British National Health Service, is not operational. Rather, it is meaningful to say: "It is our aim to make sure that no patient coming into emergency will go for more than three minutes without being seen by a qualified triage nurse." (P. 231)

Patton (1982) makes the distinction of separating the concept (the goal) from the measurement of it (the objective). We find this a useful way to think about the differences between the two. If you are still unclear, look carefully at the examples of objectives that follow.

1. To increase admissions from minority clients by five percent per year in each of the next three years.
2. To reduce the number of recidivists by 20 percent by June 30, 1998.
3. To have 50 percent of all clients still attending weekly AA meetings six months after the end of treatment.
4. To provide two thousand individual counseling sessions to clientele by the end of the calendar year.

When objectives are properly developed, they leave little doubt about what will be done and the date when its accomplishment can be expected. To be useful, objectives must specify events or activities that can be independently determined. In the fourth example above, for instance, it should be relatively easy to establish whether the program came close to providing the two thousand individual counseling sessions.

Writing Specific Program Objectives

To write an objective that provides some measure of accountability (so that it can be determined whether or not the objective was met), think in terms of activities that can be counted or observed. The objective should state what will be accomplished and when it can be expected. A model for writing specific objectives is as follows:

To	*increase*	*admissions 10 percent*	by *June 30, 1998.*
	(verb)	(specific target)	(date)

Some examples of verbs that are useful when writing objectives are:

To increase, add, develop, expand, enlarge
To decrease, reduce, lessen, diminish
To promote, advertise, publicize
To start, create, initiate, begin, establish

However, the choice of the verb may not be as critical as ensuring that the reader can visualize a measurable result. The use of vague terms can make it difficult to determine if the results were obtained. Avoid such language as is contained in the following program objectives:

To help clients discover healthier relationships with others.
To help clients develop an appreciation of etiquette.
To help students become better citizens.
To assist clients in getting their lives back together.
To increase the community's support of _____.
To improve clients' understanding of themselves.
To help families learn about alcohol and alcoholism.

All of the above objectives share the same problem—they lack specificity. They do not inform as to how much has to be learned, developed, or understood. (How would we know if clients had improved their understanding of themselves?) Also, they do not provide any indication of dates when these events will be accomplished. There is also no way of knowing exactly when the objective should be accomplished—the target event that should allow independent verification is too vague or absent.

Sometimes agency directors and program managers, in an effort to make their programs look good, write objectives that will be too easily achieved. Monitoring bodies can contribute to this situation. We once saw an evaluation form that contained these two questions: "Did the project achieve its objectives?" and "How many of the project's objectives were realized?" Every program manager would like to say that he or she accomplished 100 percent of the program's objectives. If there is no assessment of the quality of these objectives, program managers may write only objectives that they know they can meet. Setting objectives too low results only in pointless "busywork." If a program provided 2,200 units of individual counseling one year, then it should be expected to exceed that number in the next year. (The exception to this rule is when

Table 3.1
Client Utilization Data, Acceptall Counseling Services, Inc.

Variable	1994	1995	1996	1997	1990 Census
Widowed	3%	3.6%	2.5%	2.3%	4.95%
Over 60 years old	4%	4.5%	5.5%	5.2%	14.75%
Minority	5%	5.5%	6.3%	6.5%	13.25%

the program expects to lose a significant amount of staff, funding, or other resources.) Objectives should be set high enough to challenge the staff. They should not be impossible to obtain, but they ought to cause the staff to stretch a bit, to work a little harder, or to find more creative ways of solving their problems.

Once program objectives have been developed, monitoring for managerial purposes is possible. When objectives are being developed for new programs, there may be a natural tendency to make conservative estimates of what can be accomplished. Rather than overestimate the number of clients who can be served in a year, program managers may be more likely to underestimate what can be done. These objectives can be tempered by reality if data exist for the start-up phase of other formerly "new" programs. In the absence of such data, educated guesses are appropriate.

However, program monitoring really comes into play when programs have begun to generate service data. In the example from a counseling agency given in table 3.1, it is possible to identify groups that are not getting their "fair share" of the agency's resources.

As can be seen from the table, widowed persons, those over the age of sixty, and minorities are not represented in the agency clientele to the extent that would be expected from their proportions in the population. With just this much information, a program manager could develop the following objectives:

- **Objective 1:** To increase the percentage of widowed persons served by the program to 5 percent of the total clientele by December 31, 1998.
- **Objective 2:** Through special outreach efforts, to increase the number of older adults served by the program until 15 percent of the program's clients are sixty or older. This objective to be reached by July 1, 1998.
- **Objective 3:** By January 1, 1998, to double the number of minority clients served by the program in 1995.

With these objectives in place, the program manager and the program's staff now have a clear set of expectations for their future efforts. Once these objectives are met, new ones can be developed. If they are not met, corrective actions may be needed (providing there were no extenuating factors to explain the nonperformance). The setting of objectives provides a basis against which the program's accomplishment can be examined.

Because they are concerned with the logistical problems associated with getting programs started, program managers and agency administrators often write such program objectives as:

To hire a new receptionist for the XYZ program by July 10.
To write position descriptions for the six new program staff by August 1.
To secure another 4,000 square feet of office space downtown.

While these objectives may be viewed as being crucial to the success of a program, they are poor program objectives because they do not address the *performance* of the program. All of us understand that programs must have staff, office space, office furniture, and telephones. Having all of these things, however, does not necessarily make a quality program. Having a receptionist is not directly related to improving services provided to clients. Staff might, for instance, take advantage of the fact that a receptionist can intercept phone calls and extend their sixty minute lunch period to an hour and a half or longer each day. With the addition of a receptionist, clients could get less, rather than more, of a therapist's attention.

Administrators must think about such matters as hiring a new receptionist or caseworker or purchasing a new computer; however, this type of objective does not inform as to whether a program is performing as intended. For program monitoring purposes, objectives should address the consumers served, potential consumers, and products of a program—not what it takes to implement a program. Here's an illustration of this point.

Several years ago, a couple attended an open house at the school where their son was a seventh grade student. They were eager to meet their son's music appreciation teacher. Their son had been inundated by music word puzzles (where musical expressions were spelled backward and on the diagonal), and sometimes the boy spent an hour or more on a puzzle. The terms were often so esoteric that they couldn't help but wonder why it was necessary to learn them.

The music teacher, after introducing himself, said that all his students were "good" students and that they would all be getting A's or B's. He didn't seem to care whether the word puzzles were completed or not. He went on to say that he wanted students to "come alive" and interact with him. "One day," he said, "I brought a tennis ball to class, and we spent the entire period just bouncing the ball around." The couple left the open house with the strong impression that having a music teacher present in the classroom was no guarantee that the seventh graders would learn anything at all about music.

What Should Be Monitored?

Program monitoring is properly used to check a program's progress in meeting certain objectives (for example, increasing the number of minority admissions). In this sense, it is analogous to being told by your physician what kinds of things to monitor to maintain health. For instance, persons with a diagnosis of diabetes must monitor the amount of sugars and carbohydrates they consume. Persons with hypertension are told to monitor their salt intake. However, managers need not wait for their programs to become "ill" before employing program monitoring.

Program monitoring can be used most effectively in a diagnostic sense. Managers can use program monitoring to look for "symptoms" that would help them diagnose potential problems. What kinds of problems is difficult to state succinctly because of the enormous diversity in human service programs. They range from small, one-person programs to programs that employ hundreds of staff. Programs administered by the same agency in different locations may bear only a faint resemblance to one another. Every program can be expected to have a somewhat unique set of problems. Even similar programs are likely to have different problems. This is due to differences in staff composition, local (and often informal) policies and procedures, relationships with other professionals and agencies within the community, the guidance and leadership of the agency administrator, the amount of financial support, and such factors as the interest and involvement of the board of directors.

Veney and Kaluzny (1984) summarized the data appropriate for monitoring as inputs, process, and outputs. They described inputs as consisting of the resources by which the program is carried out. Resources include such categories as project staff, office space, and office equipment and supplies. With regard to inputs, the important thing to monitor is the amount budgeted for a program against what is actually used or allocated. For process, it is important to monitor the activities that were intended to be carried out during program implementation. Outputs are the results of the program—what the program actually produces.

Using this scheme, a manager might check to make sure that a program is not overspending its budget (or that it is getting all that it is entitled to); that planned activities are being conducted on a timely basis; and that regular accounting is being made of the number of service units produced (such as meals provided or other quantifiable products). Thus, a manager would know there were problems if the agency spent 75 percent of its budget by the half-year mark, if scheduled program activities were not being performed, or if the program started off providing 300 service units during the first month but fell off to only 125 service units during the second month.

Monitoring inputs, process, and outputs gives the program manager basic information needed to manage programs. However, this information may not be complete enough to allow a manager to "fine-tune" a program. A program could be meeting expectations in terms of its budget expenditures, its activities, and the number of products that were expected and still not be doing the job it was designed to do in terms of serving all facets of the population or community. This could come about because too little time was devoted to planning prior to program implementation, because of lack of management, or because of other reasons.

What other informational items might be helpful to monitor? For one, referral sources. The conscientious manager should monitor where referrals are coming from and in what proportion. It may be perfectly acceptable for a private counseling agency to have 92 percent of its clients self-referred. On the other hand, public agencies may want to see referrals coming from a broad spectrum of the community. The program manager in a public agency who notes that over a three month period of time no referrals have come from the criminal justice system may want to undertake some special efforts to insure that professionals in that system, who are in a position to refer, know whom to contact and how to make a referral. Similarly, there might be concern if physicians, clergy, or other human service agencies are not referring to the program—or are not referring in the proportion that one might expect.

A more refined level of program monitoring would examine the number of clients who drop out of the program. How many clients complete only one or two sessions? What proportion drop out by the third session? How many clients notify the program staff that they will not be returning? It is also important to know such things as how long it takes for clients to receive service from the time of their initial contact or application. Managers should know how many clients are on their waiting lists so that scheduling and programming can be planned accordingly.

Besides using program monitoring to determine if the obvious segments of the population are being served (older adults, low-income persons, minorities), program managers can determine if clients from remote geographical areas and those with special needs (such as persons who are mentally retarded or have physical handicaps) are being served. Additionally, program monitoring can inform as to whether there is an increase of clients with certain types of problems or diagnoses. If, for example, there is a significant increase in the number of clients reporting sexual abuse, this may necessitate training for the staff or require some other modification in the program. (Perhaps a support group for victims of sexual trauma should be started.) The discovery of a substantial number of clients addicted to crack cocaine may require either program modification or at least closer working ties with other agencies in the community. Examining client data by area of residence may indicate the need for a new satellite office.

Sorensen et al. (1987) have developed a set of twenty-five key performance indicators in four major areas (revenue, client, staff, and service mix) to assist managers and policymakers in assessing the performance of their programs relative to others. A sampling of these indicators includes: revenue per client, revenue collected as a percent of total charges, percent of severely mentally ill, average number of service units per F.T.E. (full-time equivalency), average caseload by program, total cost per unit of service, and total client turnover.

As management's use of program information increases, additional items, such as productivity of individual members of the staff, can be added to the items being monitored. As program managers make greater use of program information, oftentimes it becomes necessary to develop (or purchase) more sophisticated ways of managing data. Although the term **management information systems** can be applied to simple manual tabulations of service data, it has generally come to be associated with computerized systems. (For a good overview on how computers can benefit the social services, see Pardeck and Murphy, 1989, or Nurius and Hudson, 1993.)

Management information systems depend upon source documents (sometimes called service tickets) that record transactions such as the service a client received, the number of hours of service received or service units provided, the staff member involved, the location, the date, and so on (see Box 3.2). This information is useful for billing purposes as well as for understanding staff and program productivity.

Service tickets can be linked to a client's file containing the initial application data (sometimes called a "face sheet") or other forms containing the diagnosis and other pertinent information. Computerized

---

BOX 3.2
Example of a Service Ticket

McDowell Counseling Center

Service Ticket 10456   Today's Date _____
Therapist # _____   Client #_____
Time spent with client _____ hrs./_____ minutes
Program:_____
 01 Individual and Family Counseling
 02 Group Counseling
 03 Crisis Counseling (hotline only)
 04 Diagnostic Assessment
 05 Case Management
 06 Case Consultation
 07 Community Education
 08 Psychiatric Consultation
 09 Client Cancellation/No-Show
Next appointment date: Fee paid today $_____ . _____

---

information systems allow for the most sophisticated monitoring of service utilization because of the ease with which the computer can process large quantities of data. Examples of program monitoring questions that a management information system could answer are:

1. How many service units, on average, did clients with the diagnosis of bipolar disorder receive? (Or, what was the average length of stay for patients with bipolar disorder?)
2. Which unit produced the most counseling during the last quarter? (Alternatively, which worker was the least productive last pay period?)
3. What percent of the clients were able to pay the full fee?
4. Of those clients referred for services last month, how many were referred by the criminal justice system?
5. How many cancellations (or no-shows) were there last month? What were the characteristics of those who canceled and gave no notification? (Were they single mothers with small children or unemployed persons with no transportation?)

It should be noted that program monitoring data, while useful for some management purposes, does not necessarily inform as to the *quality* of care provided to the various groups of clients using the agency's services. While you may be pleased with a program because poor or minority clients were well represented in the clientele, this does not guarantee that the services they received actually helped them. Your program could be serving a large number of persons inadequately or inappropriately. By examining only the characteristics of those clients being served, you still have very little idea about how "good" the program is. When you want to know if the clients are better off as a result of being served by the program, then you need to shift from program monitoring to program evaluation models.

QUALITY ASSURANCE

Quality assurance is another basic form of evaluation that usually involves determining compliance with some set of standards. The term is often associated with ongoing reviews of medical or clinical care records, although more may be involved than this. Quality assurance aims to identify and correct deficiencies occurring in the process of providing care to consumers of services.

Certain services have well-established federal and state regulations. Medicare, for instance, has specific requirements for certified home health care. Agencies providing this service may also wish to meet the accreditation standards of organizations such as the National League for Nursing, the National Homecaring Council, and the Joint Commission on Accreditation of Healthcare Organizations (Eustis, Kane, and Fischer, 1993).

Accreditation standards exist for many, if not most, human services. By way of example, since April 1987, all psychiatric hospitals in the United States must meet the standards developed by the Joint Commission of Accreditation of Health Organizations (JCAHO). Some residential treatment agencies also seek to meet JCAHO's standards as well as those of other accrediting organizations such as the Commission on the Accreditation of Rehabilitation Facilities.

Typically, quality assurance standards require agencies to document for all their clients such information as:

- Presenting problem/diagnosis
- Treatment plan
- Frequency and length of treatment episodes
- Service modality/provider
- Drug prescriptions
- Discharge plans

From this information, reviewers can determine if admissions were appropriate, treatment was consistent with generally accepted practice, the least expensive alternative resources were used, and continuity of care and reasonable treatment follow-up were provided. Known in some agencies as "utilization review," these efforts are increasingly concerned with such issues as length of stay (in treatment) and ensuring that resource usage is fiscally justified.

Unfortunately, many social and human service organizations have considered this "medical model" of quality assurance to be synonymous with program evaluation. All too often, quality assurance has been conceptualized as and limited to checking whether a sampling of reviewed cases was essentially in conformity with accepted standards of care. Such efforts, however, do not indicate the extent to which a program is successful—whether clients improve as a result of intervention—or whether a program is worth funding again next year. Quality assurance efforts, by and large, focus almost exclusively on the process of treatment rather than on treatment outcome.

Because of the confusion that exists, it is necessary to briefly highlight the differences between quality assurance and program outcome evaluation as presented in the remainder of this book. First, quality assurance efforts often stem from legislative mandate. In 1972, amendments to the Social Security Act (P.L. 92–603) established Professional Standards Review Organizations (PSROs). The intent of this legislation was to establish peer review systems to assure that federal and state expenditures of Medicare, Medicaid, and the Maternal and Child Health Programs were spent on "medically necessary and high quality care" (Tash and Stahler, 1984). Second, clinicians tend to be involved in quality assurance efforts (peer reviews), whereas program evaluators are usually not a provider of the care that is being evaluated. Third, in quality assurance, recommendations are customarily relayed back to clinicians in order to improve the record-keeping process, whereas evaluation findings may or may not be given as feedback to the clinical staff and are more often used at the administrative level. Fourth, quality assurance often relies upon the expert opinion of peer reviewers and consensus that a sample of records met expected standards. Program evaluation methodologies tend to rely much less on peer review and more on quantitative data, research designs, the formal testing of hypotheses, and statistical analysis (Tash, Stahler, and Rappaport, 1982).

Having gone to all this trouble to convince you that quality assurance is not the same as program outcome evaluation, we would not want to leave you with the impression that quality assurance is a waste of time—it is not. It provides a degree of consistency and uniformity by

74

promoting adherence to clinical guidelines. When quality assurance standards are well established, and interventions relatively dependable and constant, the program evaluator has an easier time understanding the positive and negative effects of an intervention and such problems as clients who recidivate or relapse.

Even if quality assurance is not required within an agency, the conscientious manager may want to implement these activities in some form. Coulton (1987) has noted, "A successful organization continually looks for, finds, and solves problems. In this context, quality assurance—with its cycle of monitoring, in-depth problem analysis, and corrective action—serves as a self-correcting function within an organization" (p. 443). It is important for every agency providing direct intervention to clients to be able to identify such problems as: a large percentage of cases without treatment plans; initial assessments not providing enough information to substantiate diagnoses; inappropriate referrals or discharges; or an increase in discharges against clinical advice.

Some human service professionals resent the amount of time it takes to document what they have already done. Especially when caseloads are large, paperwork is an anathema. Workers may feel that time spent on paperwork is time taken away from needy clients. However, viewed from a manager's perspective, this "paperwork" is needed for a variety of reasons:

1. To protect clients from unethical or inappropriate treatment. Consider these "horror stories" of two consulting physicians whose contracts were canceled by different mental health agencies. At one center, the utilization review picked up a pattern of a physician overmedicating clients and using strange combinations of drugs that didn't seem to provide any benefit. Staff at the other center found that their consulting psychiatrist was diagnosing an inordinate number of clients as multiple personalities. In a more positive sense, quality assurance activities help to demonstrate that the organization cares about the services provided.
2. To protect staff from charges of inappropriate treatment or incompetence. (In this litigious society, the documentation of services rendered is some protection against unfair or untruthful claims.) Quality assurance data also can be used to identify reasons for patient dissatisfaction with services. Satisfied clients always help to improve the marketability of programs and services.
3. To recover reimbursements from insurance companies and other third parties. (As noted earlier, quality assurance activities are required by Medicare, Medicaid, and other third-party payors.)

75

4. To better plan for effective and efficient utilization of staff and agency resources. (Having such information as the average length of stay or the numbers of patients with certain diagnoses can help program managers evaluate special and unmet needs as well as better supervise staff whose cases exceed the average length of stay.)

Quality assurance efforts in an agency may be elaborate or fairly elementary. Box 3.3 provides a short checklist employed by the quality assurance office of a state social services department. Routinely, this office randomly selects cases from each of its district offices, reviews them, and where necessary asks for the records to be amended or corrected. Cases with deficiencies are clearly noted and returned to the caseworker's supervisor. Supervisors must then see that problems are corrected and report to the quality assurance office.

Once data such as this are collected on a regular basis, program evaluators and researchers can use it to explore various hypotheses— for instance, that employees in one division (for example, adoptions) obtain higher quality assurance ratings than those in another (such as adult protective services). We even went a step further and utilized this data and other information available to us to investigate whether those with social work degrees made better employees for the department than those without (Dhooper, Royse, and Wolfe, 1990).

IMPROVING QUALITY—RECENT THEMES

Green and Attkisson noted as early as 1984 that while program evaluation and quality assurance were distinctly different approaches, they were converging. They observed that quality assurance had embraced the criteria of efficiency or cost effectiveness of services (cost-containment in the medical field) and adequacy of services relative to the needs present in the population. At the same time, program evaluators were becoming more comfortable with incorporating qualitative methods into their evaluations.

In the last few years there has been a resurgence of interest in the quality of goods and services available to American consumers. Japanese industries, particularly automobile manufacturers, have popularized and demonstrated enormous success with a concept known as "Total Quality Management." The same concern with quality is increasingly being discussed in the human services (see, for instance, Janes, 1993; O'Hair and Meissner, 1993; Mawhinney, 1992; Fountain, 1992; and Rago and Reid, 1991).

BOX 3.3
Casework Evaluation Form

	YES	NO
1. Was a thorough, family-based assessment completed that reflects the family's needs for ongoing services?	_____	_____
2. Is a current, family-based treatment plan in the case record that is specific enough to be utilized in providing services?	_____	_____
3. Does service delivery follow the treatment plan?	_____	_____
4. Are types, frequency, and location of professional/family contacts appropriate?	_____	_____
5. Are problem-solving strategies used during family contacts that indicate good casework skills and knowledge?	_____	_____
6. Does the professional use identified resources through collateral contacts with service providers?	_____	_____
7. Does the running record clearly document casework activity and case progress?	_____	_____
8. Is the case being managed according to present policies and procedures?	_____	_____
9. Has the professional assured the safety of the adults/child(ren) in their current living arrangement?	_____	_____
10. Are the family's perceptions and preferences included in the provision of social services when possible?	_____	_____
11. Are services directed toward strengthening the family and preventing out-of-home placements?	_____	_____

(This form is scored as follows: 1 point is awarded for each "Yes" and a 0 is given for each "No." The quality of the casework is rated "Excellent" if there are 11 points; "Good" if there are 7 to 10 points; "Fair" if there are 3 to 6 points; and "Poor" if there are only 1 or 2 points.)

Total Quality Management is based upon a series of principles developed by William Deming. One major aim is to reduce variation from every process so that greater consistency of effort is obtained. Quality is defined by the customer, and improvement focuses on what customers want and need. However, Total Quality Management is not a one-shot effort and must come from top management's commitment to improvement. It often requires a change in thinking that encourages participation in the planning process by all staff members. Deming suggests that employees must be given freedom to dissent and stresses the importance of eliminating all barriers to communication. The organization must create an environment that fosters disclosure without penalty by all members of an organization (Maiden, 1993).

Sometimes known as Continuous Quality Improvement, Total Quality Management emphasizes client satisfaction surveys and uses feedback to make refinements. While we'll talk much more about such methods in a later chapter, it should be pointed out that much of the material we have covered so far (needs assessment, mission statements, goals and objectives, process evaluation, and program monitoring) is consistent with a Total Quality Management orientation. We'll all be hearing more about Total Quality Management in the coming years as the concept sweeps through social and human services.

It is beyond the scope of this text to outline a quality assurance program to fit your agency. Rather, the purpose of this discussion has been to help you understand how quality assurance can be used for program improvement (for example, to identify employees who tend to make inappropriate diagnoses or treatment plans, or whose interventions are not consistent with expectations or accepted practice; to identify the need for inservice or continuing education; and to provide other useful data for management decisions).

FINAL THOUGHTS

Formative evaluation, process evaluation, program monitoring, and quality assurance have in common a focus on improving programs. Because of their shared concern, it should be an obligation of every practitioner and every manager to learn more about and support these qualitative forms of evaluation within their agencies or practices.

To improve a program's quality, we cannot focus on only one portion of the process, such as the product at exit. We must examine *every* aspect of the program—perhaps beginning with goals for the program and the mix of appropriate and inappropriate admissions.

Depending upon the age, complexity, and sophistication of the agency whose program you have been asked to evaluate, you may not find mission statements or statements of program goals and objectives. In fact, your first act as an evaluator may be to assist the agency to develop mission statements and program goals. You may find yourself writing goals and objectives simply because they've never been done and no one else has any experience writing them.

Keep in mind that a program can have more than one goal, and each goal can have multiple objectives. For instance, I once heard of a mental health agency that had purchased a fast food restaurant. This purchase enabled the agency to employ their clients with chronic mental illness while providing them with necessary training and income to become employable in a competitive job market. The restaurant also brought in needed operational income to the agency. Each of these goals would be evaluated independently (with different criteria).

Patton (1982) has made several astute observations about management information systems. He noted that "if there is nothing you are trying to find out, there is nothing you will find out" (p. 229). He suggested that a management information system is not an "endpoint" but a beginning point for raising issues for additional study. Management information systems only provide data—they do not make decisions. An evaluation doesn't occur until someone uses data to answer some questions.

Finally, much of what Deming has taught about how organizations continuously improve can be summarized in four words: Plan, Do, Check, Act. In the PDCA or Deming cycle, *plan* means study a program or process by collecting data and deciding what would improve it. In the *do* step, the plan is implemented (sometimes on a small scale). In the third phase, staff *check* the results obtained so that they can make the necessary changes (*act*) in the program or process. Whenever we are in a position to provide formative or process evaluation, program monitoring, or quality assurance, we would do well to remember these four simple guides.

QUESTIONS FOR CLASS DISCUSSION

1. What is wrong with the following objectives?
   a. To improve statewide planning capacity and capability.
   b. To maximize collections from first and third party payors.
   c. To improve the skills of current staff through appropriate in-service training.
   d. To improve staff/patient ratios in state psychiatric hospitals.
   e. To participate more actively in economic development activities.

2. Rewrite the following objectives to improve them.
   a. The Free Clinic will facilitate early initiation of prenatal care by maintaining relations with local physicians and other agencies to facilitate referrals to the clinic.
   b. The Free Clinic will distribute brochures and posters describing the need for early prenatal care and the location of these services.
   c. For high risk patients, the Free Clinic will perform follow-up counseling as needed.
   d. The chronically mentally ill population will be served by a new "clubhouse" after-care program to reduce inpatient hospitalizations.
   e. By the end of eight weeks, all group members will have developed tools to help with panic attacks and flashbacks.
3. Discuss how a board of directors would know when a program is in need of a formative evaluation.
4. Tell what you know about the various ways in which social and human service agencies in your community conduct quality assurance and program monitoring activities.
5. Discuss the extent that social and human service agencies with which your class is familiar utilize computerized management information systems. What are their advantages and disadvantages?
6. Briefly describe a local social or human service program to the class. Discuss information that would be useful for program monitoring.
7. Refer to table 3.1. What possible explanations could there be for certain populations utilizing services less than might be expected? Could it be argued that some populations have a greater need for services than their proportion in a community's total population?
8. Discuss your experience with quality assurance programs. Viewed from a management perspective, what do you believe to be the benefits of quality assurance?

MINI-PROJECTS: EXPERIENCING EVALUATION FIRSTHAND

1. Choose a human service program with which you are familiar and then do the following:
   a. Briefly describe the program.
   b. Write at least one program goal.
   c. Write three specific program objectives.
2. Write a mission statement for a fictitious agency of your choosing.
3. Imagine that a friend asks you to conduct a formative evaluation

of the agency where you now work or intern as a practicum student. What sort of recommendations would you expect? List at least six realistic recommendations that could apply to this agency.

4. Briefly describe the quality assurance procedures of a social or human service agency with which you are familiar. Draft a short paper outlining how these procedures could be improved.

5. Obtain a monthly, quarterly, or yearly report from a social or human services agency. What additional information would be useful if you were a program monitor for that program? What information is missing and should be incorporated in future reports? Draft a set of recommendations based upon your reading of the reports.

6. Read one of the articles from the References and Resources section and write a short reaction paper.

REFERENCES AND RESOURCES

Below, P.J., Morrisey, G.L., and Acomb, B.L. (1987). *The executive guide to strategic planning.* San Francisco, CA: Jossey-Bass.

Chambers, F. (1994). Removing confusion about formative and summative evaluation: Purpose versus time. *Evaluation and Program Planning,* 17 (1), 9–12.

Chelimsky, E. (1985). *Program evaluation: Patterns and directions.* Washington, DC: American Society for Public Administration.

Commission on Accreditation of Rehabilitation Facilities. (1990). *Standards manual for organizations serving people with disabilities.* Tucson, AZ: CARF.

Coulton, C.J. (1987). Quality assurance. In S.M. Rosen, D. Fanshel, and M.E. Lutz (eds.), *Encyclopedia of social work.* Silver Spring, MD: National Association of Social Workers.

Dehar, M., Casswell, S., and Duignan, P. (1993). Formative and process evaluation of health promotion and disease prevention programs. *Evaluation Review,* 17 (2), 204–220

Demers, A., and Renaud, L. (1992). A formative evaluation of a nutritional marketing project in city-center restaurants. *Evaluation Review,* 16 (6), 634–649.

Dhooper, S.S., Royse, D., and Wolfe, L.C. (1990). Does social work education make a difference? *Social Work,* 35 (1), 57–61.

Drucker, Peter. (1980). The deadly sins in public administration. *Public Administration Review,* 40 (2), 103–106.

Dyme, B.S., Blaine, J.N., Bank, J.M., and Clark, W.L. (1993). Total quality management in contracted EAPs: A vendor's perspective. *Employee Assistance Quarterly,* 8 (4), 121–140.

Eustis, N.N., Kane, R.A., and Fischer, L.R. (1993). Home care quality and the home care worker: Beyond quality assurance as usual. *Gerontologist,* 33 (1), 64–73.

81

Evaluation guidebook: Demonstration partnership program projects. (1992). U.S. Dept. of Health and Human Services, Administration for Children and Families, Office of Community Services. Washington, DC: U.S. Government Printing Office.

Finnegan, J.R., Rooney, B., Viswanath, K., Elmer, P., Graves, K., Baxter, J., Hertog, J., Mullis, R., and Potter, J. (1992). Process evaluation of a home-based program to reduce diet-related cancer risk: The "Win at Home" series. *Health Education Quarterly,* 19 (2), 233–248.

Fountain, D.L. (1992). Avoiding the quality assurance boondoggle in drug treatment programs through total quality management. *Journal of Substance Abuse Treatment,* 9, 355–364.

Green, R.S., and Attkisson, C.C. (1984). Quality assurance and program evaluation: Similarities and differences. *American Behavioral Scientist,* 27 (5), 552–582.

Halvorson, H.W., Cohen, S.J., Brekke, K.L., McClatchey, M.W., and Cohen, M.W. (1993). Process evaluation of a system (Partners for Prevention) for prevention-oriented primary care. *Evaluation and the Health Professions,* 16 (1), 96–105.

Janes, R.W. (1993). Total quality management: Can it work in federal probation? *Federal Probation,* 57 (4), 28–33.

Joint Commission on Accreditation of Healthcare Organizations. (1988). *The Joint Commission guide to quality assurance.* Chicago, IL: JCAHO.

Joint Commission on Accreditation of Healthcare Organizations. (1990). *Accreditation manual for hospitals.* Chicago, IL: JCAHO.

Joint Commission on Accreditation of Healthcare Organizations. (1991). *An introduction to quality improvement in health care: The transition from quality assurance to continuous quality improvement.* Chicago, IL: JCAHO.

Joyce, L. (1989). Giving feedback in formative evaluation: A nondirective strategy. In R.F. Conner and M. Hendricks (eds.), *International innovations in evaluation methodology.* New Directions for Program Evaluation, no. 42. San Francisco, CA: Jossey-Bass.

Kamis-Gould, E., Brame, J., Campbell, J., Pascall, L., Schlosser, L., and Bard, R. (1991). A functional model of quality assurance for psychiatric hospitals and corresponding staff requirements. *Evaluation and Program Planning,* 14, 147–155.

Kaskutas, L., Morgan, P., and Vaeth, P. (1992). Structural impediments in the development of a community-based drug prevention program for youth: Preliminary analysis from a qualitative formative evaluation study. *International Quarterly of Community Health Education,* 12 (3), 169–182.

Kinzie, J.D., Maricle, R.A., Bloom, J.D., Leung, P.K., Goetz, R.R., Singer, C.M., and Hamilton, N.G. (1992). Improving quality assurance through psychiatric mortality and morbidity conferences in a university hospital. *Hospital and Community Psychiatry,* 43 (5), 470–474.

Kuechler, C.F., Velasquez, J.S., and White, M.S. (1988). An assessment of human services program outcome measures: Are they credible, feasible, useful? *Administration in Social Work,* 12 (3), 71–89.

Landsberg, G. (1985). Quality assurance activities in community mental health centers: Changes over time. *Community Mental Health Journal,* 21 (3), 189–197.

Maiden, R.P., (1993). Principles of total quality management and their application to employee assistance programs: A critical analysis. *Employee Assistance Quarterly,* 8 (4), 11–40.

Mawhinney, T.C. (1992). Total quality management and organizational behavior management: An integration for continual improvement. *Journal of Applied Behavior Analysis,* 25 (3), 525–543.

Mayer, J.P., Blakely, C.H., and Johnson, C.D. (1990). Formative evaluation of a community-based maternity services program for the uninsured. *Family Community Health,* 13 (3), 18–26.

Meisenheimer, C.G. (1985). *Quality assurance: A complete guide to effective programs.* Rockville, MD: Aspen Systems.

Morris, L.L., and Fitz-Gibbon, C.T. (1978a). *Evaluator's handbook.* Beverly Hills, CA: Sage.

Morris, L.L., and Fitz-Gibbon, C.T. (1978b). *How to measure program implementation.* Beverly Hills, CA: Sage.

Moskowitz, J.M. (1989). Preliminary guidelines for reporting outcome evaluation studies of health promotion and disease prevention programs. *Evaluating health prevention programs.* New Directions for Program Evaluation, no. 43. San Francisco, CA: Jossey-Bass.

Nevo, D. (1989). Expert opinion in program evaluation. In R.F. Conner and M. Hendricks (eds.), *International innovations in evaluation methodology.* New Directions for Program Evaluation, no. 42. San Francisco, CA: Jossey-Bass.

Nurius, P., and Hudson, W. (1993). *Human services practice, evaluation, and computers.* Pacific Grove, CA: Brooks/Cole.

O'Hair, J.R., and Meissner, P.Y. (1993). Employee assistance program total quality management in government regulated industries: The Westinghouse experience. *Employee Assistance Quarterly,* 8 (4), 77–100.

Pardeck, J.T., and Murphy, J.W. (1989). *Computers in human services: An overview for clinical and welfare services.* New York: Harwood Academic Publishers.

Patton, M.Q. (1982). *Practical evaluation.* Beverly Hills, CA: Sage.

Rago, W.V., and Reid, W.H. (1991). Total quality management strategies in mental health systems. *Journal of Mental Health Administration,* 18 (3), 253–263.

Segal, S.P., and Hwang, S. (1994). Licensure of sheltered-care facilities: Does it assure quality? *Social Work,* 39 (1), 124–131.

Smith, M.E. (1987). A guide to the use of simple process measures. *Evaluation and Program Planning,* 10 (3), 219–225.

Sorensen, J.E., Zelman, W., Hanbery, G.W., and Kucic, A.R. (1987). Managing mental health organizations with 25 key performance indicators. *Evaluation and Program Planning,* 10 (3), 239–247.

Sugarman, B. (1988). The well-managed human service organization: Criteria for a management audit. *Administration in Social Work,* 12 (4), 17–27.

Tash, W.R., and Stahler, G.J. (1984). Current status of quality assurance in mental health. *American Behavioral Scientist, 27* (5), 608–630.

Tash, W.R., Stahler, G.J., and Rappaport, H. (1982). Evaluating quality assurance programs. In G.J. Stahler and W.R. Tash (eds.), *Innovative approaches to mental health evaluation.* New York: Academic Press.

Velasquez, J.S., Kuechler, C.F., and White, M.S. (1986). Use of formative evaluation in a human services department. *Administration in Social Work, 10* (2), 67–77.

Veney, J.E., and Kaluzny, A.D. (1984). *Evaluation and decision making for health services programs.* Englewood Cliffs, NJ: Prentice-Hall.

Witte, K., Givens, V.K., Peterson, T.R., Todd, J.D., Vallabhan, S., Becktold, M.G., Stephenson, M.T., Hyde, M.K., Plugge, C.D., and Jarrett, R. (1993). Preventing tractor-related injuries and deaths in rural populations: Using persuasive health message frameworks in formative evaluation research. *International Quarterly of Community Health Education, 13* (3), 219–251.

FOUR

Goal Attainment Scaling and Client Satisfaction Studies

A schema for thinking about evaluation designs in terms of a qualitative-quantitative continuum was outlined in the Preface. Quantitative research and evaluation efforts are usually distinguished by their reliance upon counting, measuring, and analyzing numerical values. Qualitative efforts, by contrast, may involve some counting or percentages, but typically involve little or no use of statistics. Qualitative approaches to evaluating a program, such as convening a focus group of eight to ten clients, tend not to address issues that would concern a social scientist, such as the representativeness of a sample or the likelihood that the results would be replicated.

"Pure" evaluation approaches—those that are 100 percent qualitative or 100 percent quantitative—probably are less common than most people would think. Under the banner of quality assurance, for instance, sophisticated samples might be drawn and statistical testing of hypotheses conducted. Similarly, a process evaluator might survey clients using a scale or a questionnaire. However, qualitative approaches usually have a different "feel" in terms of the nature of the questions they seek to answer and in what is valued as data.

With all that as a backdrop, we can now say that some evaluation approaches, like goal attainment scaling and client satisfaction, draw from both the qualitative and quantitative perspectives and can be understood as possessing characteristics as well as strengths and weaknesses of both.

There is no single model, design, or "recipe" to follow in planning the best way to evaluate a social or human service program. While we, as evaluators, might have a preference for a particular approach, each program and evaluative situation brings a unique set of considerations which influence the choice of an evaluation design. In addition to the agency constraints associated with recruiting the assistance of staff and clients and the amount of time and monetary resources available, the very nature of the questions asked about the program have an effect upon the evaluation design. Just as there will be occasions when randomization cannot be employed or when suitable control groups cannot be located, there will also be occasions when questions arise about the effectiveness of an intervention relative to its cost. The director or board of directors may want to know, for example, if clients can achieve the same level of improvement with a less expensive intervention.

On other occasions, your supervisor may not be sure what he or she wants in an evaluation, but directs *you* to start an evaluation process in the next week or two. This happens.

GOAL ATTAINMENT SCALING (GAS)

Not long ago a phone call came in from a frantic former student who had taken a position in a rural part of the state. The executive director of his agency asked him to design a process by which a community mental health agency with numerous employees in several counties could begin evaluating its services.

"What do I do?" he said. "Where do I begin?"

"Can you start with a single program and then slowly bring in other programs?"

"I don't think so," he said. "The director wants something to use across the whole agency . . . and as soon as possible. I'm scheduled to make a presentation to staff next week."

As we talked, it became clear that there were few resources available to him. The agency didn't use standardized instruments like the Brief Symptom Inventory or the CES-D for outcome measures, and their quality assurance process consisted of checking to see that agency forms were completed, signed, and dated. Because he had to implement something quickly, we recommended that he consider Goal Attainment Scaling

(GAS). GAS would not have been our first choice of an evaluation approach (for reasons we'll explain later), but it seemed ideal for his situation.

Goal Attainment Scaling orginated in the field of mental health in the 1960s and has been used in other areas and with many different populations, such as brain-injured patients in rehabilitation hospitals, geriatric patients, and infants with motor delays. It is based on quantifying the individualized goals set with clients during treatment and requires the following:

1. *Identification of problem areas and defining goals.* Any number of problem areas and goals can be determined. Kiresuk, Smith, and Cardillo (1994) recommend at least three goals. However, in several studies the average number of goals scaled was five to six (Stolee, Rockwood, Fox, and Streiner, 1992; Simeonsson, Bailey, Huntington, and Brandon, 1991). Certainly, the number of problems brought by clients differ greatly. Problems chosen for GAS should be those most significant to the client and those that intervention is most likely to change.

2. *Scaling each goal from − 2 to + 2.* Each goal must be operationalized in observable behavioral terms. This step requires specifying a range of potential outcomes in an ordinal scale of five levels, where a + 2 outcome represents achieving much more than expected, + 1 somewhat more than expected. The 0 position represents an achievement of an expected outcome, − 1 portrays achieving somewhat less than expected, and − 2 much less than expected. A brief title is given to each goal.

Important to the GAS process is that the therapist and client routinely refer to the operationalized goals in order to assess progress. Progress toward meeting the desired goals should be monitored continuously during intervention, especially as the client nears termination.

CASE EXAMPLE OF
GOAL ATTAINMENT SCALING (GAS)

To illustrate how GAS could be used with a client, imagine that a twenty-six-year-old woman, who we will name Roberta, schedules an appointment with you at a counseling center. The first thing you notice about Roberta is that she is obese. She explains that she's unhappy and doesn't like herself. She believes that part of her problem is that she lives at home with overbearing parents who keep her from having friends and meeting people.

Roberta has lost 150 pounds or more on several occasions but can't keep the weight off because she stays home and eats when she's unhappy. She wants very much to get her own apartment but has no job. She's never worked and has only a high school diploma. You determine that she has no marketable job skills. However, a restaurant in her neighborhood has been advertising for counter help. Roberta has almost applied on several occasions, but chickened out each time.

Even though several other issues may need to be explored, Roberta wants to work on the two problems distressing her the most: her inability to secure the means to live independently and to lose weight. She appears to be motivated and capable of achieving her desired outcomes.

During the second session, the two of you create the chart in Box 4.1. Note how the intangible concepts "Financial independence" and "Weight loss" have been operationalized as varying along a continuum which reflects both the best case and worst case scenarios.

BOX 4.1
Goal Attainment Follow-Up Guide
Goal: To Improve Self-Esteem

Level	Goal 1 Financial Independence	Goal 2 Weight Loss
Most unfavorable outcome (–2)	Not working, continuing to live with parents	Gains weight
Less than expected outcome (–1)	Obtains part-time job	Loses less than 34 lbs
Expected outcome (0)	Obtains full-time job paying minimum wage	Loses 35–75 lbs
More than expected outcome (+1)	Obtains a full-time job paying slightly better than minimum wage	Loses 76–100 lbs
Most favorable treatment outcome (+2)	Obtains a full-time job with fringe benefits that pays much more than minimum wage	Loses 101–150 lbs

---

BOX 4.2
Vague Goal Statements

Outcome Level

Much less than expected	Feels worthless
Somewhat less than expected	Views self as having more deficits than assets
Expected outcome	Views self as having strengths and weaknesses in balance
Somewhat more than expected outcome	Views self as having more assets than deficits
Much more than expected	Feels positive about self

Six months later, Roberta has achieved her goal (expected outcome) of financial independence. She has obtained full-time employment at a fast food restaurant and is living in her own apartment. Additionally, she's enrolled in a weight loss program and has shed sixty-five pounds. Roberta reports being much happier, and she's thinking about enrolling in college.

From an evaluator's standpoint, the identified goal statements must be concrete and observable or measurable. They should not be subjective. The documentation and determination of progress or lack of progress should be easy to judge even if the case file were read by various professionals uninvolved with the intervention. With these criteria in mind, is Roberta's progress easy to determine? By looking at Box 4.1, can you see how it would be possible to attach a numerical value for her success level?

When goal statments are vague, persons trying to assess progress might arrive at different goal attainment scores. An example of vague goal statements is shown in Box 4.2. Shanelle was a fourteen-year-old African-American girl with low self-esteem. Could Shanelle like herself more one day than another, and could this affect an evaluation of her progress? Have you ever had a "bad hair" day or said something dumb in front of someone you were trying to impress and then been "down" the rest of the day? If you think that some days you might like yourself a lot more than others, or that someone you talk to only once a week might *not* know how you really feel about yourself, then the outcomes specified in Box 4.2 might not have a great deal of reliability. Ideally, therapists collaborate with clients in writing goal statements that are precise and measurable.

The benefits of utilizing GAS with individual clients are numerous. Its use should help set realistic expectations for treatment, facilitate clients' efforts at problem solving, increase goal direction in therapy, and perhaps even increase clients' motivation to work toward improvement.

GAS AND PROGRAM EVALUATION

The first step in using GAS as a program evaluation technique in agencies is to train staff to write relevant, realistic, and measurable goals. Kiresuk and Lund (1994) estimate that staff may require four to fourteen hours of training and that forty-five to seventy minutes per client is needed for application and quality control. About three staff hours per client is needed if in-home follow-up interviews are conducted.

Once staff are able to write measurable goal statements, an evaluator can compute composite or summary scores across clients. There are several ways this can be handled. The first way, deriving an average scale score for each client, involves adding up the outcome scores for each goal and dividing this by the number of goals or scales developed for that client. For example, Roberta would have obtained an outcome score of 0 on her financial independence goal and 0 on her weight loss goal. Adding the two zeros and dividing the answer by 2 (the number of goals) produces an average of 0, indicating that the expected goal was obtained.

Suppose that Roberta had achieved a negative average scale score. This would suggest that her progress was less than expected. A positive value would indicate greater achievement than expected.

Alternatively, Kiresuk and Sherman (1968) created a formula to produce a standard score (T-score) of 50 and a standard deviation of 10. As a first step, the outcome scores for each goal for a client are summed. To this value, 50 is added; that value is multiplied by k where:

$$k = \frac{10}{\sqrt{n - np + n^2 p}}$$

$p = .30$
n = number of scales for client

Obtaining a T-score of 50 means that the average outcome level was scored as zero (expected outcome). Higher scores than 50 indicate somewhat greater success and lower scores suggest less success.

T-scores can also be computed by adding up the individual scales, multiplying that sum by one of the following values:

10.00   when there is one scale
6.2   when there are two scales
4.56   when there are three scales
3.63   when there are four scales
3.01   when there are five scales

and then adding 50. When prediction of client outcomes is perfect, the GAS would be 50, assuming each goal is scored using the -2 to $+2$ scale.

VARIATIONS OF GOAL ATTAINMENT SCALING

Let's return to the discussion with our frantic former student. As an alternative to the $+2$ to -2 scaling originally recommended for GAS, we suggested that he use a continuum of 100 points to evaluate goal attainment in his agency. In this scheme, a value of 100 would be awarded when the hoped-for outcome was achieved. Obtaining a less than desired outcome might be assigned a value of 80, 60, or some other number depending on the percent of the goal achieved.

Using this method, average goal attainment for each client and for all the clients of all case workers in an agency could easily be computed. An average of 75, for instance, would indicate that approximately three-fourths of all clients achieved their desired goals. It would not be necessary to operationalize "more than expected" or "less than expected" outcomes, although these and other levels of outcome could be stated. A variation of GAS called Family Goal Recording (Fleuridas, Rosental, Leigh, and Leigh, 1990) assigns weights to goals, which allows for some goals to have higher priorities than others, and uses levels of achievement that add up to 100 percent.

Box 4.3 illustrates how the concept of GAS can be modified. One may make still other refinements—perhaps by inserting the category "Slight improvement" between "Less than expected" and "Optimal improvement."

With this scheme, one can multiply the importance attached to achieving the first goal (.75) and the goal outcome obtained (.75) to arrive at a figure of .56. To this is added the value obtained by multiplying the second goal's importance and the outcome obtained (.25 × .75 = .1875). This amount is added to .56 and the resulting value of .7475 (.56 + .1875) can be interpreted as the client achieved 75 percent of her desired

91

BOX 4.3

Modified Goal Attainment Follow-Up Guide

Achievement Level	Goal 1 Financial Independence Priority (.75)	Goal 2 Weight Loss Priority (.25)
Optimal improvement Level = 1.0	Obtains full-time job paying better than minimum wage and with fringe benefits	Loses 90 + lbs
Major improvement Level = .75	Obtains full-time job paying minimum wage	Loses 50–89 lbs
Less than expected improvement Level = .50	Obtains part-time job	Loses less than 49 lbs
No progress outcome Level = .00	Doesn't acquire any job; continues living with parents	Gains weight

goals. This scoring system seems easier to understand and explain than the GAS scheme.

PROBLEMS WITH GOAL ATTAINMENT SCALING

GAS has been critiqued over the years (Seaberg and Gillespie, 1977; Cytrynbaum, Ginath, Birdwell, and Brandt, 1979). Some evaluators think GAS permits too much subjectivity in the choice of goals selected. Considering the example of Roberta, we might have developed goals centering on improving her self-esteem, reducing her depression, or helping her to become more assertive with her parents. Therapists have a great deal of latitude in their *choice* of goals. Even with similar clients with identical problems, two therapists may emphasize completely different goals—with varying levels of success. What if every therapist in an agency decided to work only on the problems easily solved and ignored the difficult ones because an evaluation was being conducted?

Even if there is no system-wide bias, how many therapists may be tempted to set goals (or encourage a client to set goals) too easily obtained because they want to look good in their supervisor's eyes? How do you react to the following goals for Roberta?

- Attend at least three therapy sessions.
- Read the "Help Wanted" ads in the newspaper every day.
- Prepare a resume.
- Eliminate one candy bar from weekly grocery purchases.

Would Roberta's achieving any or *all* of these goals convince you that she is any better off as a result of the intervention?

Another problem with GAS is that a client's ability to achieve certain goals could be overestimated as well as underestimated. Would overly optimistic clinicians obtain lower success rates than pessimistic clinicians? Obviously, if some kind of goal attainment scaling is to be used as part of an agency evaluation, there needs to be someone reviewing the goals. Ottenbacher and Cusick (1990) have suggested that one way to deal with this problem is to have one therapist set the goals and another provide the treatment.

Finally, when we use the Goal Attainment Scaling as originally developed, a T-score of 50 may arise from offsetting successes and failures. Depending upon the nature of the goals, failure in one area may have many more ramifications than success in two or three minor areas. Weighing of goals—for instance, deciding that achieving financial independence is twice as important for a client as losing 50 pounds—creates real difficulties when summary T-scores are computed.

On the plus side, there is evidence that GAS has therapeutic utility in increasing clients' self-awareness and goal orientation (Malac, Smigielski, and DePompolo, 1991). And GAS has been reported to have high inter-rater reliability, adequate content validity, and high correlations with a standardized outcome measure (Stolee et at., 1992).

Smith and Cardillo (1994) conclude that the GAS score

> is a credible but unimpressive measure of an undifferentiated concept of outcome. Its modest but statistically significant relationship with other criteria of outcome indicates that it is measuring some of the same features that are assessed by the other procedures; however, like most other measures, it has no special merit when considered as a general measure of outcome. (P. 272)

We do not routinely recommend Goal Attainment Scaling or some modification of it to agencies for program evaluation. Used systematically agency-wide, it's better than not doing *any* monitoring of what clients are achieving. However, it's a little like constructing a boat out of swiss cheese—it's too porous to take you far. Program managers will find that it provides little useful information about the program itself.

CLIENT SATISFACTION STUDIES

Most professionals in the human services, if told to design a program evaluation, would begin thinking about surveying clients to determine if they liked the services they received. Such an approach is among the simplest and most frequently used measures of program evaluation and is variously known as soliciting client feedback, conducting a client satisfaction study, or exploring service acceptability.

There is much to commend the use of client satisfaction as a form of evaluation. Such approaches tend to be relatively inexpensive and easy to interpret, and they can be implemented on short notice without a great deal of planning. Furthermore, they may indicate to clients that their experiences and observations are important—further indication that someone cares about them. Whether we inquire about the accessibility of our services or the acceptability of our services, these approaches are a "client-oriented" form of evaluation. They stem from the assumption that clients provide the most valuable and accurate information available on how our program impacts their lives. Further, client satisfaction has been shown to be associated with symptom relief and improvement in a sample of outpatient psychotherapy clients, (Ankuta and Abeles, 1993). Client satisfaction, then, would seem to be a useful surrogate measure for treatment efficacy.

There is just one major problem with client satisfaction approaches. In practically every instance, the majority of respondents indicate satisfaction with services received. For example, in a national survey of recently hospitalized patients, 62 percent reported that they were "very satisfied," and another 23 percent reported being "somewhat satisfied" (Steiber, 1988b). In assessment of satisfaction with family physicians, patients were even more satisfied than they were with their hospital experiences—73 percent were "very satisfied" and 22 percent "somewhat satisfied" (Steiber, 1988a). On a 5-point scale, the average rating given by hospital patients for their overall care was 4.37 out of a possible 5.00 (Steiber and Krowinski, 1990). Most health care patients are satisfied with the care they receive—as are most individuals who are asked to respond to client satisfaction questions. This positive response bias occurs so often that Lebow (1982), in a review of twenty-six different studies, found that three quarters had satisfaction rates higher than 70 percent—even though the surveys were conducted of totally different programs, in diverse settings, using various counseling approaches and assessment methods.

High levels of satisfaction are not found just in the United States. Deane (1993) has reported that 90 percent of a sample of New Zealand psychotherapy outpatients gave a rating of three or more on all but one of eight 4-point items, indicating satisfaction with services. Ninety-five percent indicated that they would come back to the program again if they needed help and/or would recommend the program to friends who may need similar help.

Using the CSQ-8 (a standardized 8-item client satisfaction scale developed by Nguyen, Attkisson, and Stegner, 1983), Gaston and Sabourin (1992) found no differences in client satisfaction among Canadian patients receiving dynamic, eclectic, or cognitive/behavioral therapy in private psychotherapy. The mean CSQ-8 score was 28.7. Compare that value to a study conducted by Perreault and Leichner (1993) of French-speaking psychiatric outpatients in Montreal. The mean CSQ-8 in that survey was 28.4. Further, satisfaction rates varied between 87.5 percent and 98 percent when open-ended questions were used to create service dimension categories.

As Lebow (1982) has noted, high satisfaction rates tend to be obtained even when clients have little choice of facility, type of treatment, or practitioner. Studies have shown that there are no significant differences in satisfaction between voluntary and involuntary clients (Spensley, Edwards, and White, 1980).

More recently, Polowczyk, Brutus, Orvieto, Vidal, and Cipriani (1993) conducted a study of 530 patients with serious and persistent mental illness. Both trained patient surveyors and clinic receptionists interviewed patients and reported high levels of satisfaction. Those surveyed by staff responded positively (3 or higher) to questions 95 percent of the time, while those surveyed by patients responded positively 90 percent of the time. Indeed, clients often report being more pleased with treatment than one might expect them to be.

For instance, Weller (1991) reports on a combined needs assessment and satisfaction study in a representative sample of developmentally disabled clients of the Florida Department of Health and Rehabilitative Services. While the respondents in this survey were not generally capable of independent living and 97 percent of them needed the help of a surrogate to respond to the interview questions, 60 percent were "very satisfied" with residential services and 30 percent were "satisfied."

Positive client evaluations are not proof of a "good" program; in fact, Rocheleau and Mackesey (1980) suggest that a problem may be indicated if a program receives satisfaction rates of less than 70 to 75 percent. If only two-thirds of your clients are pleased with your services, then your program may warrant closer inspection.

There can be many reasons why consumer satisfaction studies tend to reveal positive findings. First of all, client feedback instruments are often "homemade" and nothing is known about their reliability or validity. (More detail on what to look for in an instrument is provided in chapter 8.) Even strongly positive client satisfaction data obtained from an instrument that lacks reliability and validity is not convincing information to evaluators and informed professionals.

A second reason that client satisfaction surveys tend to have a strong positive bias is that they usually seek feedback from clients who have remained with an agency or program. Clients who are dissatisfied with services tend to drop out early—perhaps after the first visit. Those clients who stay with a program are more likely to have had a positive experience with a therapist or with the agency's services than those who drop out. Biased samples result when only those clients having a positive experience choose to respond to a survey.

Third, not enough consideration is given to the problems associated with getting back a representative sample of questionnaires. As a rule, only about 25 to 30 percent of all those surveys mailed out can be expected to be completed and returned. Sometimes, response rates are 10 to 15 percent. How are the results to be interpreted when 85 percent of a sample do not respond? Results based on a 15 percent response rate are virtually meaningless because we would be hearing from a minority instead of a majority of the clients. It is very likely that those who respond to the client satisfaction survey might not be representative of the rest of the clients (those who didn't respond). Clients who return mailed surveys tend to have higher levels of educational attainment than those who don't return surveys. As we think about our clients, we realize that a sizable proportion are functionally illiterate. Impoverished clients who are battling every day for survival probably have more important concerns than filling out a client satisfaction questionnaire. Also, clients may move frequently and not leave forwarding addresses. In order to keep the response rate high, it may be necessary to offer a *small* incentive. If the incentive is too large, the results could be viewed as biased because of a perception that the respondents were "bought."

In order to avoid the problems associated with mailing survey instruments to clients, agencies sometimes distribute them in person and ask clients to complete the service satisfaction surveys while they are in the agency. While a higher response rate is usually guaranteed, this procedure may also threaten some clients. Feeling that their anonymity is threatened, clients may have concerns about losing benefits or not receiving future services if they say anything negative. Bias can easily creep into those procedures designed to elicit client feedback data. Consulting with client groups and involving some representatives in the planning process is advised.

Even given these problems, it is possible that the advantages associated with client satisfaction surveys will always make them attractive to managers in the social and human services.

Instead of considering a client satisfaction survey as the sole source of information about a program's performance, the trained evaluator will consider this form of evaluation as part of a more comprehensive effort. Consumer satisfaction studies often offer valuable insight into a program from a client's perspective. If you decide to conduct a client satisfaction survey, we recommend the following:

1. Use a scale that has good reliability and that has been used successfully in other studies. (See the example and references included in the next chapter.) Avoid the use of hastily designed questionnaires for which there is no psychometric information. When you use instruments that have been employed in other research or evaluation activities, oftentimes data can be found in the literature for comparison with your study. Greenfield and Attkisson (1989), for instance, present the means for a fifteen item Service Satisfaction Scale administered to patients of a university student health service and a mental health clinic, and patients in four clinics within a private nonprofit health system. Gaston and Sabourin (1992), Deane (1993), and Perreault and Leichner (1993) have all reported mean satisfaction scores for the CSQ-8. However, there is no shortage of other instruments in the literature. See, for example, the Patient Satisfaction Survey (Holcomb, Adams, Ponder, and Reitz, 1989), the Vocational Evaluation Satisfaction Survey (Sabin, Cuvo, and Musgrave, 1987), or the Sharp-V (Tanner, 1982).

2. Use the same instrument on repeated occasions and develop a local baseline of data so that departures from the norm can be observed. Conduct client satisfaction studies regularly and routinely (for example, twice or three times a year), then compare the data with the results from prior efforts. The advantage of doing this as opposed to a one-time client satisfaction study can be seen in figure 4.1.

Figure 4.1
Client Satisfaction Ratings

	Onestop Counseling, Inc.		
100%			
95%			
90%	•		
85%		•	
80%			
75%			•
70%			
65%			
	March	June	September

In this example it can be seen that the actual level of client satisfaction with services is dropping. Such a trend could be discovered only by doing more than one study. Had the evaluator conducted one study in the month of March, this decreasing satisfaction with services would not have been detected.

3. Employ at least one and possibly two open-ended questions so that the consumers of your services can alert you to any problems that you didn't suspect and couldn't anticipate. (For instance, "If you could make any improvements to this program, what one thing would you change?" Or, "What about this program do you like best and least?")

   The importance of using open-ended questions can be seen in the following example. A student who worked for the state department of social services told us of an exit interview with an adolescent in foster care. There were no problems indicated in the home where the adolescent was placed until the worker asked the next to last question: "If you could change anything about this foster home, what would you change?" At that point, the teen-ager began detailing how uncomfortable she felt when the foster father came into her bedroom at night and sat on her bed.

   Closed-ended questions, particularly in those rating scales that provide an overall measure of satisfaction, may be constructed in ways that skirt or miss altogether major sources of dissatisfaction within a specific program. Open-ended questions can allow consumers to address problems that evaluators may not have anticipated.

4. Use a "ballot box" approach where one week is set aside when every client (old and new) entering the agency is given a brief questionnaire and asked to complete it while waiting for the scheduled

appointment. Oftentimes, client satisfaction studies have focused not on active clients but on those who have completed the program or who are no longer receiving services. It is necessary to learn about clients' experiences in every phase of the program. (If a significant proportion of the agency's clients are illiterate, written questionnaires should be accompanied by procedures that will insure that a clerical person, friend, or family member reads the questions to the client.

To the extent that the evaluator uses questionnaires with unknown reliability and validity and open-ended questions that allow the respondent to describe his or her experiences with the program, the client feedback study can be thought of as being more qualitative than quantitative. When stronger instruments are used in conjunction with statistical procedures and representative samples of clients, the evaluation takes on more of a quantitative "feel"—even if some open-ended questions are also used.

A good portion of the mental work that has to be done prior to conducting a program evaluation involves conceptualizing the effort. Some individuals seem to gravitate naturally toward the more qualitative approaches and others toward the more quantitative. Still others stand in the middle of the road and don't know which way to turn. Regardless of their orientation on the qualitative-quantitative continuum, many have found a model proposed by Robert Hammond (1975) to be useful for identifying foci when planning and structuring evaluations.

THE HAMMOND MODEL

Hammond identified several major elements that can be helpful in thinking about who and what to evaluate. His model starts with the identification of a **population** (those individuals who are involved in or influenced by the program). Note that the population is not limited just to *clients* served by the program. The broad definition employed here suggests to the evaluator that *staff* also constitute a population of persons involved with the program who could be the source of pertinent information about a program. The *administration* also is an appropriate focus of some evaluation efforts.

A program operates in an **environment**. This environment is defined by the program's *intents* (the purposes, goals, or objectives established for it); by the *methods* (or interventions) used; and by the *resources* (people, money, space, materials, and equipment) available to the program.

99

Figure 4.2
Schematic of the Hammond Model

Population	Environment	Behavior
Clients	Intents	Performance
Staff	Methods	Opinion
Administration	Resources	

Once these program elements have been defined, the evaluator can begin to consider questions that can be grouped as to whether they relate to areas of *opinion* (judgments and beliefs) or behavioral *performance.*

With this model the evaluator can decide to be very comprehensive and to cover all of the population and environmental elements with regard to both opinions and performance. Or, more realistically, the evaluator may decide upon a more narrow evaluation. Using this approach the evaluator could, for example, survey *clients* regarding their *opinions* of the *methods* used by the program staff. Or, the evaluator might examine the *clients' performance* (outcomes) within a selected program (*method*).

The Hammond Model can help evaluators get an overview of the essential elements comprising a program so that a variety of ways to approach an evaluation can be seen. An evaluator should attempt to conduct as comprehensive an evaluation as is feasible. While it is possible to conduct a program evaluation involving only the staff and not the clients, the value of the Hammond Model is that it suggests that clients as well as administrators have important information or perspectives on the program. When the evaluator selects a narrow perspective, there is always some information about the program that is lost or not examined—potentially valuable information. Perhaps there are times when the evaluator ought to expand Hammond's list and ask volunteers for their opinions or suggestions. The argument for doing as comprehensive an evaluation as can be afforded is seen in the following example (which is mostly true and has been only slightly embellished).

A new program manager wanted to make an emergency mental health program a superlative program—one which all the citizens in the community could point to with pride. The first week she examined the client utilization data and made a number of recommendations that would provide better information for monitoring purposes. She trained her staff to keep timely and accurate records of the amount of services provided.

After a couple of months, she began an outcome evaluation of the program. Whenever sessions of emergency counseling were completed, the staff were to ask consumers if they would talk with the director as part of a program evaluation. The director picked up the calls or met individually with the clients and asked a series of questions about whether the counseling had been beneficial. Although she wasn't able to talk with every client, the director began the process of gathering data to help her understand the clients' experiences with her program.

Even with these measures in place, the director was not entirely satisfied that the program was as good as it could be. As she thought about what might make the program a better one, it occurred to her that it relied too heavily upon volunteers. The paid staff generally worked the "day" hours and were not on-site after 6:00 P.M., unless they were called in to handle an emergency. Approximately thirty-five volunteers augmented the paid staff, volunteering between four to eight hours a week (usually in the evening).

The program director was successful in obtaining additional funding that allowed her to reassign full-time staff so that a qualified mental health professional was on-site twenty-four hours a day. Evening coverage was no longer the prime responsibility of volunteers. This change of policy would help, she reasoned, to insure that clients got "quality service" during the evening as well as during the day hours.

One night shortly after the new policy was implemented, the full-time staff person on duty was surprised to see a man walk into the emergency unit with a bag of groceries. There was a loaf of French bread extending out of the sack, and she could see a bottle of wine, some cheese, and a radio. The man informed the staff person that he was the Thursday night volunteer scheduled to be "on duty" and that she could go home. He became very animated when he found out that a full-time staff person would be on duty all evening. A few minutes later a woman drove up in the parking lot and he ran out to meet her. After some discussion with her friend, she marched inside and demanded to know why a paid staff person was needed on "their night." The two volunteers insisted that they had not been notified of the new policy and informed the staff, as they picked up the groceries and radio, that they would *not* be volunteering anymore!

The program director learned that the two individuals had driven from distant locations to "volunteer" and had been "volunteering" for several years—always on the same evening and with each other. Were they volunteering to be of service to humankind or to provide themselves with an opportunity to get away from their spouses? During their romantic interludes would they answer the crisis phone? Were clients getting the volunteers' undivided attention?

Many evaluation efforts probably would not have discovered this problem. It was only because of the program director's dogged pursuit of "quality" service that the staffing assignments were rearranged to rely less heavily upon volunteers during evening hours.

As a general rule, the more people the evaluator can talk with (including volunteers or the volunteer coordinator), the greater the likelihood that discoveries will be made about areas where the program can be improved. Get input from a variety of sources and be as comprehensive as possible when planning a program evaluation. Program evaluation should not be considered a "one-shot" episode. It should be an ongoing process that continually provides useful information from an assortment of sources to program managers.

CHAPTER RECAP

This chapter has introduced several different evaluation designs that are available to you as a program evaluator. Your choice of an evaluation design will depend upon the resources you have, the constraints within the agency, as well as what is pragmatically possible.

The difference between the competent and incompetent evaluator is that the competent evaluator knows what data will be produced, has plans for the analytical or statistical procedures that will be used, and understands the limitations of the chosen evaluation design. The incompetent evaluator is not sure what data will be produced, how it can be interpreted, or what can be done to make up for limitations in the data. The incompetent evaluator is not able to plan ahead and anticipate what might happen with the use of a given procedure or instrument.

When planning an evaluation, ask yourself such questions as:

1. What could go wrong with this data collection procedure? (Then strengthen or improve the procedure; collect data from more than one source.)
2. If the intervention is successful, how might the critics of the program explain it away? Conversely, if the intervention does not appear to be successful, how would I explain that?
3. What is the weakest aspect of this evaluation design?
4. What would make the evaluation more convincing?

As you answer these questions, ways to strengthen and improve your procedures will become apparent. You may want to build in safeguards that will take "ammunition" away from any potential critics or skeptics. And, as a result, you will have a stronger and more compelling evaluation.

Ultimately, the evaluation design you use will be based on several considerations: the amount of time you have in which to conduct the evaluation, the cost in materials and personnel, the administrative and political constraints, the purpose of the evaluation, and the concern that the results be reliable and valid. Muscatello (1988) described these and several other factors in a discussion on choosing which program to evaluate and assessing the difficulty associated with evaluating any program.

Finally, Wholey (1987) identified four problems that prevent an evaluation from being used to improve program performance:

1. Lack of definition (of the problem to be addressed, the intervention, the expected outcomes or impact).
2. Lack of a clear logic of testable assumptions.
3. Lack of agreement on evaluation priorities and intended uses of the evaluation.
4. Inability or unwillingness to act on the basis of evaluative information.

Evaluators may not always be able to convince policymakers to act on the findings produced in their evaluation reports. However, by attending to the first three points made by Muscatello and trying to think like a "competent" evaluator, you will go a long way toward insuring that your evaluation product will make a useful contribution.

QUESTIONS FOR CLASS DISCUSSION

1. How is Goal Attainment Scaling affected by subjectivity?
2. What are the advantages and disadvantages of using GAS or some modification of it to evaluate an outpatient mental health counseling program?
3. If you were a manager thinking about implementing GAS or Family Goal Recording, what problems might arise with your staff?
4. Although it is known that client satisfaction studies typically are positively biased, discuss why this form of evaluation is used so often in evaluating university faculty.
5. Knowing what you now know about client satisfaction studies, argue for and against their place in a comprehensive program evaluation.

MINI-PROJECTS:
EXPERIENCING EVALUATION FIRSTHAND

1. You have been hired to conduct an evaluation of a hospice program. How will you determine if this is a "good" hospice program? Unlike most social and human service programs, it is unrealistic to expect that the clients of the hospice program will improve. Because they are terminally ill, most of them die within several months after becoming clients. Devise an evaluation plan using a design discussed in this chapter.
2. Collect as many client satisfaction forms as you can at school, work, fast food restaurants, or other sources. Examine them and determine how many questionnaires have similar or identical items. Select the best of all the items and create your own questionnaire to replace one currently being used.
3. If you are working or interning in an agency that provides direct services to clients, devise Goal Attainment follow-up guides for two different clients. Write a short paper describing the ease or difficulty you experienced. Without identifying the clients by name, include the guides you created.

REFERENCES AND RESOURCES

Ankuta, G.Y., and Abeles, N. (1993). Client satisfaction, clinical significance, and meaningful change in psychotherapy. *Professional Psychology: Research and Practice*, 24 (1), 70–74.

Cytrynbaum, S., Ginath, Y., Birdwell, J., and Brandt, L. (1979). Goal attainment scaling: A critical review. *Evaluation Quarterly*, 3, 5–40.

Deane, F.P. (1993). Client satisfaction with psychotherapy in two outpatient clinics in New Zealand. *Evaluation and Program Planning*, 16, 87–94.

Fleuridas, C., Rosenthal, D.M., Leigh, G.K., and Leigh, T.E. (1990). Family goal recording: An adaptation of goal attainment scaling for enhancing family therapy and assessment. *Journal of Marital and Family Therapy*, 16 (4), 389–406.

Gaston, L., and Sabourin, S. (1992). Client satisfaction and social desirability in psychotherapy. *Evaluation and Program Planning*, 15, 227–231.

Greenfield, T.K., and Attkisson, C.C. (1989). Steps toward a multifactorial satisfaction scale for primary care and mental health services. *Evaluation and Program Planning*, 12.

Hammond, R.L. (1975). Establishing priorities for information and design specifications for evaluating community education programs. *Community Education Journal*, March/April.

Holcomb, W.R., Adams, N.A., Ponder, H.M., and Reitz, R. (1989). The development and construction validation of a consumer satisfaction questionnaire for psychiatric inpatients. *Evaluation and Program Planning*, 12, 189–194.

Janikowski, T.P., Bordieri, J.E., and Musgrave, J. (1991). Dimensions of client satisfaction with vocational evaluation services. *Vocational Evaluation and Work Adjustment Bulletin*, 24(2), 43–48.

Joyce, B.M., Rockwood, K.J., and Mate-Kole, C.C. (1994). Use of goal attainment scaling in brain injury in a rehabilitation hospital. *American Journal of Physical Medicine and Rehabilitation*, 73(1), 10–14.

Kiresuk, T.J., and Lund, S.H. (1994). Implementing goal attainment scaling. In Thomas J. Kiresuk, Aaron Smith, and Joseph E. Cardillo (eds.), *Goal attainment scaling: Applications, theory, and measurement*. Hillsdale, NJ: Erlbaum.

Kiresuk, T.J., and Sherman, R.E. (1968). Goal attainment scaling: A general method for evaluating community mental health programs. *Community Mental Health Journal*, 4, 443–453.

Kiresuk, T.J., Smith, A., and Cardillo, J.E. (1994). *Goal attainment scaling: Applications, theory, and measurement*. Hillsdale, NJ: Erlbaum.

Lebow, J.L. (1982). Consumer satisfaction with mental health treatment. *Psychological Bulletin*, 91(2), 244–259.

Lebow, J.L. (1987). Acceptability as a simple measure in mental health program evaluation. *Evaluation and Program Planning*, 10(3), 191–195.

Malec, J.F., Smigielski, J.S., and DePompolo, R.W. (1991). Goal attainment scaling and outcome measurement in postacute brain injury rehabilitation. *Archives of Physical Medicine Rehabilitation*, 72, 138–143.

Muscatello, D.B. (1988). Developing an agenda that works: The right choice at the right time. *Evaluation utilization*. New Directions for Program Evaluation, no. 39. San Francisco, CA: Jossey-Bass.

Nehls, N. (1991). Borderline personality disorder and group therapy.*Archives of Psychiatric Nursing*, 5(3), 137–146.

Nguyen, T.D., Attkisson, C.C., and Stegner, B.L. (1983). Assessment of patient satisfaction: Development and refinement of a service evaluation questionnaire. *Evaluation and Program Planning* 6, 299–314.

Ottenbacker, K.J., and Cusick, A. (1990). Goal attainment scaling as a method of clinical service evaluation. *American Journal of Occupational Therapy*, 44, 519–525.

Palisano, R.J., Haley, S.M., and Brown, D.A. (1992). Goal attainment scaling as a measure of change in infants with motor delays. *Physical Therapy*, 72 (6), 432–437.

Perreault, M., and Leichner, P. (1993). Patient satisfaction with outpatient psychiatric services: Qualitative and quantitative assessments. *Evaluation and Program Planning*, 16, 109–118.

Polowczyk, D., Brutus, M., Orvieto, A.A., Vidal, J., and Cipriana, D. (1993). Comparison of patient and staff surveys of consumer satisfaction. *Hospital and Community Psychiatry*, 44(6), 589–591.

Rocheleau, B., & Mackesey, T. (1980). What, consumer feedback surveys again? *Evaluation and the Health Professions*, 3(4), 405–419.

Royse, D. (1985). Client satisfaction with the helping process: A review for the pastoral counselor. *Journal of Pastoral Care*, 39(1), 3–11.

Russell, M. (1990). Consumer satisfaction: An investigation of contributing factors. *Journal of Social Service Research*, 13(4), 43–56.

Sabin, M.C., Cuvo, A.J., and Musgrave, J.R. (1987). Developing a client satisfaction scale in a vocational evaluation setting. *Vocational Evaluation and Work Adjustment Bulletin*, 107–113.

Seaberg, J.R., and Gillespie, D.F. (1977). Goal attainment scaling: A critique. *Social Work Research and Abstracts*, 13, 4–11.

Simeonsson, R.J., Bailey, D.B., Huntington, G.S., and Brandon, L. (1991). Scaling and attainment of goals in family-focused early intervention. *Community Mental Health Journal*, 27(1), 77–83.

Smith, A., and Cardillo, J.E. (1994). Perspectives on validity. In Thomas J. Kiresuk, Aaron Smith, and Joseph E. Cardillo (eds.), *Goal attainment scaling: Applications, theory, and measurement*. Hillsdale, NJ: Erlbaum.

Spensley, J., Edwards, D., and White, E. (1980). Patient satisfaction and involuntary treatment. *American Journal of Orthopsychiatry*, 50(4), 725–727.

Steiber, S.R. (1988a). Making use of patient survey data. *Health Care Strategic Management*. 7(3), 12–14.

Steiber, S.R. (1988b). How consumers perceive health care quality. *Hospitals* 62(7), 84.

Steiber, S.R., and Krowinski, W. (1990). *Measuring and managing patient satisfaction*. Chicago, IL: American Hospital Association.

Stolee, P., Rockwood, K., Fox, R.A., and Streiner, D.L. (1992). The use of goal attainment scaling in a geriatric care setting. *Journal of the American Geriatrics Society*, 40, 574–578.

Tanner, B.A. (1982). A multi-dimensional client satisfaction instrument. *Evaluation and Program Planning*, 5, 161–167.

Weller, B. (1991). Client satisfaction with developmental disabilities services. *Population and Environment: A Journal of Interdisciplinary Studies*, 13(2), 121–139.

Wholey, J.S. (1987). *Using program theory in evaluation*. New Directions for Program Evaluation, no. 33. San Francisco, CA: Jossey-Bass.

FIVE

Single System Research Designs

We have been moving by incremental steps toward evaluation methodologies that are distinctly quantitative. In this chapter and those that follow, we are concerned with systematic approaches that lend themselves to replication by others. Replication strengthens credibility by demonstrating that one's measurements *do* accurately reflect reality.

One methodology that is increasingly being adopted within the human services is called **Single System Research Designs**, or SSRDs (see Alter and Evens, 1990; Barlow and Hersen, 1984; Bloom, 1993; Bloom and Fischer, 1994; Jayaratne and Levy, 1979; Kazdin, 1982; and Krishef, 1991). SSRDs are also known as interrupted time series designs, single case experimental designs, and idiographic research designs. The fundamentals of SSRDs are relatively simple, with only two requirements.

1. The program evaluator must be able to select one or more reliable and valid measures of some social problem or program outcome.
2. The evaluator must repeatedly assess this outcome measure over time.

We will address each of these requirements separately, and then discuss the various ways in which they can be applied to evaluate programs, working from relatively simple applications to more complex ones.

107

Although sometimes referred to as single case or single subject designs, SSRDs are more accurately labeled single system designs, because they can be used with virtually any level of investigation, from clinical work with individual clients to national social policies. In program evaluation, the unit of analysis is usually some aggregated measure obtained from large numbers of people. For example, absenteeism of workers at an agency can be measured as a percentage of days actually worked versus those scheduled to be worked, the numbers of homeless persons for whom workers found shelter, the number of home visits made by workers, and so on.

At the level of policy evaluation, city, state, or federal statistics can be useful indicators of program outcomes. Crime, poverty, or unemployment statistics can be used as outcome measures for program evaluation. If such measures are repeatedly assessed over time, and you can have confidence that these measures are reasonably accurate, then program evaluation using SSRDs becomes feasible.

SELECTING OUTCOME MEASURES

Outcome measures useful for single system research must possess several features. Among these are the properties of reliability, validity, and sensitivity to change. Reliability has several dimensions. First is consistency. If multiple measures are taken of a program, when nothing about the program has *really* changed, then the measure should yield the same information on each application. Second, the measure should be fairly easy to gather. Agency records and other archival material can be useful, if retrospective, sources of data applicable for SSRDs. Alternatively, program evaluators can make prospective plans to gather additional, nonservice-related information specifically intended for evaluation purposes. If two people independently extract data from records, or prospectively gather or score the same data, their figures should agree. Data lacking good interrater agreement are suspect.

If standardized instruments are used, they should be relatively brief, easy to score, and understandable, and they should clearly pertain to the agency's mission. The Minnesota Multiphasic Personality Inventory (MMPI) is one measure that violates these principles. It consists of over four hundred questions and is awkward to hand score (but can be machine scored for a considerable fee). Few agencies are in the business of "personality change" per se, and with repeated administrations, clients' MMPI scores tend to drift for reasons unrelated to program efficacy (Kelley, Jacobs, and Farr, 1994). Thus, the MMPI does not lend itself to most forms of program evaluation.

The most direct approach to selecting an outcome measure is to ask "What is the agency's mission?" As we discussed in Chapter 3, most agencies have a mission statement, charter, or charge. If not, ask the agency director and other professional staff the above question. Usually the response will allow you to identify the agency's mission. For example, an agency charged with providing child protective services may have several goals. One goal may be to *prevent* child abuse from occurring; a second may be to intervene so that child abuse does not recur after initially being brought to the attention of the agency. A foster care and adoption agency may have as its goal the placement of children in suitable foster homes, or with adoptive families. A psychiatric service would be interested in working with clients to ameliorate behavioral, cognitive, and affective symptoms. A voter registration drive would aim to sign up unregistered voters and help them get to the polls. In intensive family preservation programs, the goal is to avert imminent family breakup, usually because of the risk of abuse or neglect.

In each of these examples, outcome measures seem to be clear. "Official" reports of child abuse or domestic violence may be useful outcome measures for child protective service agencies, whereas the numbers of children placed in foster care or with adoptive families each month or year by year are natural outcome indicators for those providing foster care and adoption services (see Briggs, 1994, for one such example). Measures of psychiatric symptomatology that can be repeatedly administered are useful for evaluating change in clients at a mental health agency; the numbers of new voters registered and the numbers of these new registrants who actually cast ballots would be good indicators of the efficacy of a voter registration drive. In general, the closer you can keep your choice of outcome measure to the *real* issue being addressed by the agency, the better.

For example, suppose an agency serves women who have a history of abusing their children. Drawing upon research that shows that abusive mothers tend to be more socially insular—they are alone with their children a great deal of the time with little adult contact, or they lack a social support network—an agency may devise an intervention that is aimed at expanding the social networks of these mothers in the hope that this will reduce the potential for abuse. A program evaluation could be undertaken of this approach, using a standardized measure of social insularity as an outcome measure. Note, however, that the concept of reducing social insularity is somewhat removed from the *core* mission of the agency—preventing child abuse. A program evaluation that shows reductions in social insularity but lacks data on incidents of child abuse could be faulted for not having *direct* evidence that the agency was accomplishing its mission. If indirect indicators are used, it is best to complement them with more direct ones. For a program outcome measure to be valid it should provide an *accurate* indicator of what it is supposed to be measuring. For example, a written client self-report measure of drug abuse is not as direct (or as valid) an outcome measure as periodic random urine tests for illicit substances.

Often we must acknowledge from the outset that outcome measures are flawed. *Reports* of domestic violence do not capture all occurrences of violent episodes. This is also true for child abuse and neglect reports, allegations of rape, and so on. Brief mental status examinations provide a measure of cognitive functioning of persons with chronic mental illness but are not a measure of their actual *thinking*. So, for practical purposes, we must do the best that we can with the available range of measures. Of course, this means choosing the *best* available indicators. It is professionally irresponsible to not make use of the best measures that are currently supported by empirical research, practical, low cost, reliable, and valid. (More information on how to locate and evaluate instruments for program evaluation is contained in chapter 8.)

The well-known *Michigan Alcoholism Screening Test* (MAST) is a valid tool to help assess clients, but it is a poor measure for program evaluation. Why? Consider the following items taken from the MAST:

> 8. Have you ever attended a meeting of Alcoholics Anonymous (AA)? (Yes or No)
>
> 17. Have you ever been told you have liver trouble? (Yes or No)

While good initial screening questions, these MAST items are not useful for program evaluation because they are not sensitive to *change*. Even a recovering alcoholic who had not touched a drop of booze in ten years would not show improvement (change in a positive direction) by answering such questions (and there are many like these on the MAST), because they will not change. To undertake a program evaluation using SSRDs requires that you familiarize yourself with the state of the art outcome measures applicable to your agency, have the skills to choose the best ones (or seek skilled consultation in making such selections), and make use of them appropriately.

CONDUCTING NEEDS ASSESSMENTS

Single system research designs can make invaluable contributions to a needs assessment process. If, for instance, members of a local community were concerned with an apparently growing number of burglaries in their neighborhood, they could petition or lobby the city government to provide greater police protection through increased patrols and decreased response time. Depending upon political influence and available resources, such increased police protection may or may not be forthcoming.

One way to increase the likelihood of community complaints being attended to is to systematically gather data *over time* that will corroborate (or refute) perceptions of an increase in burglaries. The police department has records of burglaries going back for several years. These can be compiled by citizens, and the numbers of burglaries occurring within a given neighborhood on a month-by-month basis can be plotted on a graph. The visual portrayal of data is a more powerful method of illustrating an increase in burglaries than a column of numbers. Compare table 5.1 with figure 5.1, and imagine presenting these illustrations at a City Coun-

Table 5.1
Burglaries within the Rocksprings Neighborhood during the Past Two Years

Year and Month		Number of Burglaries
1995	January	9
	February	10
	March	8
	April	10
	May	8
	June	10
	July	11
	August	10
	September	12
	October	11
	November	13
	December	12
1996	January	8
	February	11
	March	9
	April	14
	May	9
	June	10
	July	13
	August	10
	September	14
	October	13
	November	14
	December	14

Figure 5.1
Burglaries in the Rocksprings Neighborhood during the Past Two Years

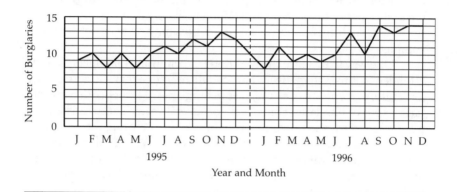

cil meeting. Which do you think makes a more compelling argument for increasing police protection?

SSRDs have their own schematic code to describe their features. An **A** refers to a baseline phase, a period where reliable and valid data are gathered in a systematic manner that extends over some time frame *in the absence of a particular intervention*. A **B** refers to a design phase when the same reliable and valid data are gathered in a manner similar to that used in an **A** phase *during or after a particular intervention is implemented*. A **C** could refer to still a different phase. Thus, using these symbols, assessing a problem or situation over time is called an **A** design (baseline only); an **A-B** design consists of a baseline phase followed by a period of intervention; an **A-B-A** study examines what happens when an intervention follows a baseline period, and then that intervention is removed, followed by a second baseline phase. Similarly, an **A-B-A-B** design consists of alternating baseline-intervention-baseline-intervention phases; and a **B-A-B** design involves recording data while an intervention is in place, again after it has been removed, and yet again after its reinstatement. An **A-B-A-C** design allows for a possible comparison of the efficacy of intervention **B** versus intervention **C**, and so forth. The numbers of possible permutations are lengthy, but in practice most SSRDs used in program evaluation are relatively simple.

A common question is, "How many data points do I need for each phase?" The answer is, "The more the better." Two are better than one; three better than two, and so forth. Any two points can be connected to depict a line, but it takes a minimum of three data points to infer a trend, and more are better. One well-respected journal that publishes research using SSRDs almost exclusively (*Journal of Applied Behavior Analysis*) found that the modal (most common) number of data points in the individual phases of SSRDs published in *JABA* was only four. As a general standard, ask yourself, "Can I visually infer any changes occurring in the data, either within or between phases? and if so, can I be confident that my inferences are accurate?" If the answers to those questions are "Yes," then you have enough data.

The exception to this is that some methods of statistical analysis require relatively larger numbers of data points. For example, the inferential tool called "time-series analysis" (a sophisticated statistical tool sometimes accompanying the use of SSRDs) may require over 50 data points in order to calculate statistics. However, most forms of program evaluation discussed in this chapter do not make use of inferential statistics.

Figure 5.1 could be said to represent the **A** design, data gathered during a period of time without any special intervention being applied. You can see that an **A** design lends itself quite naturally to the purposes of a needs assessment "to verify that a problem either currently ignored or being treated unsuccessfully exists in sufficient degree to warrant a new or additional intervention" (Rossi and Freeman, 1985, p. 107).

Some have contended that initial baseline phases are an essential feature of SSRDs, but such is not the case (witness the design **B-A-B**). Also, note that the term *baseline* applies to single-system research designs, not to group designs. A baseline is quite literally that, a *line* or *series* of data points connected on a graph. It does not refer to the single-point-in-time measures associated with the pretreatment assessments characteristic of group designs, such as the **O-X-O** design that we'll discuss later. Data for group designs are typically gathered on single occasions, reported descriptively and inferentially using statistics, and presented in tables reporting numbers like means and percentages, not graphs of connected data points. Data gathered before intervention and investigated using group designs is best referred to as the "Pretest." Data gathered before intervention and evaluated using SSRDs are called the "Baseline."

Adolescent pregnancy is said to be a growing problem, but is it? Where are the data? Are adolescents getting pregnant more often than they were ten years ago? Take a look at figure 5.2, which plots teenage pregnancy rates from 1982 to 1990 in DeKalb County, Georgia. Just by looking at the data it seems that the numbers of pregnancies occurring among females aged ten to seventeen years old had increased from

Figure 5.2

Pregnancy Rates Per 1,000 Females 10 to 17 Years of Age, DeKalb County, GA' 1982–1990

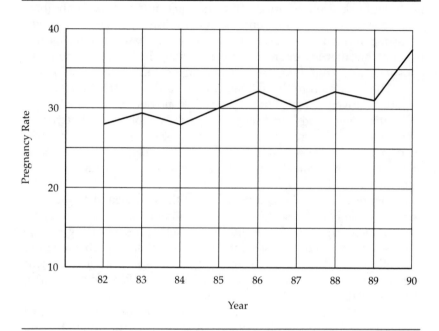

Source: McKenna and Wiesner (1994), p. 581.

about thirty to thirty-seven or thirty-eight per thousand. Another way to portray this is to note that pregnancies have increased from about 3 percent to near 3.8 percent over this nine year period (these are real data, by the way). You don't need the statistical expertise of a rocket scientist to look at figure 5.2 and figure out that there were more pregnancies in those years. Human service workers and community activists armed with graphic data like these are in a good position to argue for a need for pregnancy prevention programs in schools and related services.

FORMATIVE EVALUATION

Recall from chapter 3 that formative evaluations are used to adjust and enhance existing interventions or programs. SSRDs can be used for this purpose, as illustrated by a study conducted by J. Timothy Stocks when he was a M.S.W. intern at a group home operated by Goodwill Industries for persons with physical and mental disabilities (see Stocks, Thyer, and Kearsley, 1987). When Tim arrived at the group home to begin his internship, he found a "point" system in place, a program whereby residents earned points for performing daily living tasks (laundry, washing dishes, housekeeping, personal grooming). These points could be redeemed for extra consumable items (snacks and drinks) and privileges above and beyond what were noncontingently available to all group-home residents. This point system had been in place for over ten years, and no systematic evaluation of its usefulness had been undertaken during that time. Would the residents do their chores without contingent points being awarded by the staff? Maybe the point program could be dropped entirely, or maybe it should be improved. Tim approached the group-home manager about conducting such a study, and permission was given.

Tim and the group-home staff kept careful daily records for a week, tabulating the chores done by residents in exchange for points redeemable for privileges. This corresponded to a **B** phase, data gathered on an existing intervention. Thus he had seven data points (total numbers of points earned per day by group home residents). During week two, the group-home manager informed the residents that they no longer needed to perform chores to earn points for extra privileges. The extras would be provided irrespective of how much they helped out in the running of the group home, chores, and personal care. Tim and the staff continued to monitor the residents' performance of such tasks. They recorded data daily for another seven days, in the same manner as in the first week. This second week can be viewed as an **A** phase, gathering data in the absence of an intervention (in this case, the contingent point system). Finally, during the third week the program manager announced the restoration of the traditional point system. Privileges would once again be contingent upon earning points through the performance of chores. This can be construed as a return to the initial "**B**" phase. When graphed, the data appeared as in figure 5.3. We can see that the residents' performance of chores (as reflected by daily points accrued) underwent a significant dip during the week the point system was discontinued. Moreover, when the point system was restored, the performance of chores went back up. There appears to be a clear functional relationship between the point program and the performance of chores. As a result of this and other elements of Mr. Stocks' evaluation, the point system was altered to make it even more effective.

Figure 5.3
Average Number of Points Earned Per Day by Twelve Disabled Adult
Half-Way House Residents

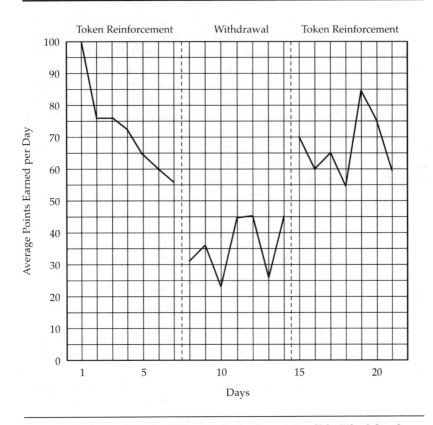

Source: Stocks, Thyer, and Kearsley (1987), p. 182. Used with permission of John Wiley & Sons, Inc.

QUALITY ASSURANCE STUDIES

Another use of the versatile SSRD is for the purpose of conducting quality assurance studies (QA). QA is most often construed as a checklist approach, reviewing paper records to determine compliance with various regulations. However, SSRD data are useful for the purposes of continued-stay utilization reviews, systematic audits of clinical records necessary to justify extended hospital stays, and outpatient treatments. Neuhring and Pascone (1986) contend that SSRDs are "capable of contributing to peer review questions, utilization reviews, clinical care evaluation stud-

116

ies, and profile analysis" (p. 359) and provide several examples of using SSRDs in peer review.

Neuhring and Pascone (1986, p. 364) show a graph depicting average length of stays on three different hospital units. Baseline phases for each unit depict the average length of stay (in months) for patients being treated at that unit. One unit had zero social workers, the second had one social worker, and the third unit had two social workers. When units one and two each added one social worker to their staff, length of stays declined. When units one and two then added discharge planning upon admission as a part of the treatment plan, length of stays declined further still. When unit three added the element of discharge planning beginning at admission to its social work program (which already had two social workers), average patient length of stays declined again. Average length of stay data were plotted on a simple graph, one for each unit, with monthly data tabulated for a two-year period. This is a fine example of making use of SSRDs, and these authors concluded that "several of the customary quality-assurance methodologies—peer review, continued stay utilization review, retrospective chart audits, clinical care evaluation studies, and profile analysis—may readily be operationalized using single-case designs" (Neuhring and Pascone, 1986, p. 364). Another example of using SSRDs in a quality assurance study is presented at the end of the next section on evaluation designs.

EVALUATION DESIGNS

In the next chapter, we describe the application of several simple group evaluation designs. The purpose of studies using evaluation designs is to answer the general question "Did our clients get better?" This can be paraphrased "Did our program achieve its goals?" "Were agency clients satisfied with the services they received?" "Are things getting better?" "Did things improve after a new policy was implemented?" Often, program evaluators want to know only if meaningful changes have occurred within a given program—not to prove that a program is responsible for observed improvements. The question "Did clients improve because of their participation in a given program?" requires considerably more complex designs. It is much more difficult to "prove" that a particular program's services were causally responsible for observed changes than to show that changes occurred. Yet, most programs do not have adequate information to answer the question "Did our clients get better?" and it is immensely useful to obtain such data. There are SSRD counterparts to simple group designs that can be used in evaluating programs, and two of these will be reviewed next.

When using the **B** design, one gathers data (outcome measures) that occurs coincident with the implementation of a new program, service, or policy. There is no preceeding baseline or no-treatment phase. Thus, one cannot compare data from a time when the program was in effect and when it was not in effect. However, the **B** design does allow one to answer the question "Did things get better when this program was implemented?" or to test the hypothesis "Implementation of Program X will be accompanied by an improvement in outcome measure Y." However, causal inference is not possible.

It is not legitimate in most cases, even with the most positive of improvements, to claim that the improvements were *caused* by Program X, because the **B** design does not allow one to rule out alternative explanations and threats to internal validity (more on these threats in chapter 6). For instance, maybe the outcome measure was improving before Program X began, and the graphed results simply reflect a previous trend in the data. Or, maybe something happened in the community coincident with the implementation of Program X, and it was this concurrent historical variable that *really* caused the observed improvements. Maybe the process of being evaluated in some way affected the outcome measure, causing it to drift in the direction of improvement. Rival explanations such as these typically remain to plague the program evaluator attempting to study various programs using the **B** design. Nevertheless, this simple approach is *very useful* when programs have *no data at all* to show that things are getting better (much less data permitting causal inferences). It is also the design of choice if it is not logistically feasible or ethically appropriate to delay implementation of a new program in order to gather baseline data. So, go ahead and use the **B** design, but be modest about your conclusions.

The next logical improvement to the **B** design is the **A-B** design, which was used by two social workers to evaluate a new public policy regarding the use of safety belts. Impressive statitics illustrate the immense carnage on our nation's highways because of motor vehicle accidents. Equally good data have shown that one's risk of being seriously injured or killed can be cut in half if one is wearing a safety belt when an accident occurs. Hoping to reduce injuries and deaths, a large number of states have enacted mandatory safety-belt use laws (MUL) requiring drivers (and sometimes passengers) to wear a safety belt. In September 1988, the state of Georgia implemented a rather weak MUL: Drivers could be cited for not being belted only if they are stopped for an unrelated offense (e.g., speeding), and the fines were small (maxmum of $25).

Margaret Robertson, a M.S.W. student at the University of Georgia, obtained monthly statistics on the numbers of injuries and fatalities per month and the death rate per 100 million miles driven for the twelve months before and after the implementation of the Georgia MUL. Ms. Robertson hypothesized that, if the MUL were effective, injuries, fatalities, and the death rate would decline in the year after the MUL was in effect. The data are presented in figures 5.4 and 5.5, which illustrate the numbers of persons seriously injured dring the twelve months before and after the MUL and the death rate per 100 million miles driven (a statistic that adjusts for the possibility that more or less driving occurred within Georgia during the two years). These data are taken from Thyer and Robertson (1993).

Figure 5.4
Number of Persons Injured in Motor Vehicle Accidents in Georgia for the Twelve Months Prior to and Following Passage of the Georgia Mandatory Safety Belt Use Law

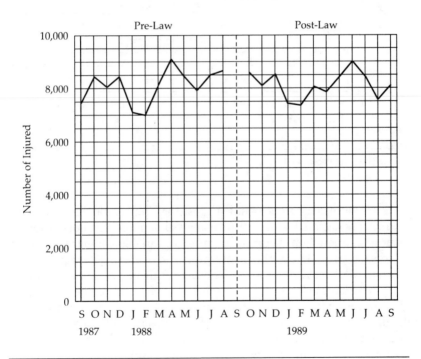

Source: Thyer and Robertson (1993), p. 510.

Figure 5.5
Death Rate per 100 Million Miles Driven in Georgia for the Twelve Months
Prior to and Following Passage of the Georgia Mandatory Safety Belt Use
Law

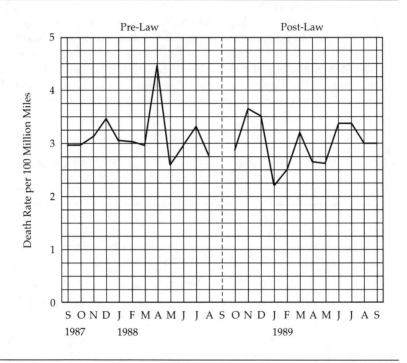

Source: Thyer and Robertson (1993), p. 510.

Visual inspection does not suggest that injuries or the death rate
appreciably declined, and statistical analysis supports the conclusion of
no post-law reduction occurring in these two variables (or in the numbers
killed each year). The authors' interpretation of these data was that the
Georgia MUL provided for ineffective contingencies. They suggested
ways in which the law could be improved so that it could become more
effective, as has been demonstrated in other states with stiffer laws man-
dating safety belt use. The benefits of empirically examining the effects
of public policies like this one are obvious. How will we know which
laws need improving if they are not regularly subjected to some form
of evaluation?

120

The **A-B** design helps to eliminate the threat that a pretreatment trend may have been present, as the baseline data can be used for comparison purposes to rule out that possibility. It also helps exclude the rival hypothesis that the very act of evaluating (measuring) somehow affected the situation, since such measurement effects would likely also occur when gathering the baseline data. The threat of some concurrent historical variable accounting for any observed improvements is not usually ruled out by the **A-B** design, hence its designation as an evaluation design, not an experimental design. If circumstances permit, use the **A-B** in lieu of the **B** design. Archival or retrospective data may be useful for developing baselines and help you evaluate many programs.

EXPERIMENTAL DESIGNS

For program evaluation purposes, an experimental SSRD can be considered a research design that permits a reasonable degree of *causal inference.* An experimental design allows the program evaluator to be relatively confident that the *program* was responsible for any observed improvements rather than some extraneous variables (threats to internal validity). In SSRDs, threats to internal validity are removed by repeatedly demonstrating a functional relationship between the introduction or the removal of an intervention and some corresponding change in the outcome measure. By definition this is not feasible in the B design. It is also possible that things may have been improving at the same time program X was implemented. In the **A-B** design, the skeptic who is faced with improvements that began immediately after a new program was initiated could contend, "Well, maybe it was just a coincidence that improvements occurred right after the program began." In many cases this criticism is justified. Lots of things occur in the natural environment, and lacking control over them means that clients in a program can be affected unbeknownst to the evaluator. Hence, the **A-B** design permits an evaluation of change (Did it improve?) but not causal inference (Did it improve *because* of the new program?).

Causal inference typically requires some type of experimental design. The simplest is called the **A-B-A** design, where a baseline phase is followed by intervention which is then deliberately or inadvertently removed, and data continues to be collected following removal of the intervention. The idea behind the **A-B-A** design is that if two consecutive meaningful changes in outcome measures can be produced, one of improvement when the program is begun and the second of deterioration when it is removed, then it is much less likely that some coincidental happening unrelated to the program was responsible for these changes. Following is a simple example taken from Thyer, Thyer, and Massa (1991).

A social worker was consulting at a local senior citizens' center where a program provided a free hot lunch to local seniors. It was noted that many of the seniors who ate lunch at the center did not wear their automobile safety belts. The center director agreed that it would be useful to help promote safety belt usage among these elderly drivers. For seven days an observer parked in the street and unobtrusively recorded safety belt use of drivers leaving the Senior Center between noon and 1:00 P.M. The outcome measure was the *percentage* of drivers exiting each day who were buckled up. Data were gathered for seven consecutive days.

The independent variable (intervention) was a female graduate social work student standing at the parking lot exit and displaying a sign to the exiting drivers. The sign read "Please Buckle Up—I Care" on one side (see Geller, Bruff, and Nimmer, 1985, for a description of this sign and its use). If drivers were wearing seat belts, the student flipped the sign over as they drove by, displaying the message "Thank You for Buckling Up." The sign was displayed from noon to 1:00 P.M., and observations of safety belt use continued as before. This fourteen-day period constituted the B phase of the study. Finally, the display of the sign was discontinued, and baseline conditions were reinstated for six consecutive days, constituting the second A phase and completing the **A-B-A** design.

To establish reliability, an observer (a M.S.W. student) independently rated over-the-shoulder safety-belt use on half of the days of the study. A very high interrater agreement was obtained between the two observers, suggesting that the recording methods were reliable. The data are depicted in figure 5.6.

During the first A phase, only 42 percent of the drivers were buckled up; during the B phase (display of the sign), safety belt use increased to 60 percent; use declined to 48 percent during the second A phase. It seems clear that safety belt use improved during the prompting condition, relative to the first baseline, and declined after the prompt was removed. It is implausible (but not impossible) to argue that these changes occurred by coincidence, hence internal validity is relatively high in this simple design.

Obviously, **A-B-A** designs have shortcomings, but this should not deter beginning program evaluators from undertaking them. They can produce useful data, and your evaluation skills will be enhanced by completing them. Don't wait until you can undertake a "perfect" program evaluation before attempting such projects. You'll never begin if you wait for the "perfect" program. Rather, think small, think simple, and

Figure 5.6
Daily Percentages of Observed Safety Belt Use among Drivers Exiting the
Senior Citizens' Center

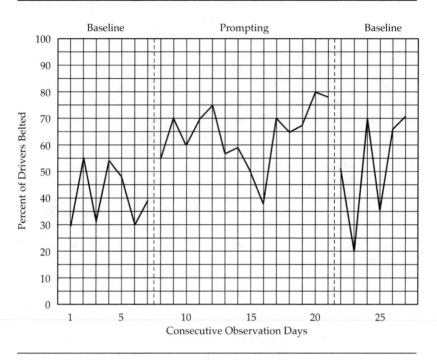

Source: Thyer, Thyer, and Massa (1991), p. 128. Reprinted with the permission of Aldine de
Gruyter, Inc.

gradually hone your program evaluation skills by undertaking succes-
sively more complicated studies. This study conducted at the Senior
Citizens' Center helped another social worker to design and complete
an evaluation of an immensely more complex project.

A doctoral student in social work, Karen Sowers-Hoag (1986), was
interested in child welfare—particularly in promoting safety-belt use
among young children. Karen arranged to provide a safety-belt use training curriculum at a local private school to children ranging in age from
4.8 to 7.1 years of age (average age = 5 years). She monitored the safety-
belt use of all children as they were picked up and driven away from
school at the end of the day for a period and found sixteen who *never*
buckled up. She formally baselined these sixteen after dividing them
into two groups of eight children. Then she trained the ones in Group

1 in her safety-belt curriculum, continuing to gather safety-belt use data on all children in both groups. After a week had passed, children in Group 2 were trained. In effect, each group received an **A-B** design, but the baselines were staggered and of differing length. The outcome measure was the percent of children in each group who buckled up as they were driven away from school each day. Highly reliable but unobtrusive observations were made of the outcome measure. The educational program was discontinued for both groups thirty-four days into the study, and follow-up observations were made over the next several months. The data Karen obtained are depicted in figure 5.7. Following a stable (and low) baseline, those in Group 1 immediately began buckling up on a consistent basis after the program began. Regular safety-belt use was maintained while the program was faded, then discontinued entirely. Group 2's baseline, initially stable, went up a bit after Group 1 (but not Group 2) received training. It was later found out that this was because a brother and sister with different last names were randomly assigned to the two different groups. There was evidently "contamination" in Group 2's baseline—the child in Group 1 influenced his sister in Group 2. Nevertheless, a clear functional relationship between training and safety-belt use appeared to occur for Group 2 as well.

This design is called a **multiple baseline design**; like the **A-B-A** design, it permits causal inference. It is not plausible to argue that Group 1 and Group 2 both changed following the implementation of the program because of some coincidental happenings in the natural environment. Possible, yes, but not very likely. *All* 158 children attending the school received safety-belt training. It can be reasonably argued that a program found effective with children who did not initially use their safety belts at all would likely be effective with the children who initially used their belt sometimes. However, it is likely that a program found to be effective in getting small children who already buckled up *sometimes* to use their safety belts *consistently* would not prove equally efficacious with children who initially never buckled up at all. (Details on the study can be found in Sowers-Hoag, Thyer, and Bailey, 1987, and in Karen Sowers-Hoag's doctoral dissertation, 1986.)

Working in a psychiatric emergency room setting, Jones, Morris, and Barnard (1986) applied an intervention program intended to increase the staff's timely completion of required civil commitment forms. These researchers also used a multiple baseline design to evaluate the intervention's effectiveness. There were three required forms, and the outcome measure was the percentage of charts that contained properly completed forms. Baselines were initiated on all three forms separately, and intervention was sequentially applied for each form in a staggered manner. After

Figure 5.7
Percentage of Safety-Belt Use by Eight Children in Group 1 and Eight Children in Group 2

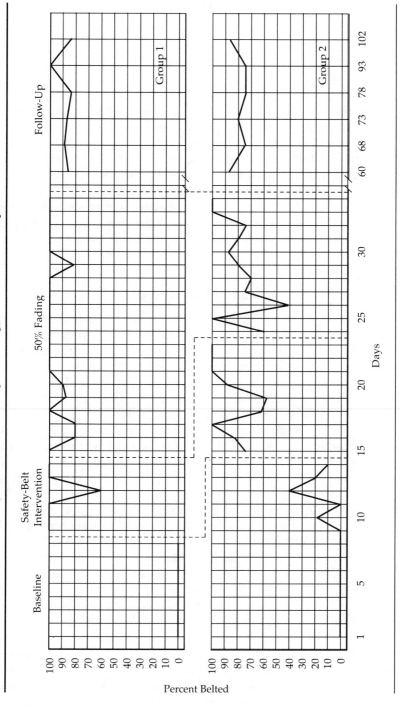

Source: Sowers-Hoag, Thyer, and Bailed (1987), p. 136. Reprinted with the permission of the Society for the Experimental Analysis of Behavior, Inc.

baseline, intervention was applied to the first required form (notices of rights), while baselines were continued on the other two forms. Then intervention was applied to the use of the second form (imminent harm applications), while the baseline was continued on the third form. Finally, intervention was begun for the third form (witness list). In each instance, the percentage of charts containing correctly completed forms dramatically improved but only after the intervention was applied. At the end of the study, with six month follow-up, virtually 100 percent of the charts contained properly completed forms. This study involved thirty-four staff members and high interrater agreement pertaining to assessing the outcome measures. The quality of the data permitted clear causal inferences that it was the intervention program (involving simple instructions and feedback) that was responsible for the improvements and not some extraneous variables.

CHAPTER RECAP

Single system research designs can be a useful tool in the methodological armamentarium of the program evaluator. Like group (nomothetic) research designs, which we'll cover in the next chapter, SSRDs can be viewed as falling along a hierarchy of sophistication, ranging from simple designs, useful in evaluating the occurrence of change, to relatively complex designs, used to determine whether or not a given program caused any observed effects. The unit of analysis in SSRDs is called a "system" In *clinical practice* the system can be a client, a family, a couple, or a small group. In *program evaluation*, the system can be conceptualized as a single program, an agency, a network of agencies, another type of organization, a city, state or even a nation. The key to using SSRDs is having a reliable and valid outcome measure that can be repeatedly assessed over time, plotting such data on a simple line graph, and interpreting the outcomes using visual inspection. In some cases, inferential statistics can be applied to SSRD data (see Bloom and Fischer, 1994, for examples), but this is not usually necessary.

Conceptually, the reasoning behind SSRDs is not difficult, although the usual evils attendant upon doing research in field settings (see Wodarski and Feldman, 1974) often complicate the otherwise elegant simplicity of these methods. Conclusions drawn from program evaluations using SSRDs usually possess limited external validity (generalizability), since almost by definition program evaluations make use of convenience samples, not randomly selected ones. This limitation, however, needs to be tempered with the recognition that program evaluations using group designs and other research methodologies are also likely to be compromised in this manner; hence, this limitation is in actuality not particularly salient. Most program evaluators are concerned with learning about a *particular program*, not with making generalizations to all programs, and SSRDs are a great tool for this purpose.

QUESTIONS FOR CLASS DISCUSSION

1. Make a list of problems in your community or on your campus. Discuss how a SSRD could be used for needs assessment with one of the problems. What data would need to be gathered? How long would the baseline need to be? How convincing would evidence from a SSRD be?
2. In relation to the social service agencies known to students in your community, brainstorm how a SSRD could be used for either formative evaluation or quality assurance. Start with a specific problem and then move to a discussion of possible interventions. What would be the outcome measure(s)? How long would the study take?
3. Could SSRDs be used in conjunction with consumer satisfaction studies? How?

MINI-PROJECTS: EXPERIENCING EVALUATION FIRSTHAND

1. For a client population with which you have worked or are working (or a fictitious population), select an outcome measure that follows from some problem they have in common. Construct a graph that could monitor their progress over time. In the accompanying paper, be sure to address the target behavior, the baseline, the type of design you would use, and any efforts you would make to improve or check the reliability of the data you obtain.
2. If you are not familiar with single system research designs, browse though back issues of the *Journal of Applied Behavior Analysis* until you find an article that interests you and describes the use of an SSRD. Summarize the findings of this article relative to the usefulness and limitations of the SSRD employed. How could the study have been improved?

REFERENCES AND RESOURCES

Alter, C., and Evens, W. (1990). *Evaluating your practice*. New York: Springer.
Barlow, D.H., and Hersen, M. (1984). *Single-case experimental designs*. New York: Pergamon.

Benbenishty, R. (1989). Combining the single-system and group approaches to evaluate treatment effectiveness on the agency level. *Journal of Social Service Research.* 12(3/4), 31–48.

Bloom, M. (ed.) (1993). *Single-system designs in the human services.* New York: Haworth.

Bloom, M., Fischer, J., and Orme, J. (1994). *Evaluating practice* (2d ed.). Englewood Cliffs, NJ: Prentice-Hall.

Bowen, G.L., Farkas, G., and Neenan, P.A. (1991). Application of time series designs to the evaluation of social services program initiatives: The recycling fund concept. *Social Work Research and Abstracts,* 27(3), 9–15.

Briar, S., and Blythe, S.J. (1985). Agency support for evaluating the outcomes of social work services. *Administration in Social Work,* 9(2), 25–36.

Briggs, H.E. (1994). Promoting adoptions by foster-parents through an inner city organization. *Research on Social Work Practice,* 4, 497–509.

DiNitto, D. (1983). Time series analysis: An application to social welfare policy. *Journal of Applied Behavioral Science,* 19, 507–518.

Geller, E.S., Bruff, C.D., and Nimmer, J.G. (1985). "Flash-for-life": Community-based prompting for safety belt promotion. *Journal of Applied Behavior Analysis,* 18, 309–314.

Horn, W.F., and Heerboth, J. (1982). Single-case experimental designs and program evaluation. *Evaluation Review,* 6, 403–424.

Jayaratne, S., and Levy, R.L. (1979). *Empirical clinical practice.* New York: Columbia University Press.

Jones, H.H., Morris, E.K., and Barnard, J.D. (1986). Increasing staff completion of civil commitment forms through instructions and graphed group performance feedback. *Journal of Organizational Behavior Management,* 7(3/4), 29–43.

Kazdin, A.E. (1982). *Single-case research designs.* New York: Oxford University Press.

Kelley, P.L., Jacobs, R.R., and Farr, J.L. (1994). Effects of multiple administrations of the MMPI for employee screening. *Personnel Psychology,* 47, 575–591.

Krishef, C.H. (1991). *Fundamental approaches to single subject design and analysis.* Malabar, FL: Krieger.

Marsh, J.C. (1981). Combining time series with interviews: Evaluating the effectiveness of a sexual assault law. In R.F. Conner (ed.); *Methodological advances in evaluation research* (pp. 93–108). Beverley Hills, CA: Sage.

Mazur-Hart, S.F., and Berman, J.J. (1977). Changing from fault to no-fault divorce: An interrupted time series analysis. *Journal of Applied Psychology,* 7, 300–312.

McKenna, M.T., and Wiesner, P.J. (1994). Evaluation of the Consesus Health Status Indicator for assessing adolescent pregnancies and births. *Public Health Reports,* 109, 579–582.

Nuehring, E.M., and Pascone, A.B. (1986). Single-subject evaluation: A tool for quality assurance. *Social Work,* 31, 359–365.

Nurius, P.S. (1983). Use of time-series analysis in the evaluation of change due to intervention. *Journal of Applied Behavioral Science,* 19, 215–228.

Rossi, P.H., and Freeman, H.E. (1985). *Evaluation: A systematic approach.* Beverly Hills, CA: Sage.

Sowers-Hoag, K.M. (1986). Promoting safety belt use among young children: An experimental analysis. Ph.D. diss., Florida State University School of Social Work.

Sowers-Hoag, K.M., Thyer, B.A., and Bailey, J.S. (1987). Promoting safety belt use among young children. *Journal of Applied Behavior Analysis,* 20, 133–138.

Stocks, J.T., Thyer, B.A., and Kearsley, M.A. (1987). Using a token economy in a community-based residential program for disabled adults: An empirical evaluations leads to program modification. *Behavioral Residential Treatment,* 1, 173–185.

Thyer, B.A., and Robertson, M. (1993). An initial evaluation of the Georgia safety belt use law: A nul MUL? *Environment and Behavior,* 25, 506–513.

Thyer, B.A., Thyer, K.E., and Massa, S. (1991). Behavioral analysis and therapy in the field of gerontology. In Paul K.H. Kim (ed.), *Serving the elderly: Skills for practice* (pp. 117–135). New York: Aldine.

Tripodi, T., and Harrington, J. (1979). Uses of time-series designs for formative program evaluation. *Journal of Social Service Research,* 3, 67–78.

Wodarski, J.S., and Feldman, R.A. (1974). Practical aspects of field research. *Clinical Social Work Journal,* 2, 182–193.

Wodarski, J.S., and Lindsey, E.W. (1987). Training social work administrators to use evaluation in daily practice. In N. Gottlieb (ed.), *Perspectives on direct practice evaluation,* (pp. 123–133). Seattle: University of Washington School of Social Work.

SIX

Group Evaluation Designs

Group evaluation designs vary in sophistication and in the degree to which they allow us to rule out other explanations and to understand the true power of an intervention to effect change. At the lowest level (pre-experimental), a design like the One-Group Pretest-Posttest resembles the **A-B** design in the previous chapter—the main difference being that One-Group Pretest-Posttest designs *must* be based on data from a collection of individuals.

At the most sophisticated level (experimental designs), group evaluation designs allow researchers and evaluators to answer questions of causality such as "Did the intervention alone improve clients' lives?" Randomized experimental designs not only provide a lens for examining the impact of interventions, but also do something that other designs can't do nearly as well—they allow evaluators to make predictions about how well the treatment may work the next time it is employed.

Group evaluation designs are sometimes called outcome, impact, effectiveness, or summative evaluation. While it could be argued that the Single System Research Designs and perhaps some of the others we've already discussed also look at outcome, by convention usually only group designs are known as outcome designs.

STARTING AN OUTCOME EVALUATION

Your agency director wants you to conduct an evaluation for the agency. The agency currently does some program monitoring and has made use of consultants for formative evaluations in previous years. Now, however, the agency director wants an outcome evaluation and wants you to coordinate this effort. Where do you begin? Although the director may strongly urge you to do an evaluation of the whole agency (or examine all of the agency's programs simultaneously), it is not recommended that the novice evaluator attempt a multi-program evaluation. Instead, a single program should be chosen as the object or target of the evaluation. The wisdom of this recommendation can be seen if we look at the programs contained in a single "yellow pages" phone listing for one moderate-sized mental health center, shown in Box 6.1.

It is hard not to notice the rich variety of programs that are provided in this agency. This assortment of programs prevents an evaluator from using any one tool or instrument to measure the same outcome for every program. One would expect the Day Treatment Unit to have a different set of outcomes than the Employee Assistance Program or the Chemical Dependency Outpatient Counseling Center. Thus, the evaluator starts an evaluation effort by selecting a single program to be the focus of the evaluation. (Later on, as you know more about evaluation, you may find the same evaluation procedure or the same instrument can be used with several programs simultaneously, but for now keep in mind that we are to evaluate one program at a time.)

Once a single program has been selected, it is possible to begin to think about criteria that would help differentiate a "good" program from a poor program. Start by thinking in terms of single indicators. For instance, with programs designed to employ the "hard-core" unemployed, success could be measured by the percentage who actually become employed. A program designed to help agoraphobics could be evaluated based upon the percentage who, after treatment, are able to leave their homes without symptoms in order to shop, work, volunteer, or play. Bereavement counseling programs should help participants become less depressed. Treatment programs for impotence should determine the percent who are still impotent after intervention.

These examples provide illustrations of the kind of indicators needed for outcome evaluation. Evaluators do not always have to come up with these indicators on their own. If the agency already has developed goal statements and objectives for the program, outcome indicators can often be obtained from reviewing these.

Once the evaluator has a firm notion of an outcome indicator (sometimes called a dependent variable), he or she can formulate a research question or hypothesis to further focus the program evaluation. For example, the evaluator might ask of a job training program, "What percent-

BOX 6.1
Yellow Pages Phone Book Listing
for the Comprehensive Mental Health
Services Agency

Main Office:
234 W. Burton Street   885-4000

Adult Counseling Clinic   885-4001

Chemical Dependency Services   885-4911
   Detoxification Center   885-4999
   Inpatient Treatment Center   885-4949
   Outpatient Counseling Center   885-4989

Child Guidance Program   885-4363

Community Support Services   885-4888
   West Side Personal Care Home   885-4212
   Campbell House   885-4175

Employee Assistance Program   885-4222

Forensic Services   885-4333

Lifestyles   885-4545

Parent's Place   885-4721

Partial Hospitalization Services   885-4110
   Our Place   885-4166
   Day Treatment Unit   885-4699

Passages   885-4677

Teen Help   885-4444

age of clients completing the program secure full-time employment within six months of graduation from the program?"

Sometimes a program director or the evaluator might propose a hypothesis instead of a research question. An example of a hypothesis might be: "The Teen Help outpatient counseling program is more effective in combating adolescent chemical dependency than the Life Adventure program." Or, "A greater percentage of the clients of Chrysalis House will be drug-free one year after completion of the program than those who complete residential treatment at Pilot House." No matter whether you tend to think in terms of hypotheses or of questions, either will provide the necessary focal point with which to begin planning an evaluation. Once a question or hypothesis has been selected to guide the outcome study, the next step is to choose an appropriate design.

If the question is simply "Did clients improve?" the evaluator does not need to be concerned with control groups and random assignment. Random assignment can be difficult, if not impossible, to impose in a social service agency. Often, intact groups already exist, and involving these individuals in an evaluation effort makes a good deal of sense. Selection of a design is affected by multiple considerations, including the type of questions you need to answer, access to data, cooperation one might expect from staff, the importance of controlling for variables that might contaminate the validity of the findings, the amount of time you have, and your technical analytical skills.

OUTCOME EVALUATION DESIGNS

Fitz-Gibbon and Morris (1987) have defined an **evaluation design** as "a plan which dictates when and from whom measurements will be gathered during the course of an evaluation" (p. 9). Evaluation designs are roughly analogous to blueprints in that they suggest a plan or model to be followed. Even though you may know nothing about building a new house, you can appreciate the carpenters' frustration if the only instructions they were given were, "Build a house." Without more elaboration, the carpenters will not know whether to begin framing for a six room house or a house with eight bedrooms. Should there be one bath or a bath adjacent to each bedroom? Will the house be brick or frame? Beyond even the basic features, there are still important details that must be worked out, such as the number of windows to be used, and their placement. To guide the carpenters as they work on the house, detailed sketches or blueprints are used. These diagrams provide guidance and direction to the carpenters in their construction.

Evaluation designs describe the key features and procedures to be followed in conducting an evaluation. They make it possible to estimate the cost of the evaluation, the length of time that will be required, and the rigorousness of the evaluation. Just as a carpenter could take a set of blueprints to another site and build a house identical to the one that had just been constructed, an evaluation design contains the necessary information to allow other evaluators to replicate or reproduce the original evaluation.

There are plenty of designs and evaluative criteria to choose from. More than twenty years ago, Suchman (1967) discussed the focus of evaluation in terms of effort, performance, adequacy, efficiency, and process. Attkisson and Broskowski (1978) defined program evaluations as having a special focus on accessibility, acceptability, comprehensiveness, integration of services, awareness, availability, continuity, and cost of services. Shipman (1989), an employee of the U.S. General Accounting Agency, described general criteria that were developed to ensure fair comparisons and comprehensive reviews of federal programs for children. Three criteria assess the need for the program: problem magnitude, problem seriousness, and duplication of services. Three criteria relate to program implementation: program fidelity, administrative efficiency, and interrelationships between the program and other programs. The last set of criteria relate to the effects of the program: achievement of intended objectives, targeting success in reaching intended clients, achievement of intended objectives, cost-effectiveness, and other effects (e.g., unforeseen or unintended effects).

Michael Patton, the author of several books on evaluation, demonstrated his creativeness by listing one hundred different types of evaluation in his 1987 text. However, unless you are particularly interested in the absolute number of variations that can be made of a small set of evaluation designs, there is little reason to contemplate, name, or enumerate all of the evaluation designs available to us. You will find it more useful to learn how to conceptualize ways of evaluating programs. Any program can be viewed from numerous perspectives and can be evaluated for various purposes.

How do you go about selecting a program evaluation design? The design follows from the research question or hypothesis and purpose of the evaluation. Evaluation designs are selected based upon what information is needed about the program. What do you want to know about the program? Oftentimes it is useful to make a list of all the relevant questions. (If this list becomes too long, it will have to be pared down to those questions that are crucial and that realistically can be addressed.)

Once it is clear what information is needed from the evaluation, the evaluator must consider the resources available and the constraints in

135

the agency. It has been our experience that the selection of an evaluation design is made a great deal easier if some of the realistic constraints under which the evaluation must operate are considered. Students and agency personnel often complain: "We can't evaluate our services. We don't have any money." Sometimes this is expressed another way: "The director is very supportive, but we don't have a computer and can't afford a consultant." Besides the problem of the cost of the evaluation, there occasionally are constraints on the type of data that the evaluator can access: "I don't know what kind of evaluation to do—the director says that we cannot recontact any of our former clients."

The amount of time allowed or available for completion of the evaluation can be another constraint. Because of the press of other concerns, an evaluation may need to be conducted and a final report prepared within three or four weeks. This constraint has a way of ruling out a number of evaluation designs.

Another consideration is the evaluation audience. On some occasions, the evaluator anticipates that the findings will be warmly received. There will be no hostility or attacks upon the evaluation methodology. Given that situation, it may not be necessary to use a very rigorous evaluation design. On other occasions, the evaluator may expect a hostile reaction to the evaluation results. Where the evaluation is expected to be attacked, the evaluator will want to provide the best possible information from the most rigorous methodology that can be applied in that setting. Fitz-Gibbon and Morris (1987) have noted, "Your task as an evaluator is to find the design that provides the most credible information in the situation you have at hand" (p. 10).

When these and other constraints have been identified, the evaluator can effectively eliminate some evaluation designs from consideration and begin to develop a plan for selection of the sample, the timing of the evaluation, and the data collection procedures. The evaluation design will dictate when and from whom measurements will be gathered during the course of an evaluation. Your task as an evaluator is to find the design that provides the most objective and convincing information that can be produced in that particular setting.

In order to reduce the confusion associated with choosing among the plethora of evaluation designs available, the designs in this chapter have been arranged in terms of the simplest (pre-experimental) designs, followed by the quasi-experimental, and then the more rigorous (experimental). Generally, the simpler designs tend to require less effort and are therefore the least expensive. Although this is not a perfect categorization scheme, thinking about designs in this way may be of benefit to beginning evaluators. Since these designs are generally covered in introductory research methods courses, they will not be presented here in great detail.

PRE-EXPERIMENTAL EVALUATION DESIGNS

The evaluation designs in this group will appeal to those of you who have any of the following constraints:

- very little budget or staff support
- very little time in which to conduct the evaluation
- very little research expertise

The designs in this section are not very rigorous and are best suited for those occasions where an evaluation is needed but those who are requiring it are not expected to be terribly fussy. In short, the evaluation will be used not so much as a fact-finding mission as to confirm or "rubber stamp" a decision that is likely to be made (e.g., to continue funding a program).

One-Group Posttest Only Design

Although it may sound impressive, this evaluation design is one of the most elementary. This design involves providing an intervention or program to a group of clients and then determining if they have changed for the better. For example, suppose you are running a smoking cessation program. The goal of the program is for participants to be completely free of all smoking by the end of the intervention. Assuming this intervention ran over a number of weeks, the evaluator could determine how many of the workshop participants had stopped smoking by the time of the last session. If you started the group with eighteen participants and nine stopped smoking by the time of the last session, then your program would have experienced a 50 percent success rate. Schematically, we can represent this design:

$$X \quad O$$

where X is the intervention for some smokers, and O represents the observation or measurement of the effect of the intervention.

This design is most suited to situations where clients' preprogram status can be ascertained without formal assessment. Note that cost, staff support, research expertise, and the amount of time required to

137

Table 6.1
Number of Participants Not Smoking by Last Session

| | Calendar Year 1995 | | | | Average Success Rate |
	Feb.	April	July	Oct.	
Number of Participants	24	21	25	18	
Number Not Smoking	9	9	12	9	
Success Rate	38%	43%	48%	50%	43%

complete the evaluation would be minimal. Since so little is involved here, the evaluator could even get the results from prior workshops and compute an average success rate for the past year (or even the past three years). This evaluative data could be displayed rather handily in a single table, as shown in table 6.1.

Of course, the problem with this design (as any smoker would know) is that "success" could be better determined if the participants were surveyed six months or a year after completion of the intervention. Oftentimes smokers quit for a brief period of time, only to start up again. However, tracking down former participants to learn if they are free of their smoking habit would involve some expenditure of possibly scarce funds. Postage would not be a large expense unless hundreds of questionnaires are to be mailed. Phone calls are not usually expensive (unless they involve long-distance tolls), but they do require staff time to place the calls. (However, these might be made by clerical staff in between other assignments.)

A problem with this design is that it is not rigorous. It will tell us very little about the differential effectiveness of the intervention. We would not know if just as many smokers were successful by quitting on their own. This is also a weak evaluation design because the workshop participants were not randomly selected from the population of all smokers. Without that random assignment, there is the possibility that your sample of participants does not represent all smokers in the community. Perhaps those who have enrolled in this program were encouraged to participate by their physicians because of smoking-related health problems. These smokers may be more willing to quit smoking than other (healthier) smokers because further smoking will be injurious. Your program may show better results with such "motivated" smokers than with those who do not currently have health problems related to smoking. Similarly, your program might be more effective with those who have quit previously than with those who have never been able to quit on their own. Since there was no control group, there is little "hard" evidence that it was your program and not some other influence that was responsible for the participants' success. (Perhaps physicians' stern warnings played a greater role than your program in any smoking cessation.)

Posttest-Only Design with Nonequivalent Groups

This design is a slight improvement over the prior design because it uses a control group. A control group is simply a comparison group. In the example of a smoking cessation program, the group of program participants is known as the experimental or treatment group. With this design, another group of smokers must be located for comparison. Ideally, this should be a similar group of smokers who are different only because they are trying to quit on their own. The evaluator compares the success rate of the workshop participants against the success rate of those smokers in the control group who were trying to quit on their own. This design might be diagrammed:

$$X \quad O_1$$
$$------$$
$$O_2$$

where X is the intervention, O_1 is the observation or measurement made of the group who received the intervention and O_2 is the measurement or observation made of the comparison group; the broken line between groups indicates the absence of nonrandom assignment.

The weaknesses of this design can be seen. For one, it may or may not be easy to identify a group of smokers trying to quit on their own, and, even if you learn that those attending the smoking cessation program have a much higher success rate than the control group, you do not know that the control group was a fair comparison. There may have been great differences between the two groups in the average number of cigarettes smoked daily. Perhaps the majority of those in your smoking cessation program were young employees of a factory in town where they expected a cash bonus at the end of the year if they could quit smoking. Although you had not intended the control group to be dissimilar from the intervention group, you discover later that the control group is much older and that they have been smoking, on the average, for thirty-seven years. It could have been more difficult for this group to stop smoking than it was for young adults who had been smoking for five years or less. Since the control and treatment groups were not equivalent, an "apple and orange" type of comparison is being made. While

139

it may be possible for you to find a control group that is more like the intervention group than the one mentioned here, the burden of trying to demonstrate the rough equivalence of the two groups is still yours.

One-Group Pretest-Posttest Design

Sometimes it is not convenient to gather a control group. We'll examine this problem later, but for now let's assume that there is not enough time prior to the starting of the intervention to coordinate a control group. However, you have been successful in locating what you consider to be a wonderful instrument to monitor the success of those participating in your program. In the situation where you can get a measurement before the intervention (this is called the **pretest**) and also get a measurement after the intervention (the **posttest**), you have the One-Group Pretest-Posttest Design. This design can be diagrammed:

$$O_1 \quad X \quad O_2$$

where the first observation (the pretest) is represented by the O_1 while the second observation (posttest) is O_2.

You could use this design when starting most new programs.

Let's say that you are going to begin a support group for women who have recently gone through a divorce. Knowing that such women are often depressed, you decide upon an intervention that is designed to reduce depression. In theory, these women should be less depressed after the ten week support group than they were when they started. After some library work, you decide to use the twenty-item depression scale (the CES-D) developed by the National Institute of Mental Health's Center for Epidemiologic Studies (Radloff, 1977) for both the pre- and posttest measures of depression.

When the group comes in for their first meeting, you explain the purpose of the pretest, respond to any questions, and then distribute the instrument. At the final meeting of the group, you administer the same depression scale a second time. Having both the pretest and posttest data, it is possible to determine what percentage of the support group showed an improvement by the end of the tenth week.

Since two measurements were obtained with a standardized instrument, success could be measured in terms of (1) any decrease in the percentage of support group members who were depressed or (2) improvements in the group's average score from pretest to posttest. This information would be valuable in terms of helping future consumers or policymakers decide whether the support group is effective. This evaluation design would meet many agencies' needs for evaluation.

However, this design is inadequate on those occasions when it becomes important to establish that it was the intervention—and the intervention only—that produced the improvement. For instance, perhaps you have observed that most persons who are depressed immediately after a divorce tend to improve with the passage of time—whether or not they get professional help. In other words, this design does not eliminate other explanations that might actually be responsible for the improvement. In many situations, it may not be necessary to rule out these alternative explanations. One therapist might say, "So what if it really was the passage of time and not the intervention? The vast majority of my clients improved in the past ten weeks and that, after all, is the reason they came here."

Because this evaluation design is not very rigorous, it cannot rule out alternative explanations, such as changes due to greater maturity (a potential explanation to be especially considered when children are involved), or the effect of repeated use of the instrument (testing), or several others. On those occasions when there is a need to rule out alternative explanations (for instance, you may want to market the intervention), you can employ more rigorous (experimental) evaluation designs. Weiss (1972) advocated the use of experimental evaluation designs in those situations where

> it is for purposes outside the immediate program that experimental design is best suited. Decisions on the order of continuation or abandonment of the program, decisions on whether to advocate nation-wide use of the program model—these require great confidence in the validity of the research, and therefore experimental design. Other types of decisions may not need such rigor, at least initially. (Pp. 66–67)

QUASI-EXPERIMENTAL AND EXPERIMENTAL EVALUATION DESIGNS

The evaluation designs described so far can be thought of as elementary or beginning designs. Campbell and Stanley (1963) call them pre-experimental designs. Methodologically, they are weak, because they cannot rule out alternative explanations for any observed changes. While the pre-experimental designs may provide information that satisfies friendly supporters of programs, they cannot provide conclusive evidence that it was the intervention alone that was responsible for changes. Fortunately, there are other, more rigorous evaluation designs available. Since the next group of designs tends to require more planning, and more extensive involvement with control groups, and may result in more data to analyze, they are more expensive and require more resources than the pre-experimental designs.

As we suggested in the Preface, program evaluation approaches can be thought of as a series of steps beginning with the simplest: formative, process, and program monitoring. The discussion of pre-experimental designs we just completed brings us another step closer to the strongest of quantitative methodologies. Quasi-experimental designs are better than the pre-experimental designs but not so good as the experimental designs for providing "hard evidence" that the intervention was responsible for the observed changes. Because they do not use randomization and may not always involve a control group, **quasi-experimental designs** draw their name from not quite being experiments.

Nonequivalent Control Group Design

The Nonequivalent Control Group Design is one of the most commonly used evaluation designs. In this design a group of persons who are similar in composition to the group receiving the intervention is used as the control in both pretest and posttest observations. This design can be diagrammed:

$$O_1 \quad X \quad O_2$$
$$\overline{ \quad \text{--} \quad }$$
$$O_3 \qquad O_4$$

where O_1 and O_3 are pretests for the intervention and control groups, respectively; O_2 and O_4 are posttests for the intervention and control groups; the broken line between groups indicates nonrandom assignment.

Suppose you are an evaluation consultant to a school principal who wants to implement a drug education program with all seventh, eighth, and ninth graders. If the principal, the parents, or the school board has determined that all of the students will receive the intervention, then it may not be possible to develop a control group from within the same school. It may be necessary to locate a control group in a different school or community.

With this design, the control group can be used to help eliminate alternative explanations. It is quite possible, for instance, that any increase in the intervention group's knowledge about drugs at the time of posttest could have occurred merely from interaction with older students or their own firsthand experience with drugs. Perhaps as seventh, eighth, and ninth graders mature, they read the newspapers to a greater extent and thus "educate" themselves about the dangers of drugs. These explanations and the effectiveness of the intervention can be understood by making comparisons to the control group. If those receiving the intervention are more knowledgeable at the time of the posttest than those in the control group, then the intervention appears to have been a success. If, however, the control group shows the same gains in knowledge about drugs as the experimental group, then you would know that it was not the intervention that was responsible but some other factor or combination of factors.

The problem with this design is that while you could establish that the seventh, eighth, and ninth graders in the control group were equivalent to those receiving the intervention in terms of knowledge about drugs at the time of pretest, students receiving the drug awareness program could simultaneously be exposed to other influences or have access to resources that were not available in the comparison school. For example, suppose that the principal in the intervention school has been especially active in getting local businesses to contribute computers to the school. Let's further suppose that while the great availability of computers in this school has nothing directly to do with the drug awareness program, use of the computers by a large majority of the student body serves to increase their reading skills. Even though you were concerned only about their scores on the instrument that measured their drug awareness, as the children in the intervention school learned to read better, they learned more on their own about the dangers of drugs. So, it may not have been the intervention program alone that was responsible for the improvement in test scores, but the double whammy of greater access to computers in addition to the drug awareness program. Conversely, if the control group showed greater improvement, it may have been the influence of factors not known to the evaluator (such as pairing every student with a volunteer reading tutor) that had the effect (as students began reading more on their own, they learned about the dangers of experimenting with illicit drugs).

It is easy to see the importance of obtaining groups that are similar not only in the skill, behavior, or characteristic being observed, but also in other major variables. What kinds of variables are important? (This question becomes especially critical if we have to go to another school to obtain a control group.) Would it be fair to compare a suburban school with an inner city school? If one school was situated in a low income, high-dropout area, would both schools need to be? How essential is it for the teachers to be similar with respect to commitment to teaching or years of experience?

Although finding a comparison group that is as alike as possible to the intervention group may be a problem at times, in other situations it presents no problem at all. For instance, the military attempts to produce companies of soldiers that are pretty similar to one another. There is a presumed equivalence in the comparison of one company of soldiers to another company. An example of this has been reported by Majchrzak (1986). Evaluating a program designed to reduce unauthorized absenteeism in the Marine Corps, she used the Nonequivalent Control Group Design because complete random assignment could not be employed. Majchrzak first matched available infantry and artillery battalions on the variables of deployment schedule, mission, regiment, and tenure of commander and then randomly assigned battalions either to a control condition or to participation in the unauthorized absenteeism prevention program. All subordinate companies were then asked to participate in the experiment. This procedure yielded twenty treatment companies and twenty control companies of Marines.

Time Series Design

Another quasi-experimental design is called the Time Series or the Interrupted Time Series Design. The advantage of this design over some of the others is that it allows the evaluator to detect trends. If there is a trend in the data (maybe children in remedial math classes begin to do better simply as a result of growing older), this gradual process would become apparent. It could be observed prior to the start of an intervention and monitored afterwards. We can use the following notation to represent this design:

$$O_1 \qquad O_2 \qquad O_3 \qquad X \qquad O_4 \qquad O_5 \qquad O_6$$

where O_1 is the first measurement, O_2 is the second measurement, and O_6 is the sixth measurement

Usually this design is depicted as having three equally spaced observations before the intervention and three (separated by the same time intervals) afterwards. However, as with other designs, this may be modified according to the needs of the evaluator. There would be nothing wrong with having four or more observations prior to the intervention and the same number (or perhaps fewer) after the intervention. The time intervals between measurements might be days, weeks, or even months. The lengths of these intervals are determined by the evaluator. This type of design relies upon **longitudinal data**. Longitudinal data are collected at several different times during the course of the study.

144

The time series designs are especially useful when finding non-equivalent control groups is a problem. These designs are often the design of choice when evaluating the impact of new legislation or policies. For instance, Shore and Maguin (1988) used a time series design to determine that the passage of a new law in Kansas that prohibited plea bargaining in Driving Under the Influence (DUI) arrests resulted in a decrease of eight fatal accidents per month during the eighteen month post-intervention period. This translated to a 20 percent reduction in the number of fatal accidents. Of course, the revision of the law alone was not responsible for the decrease. Accompanying the change in the law was widespread publicity, media coverage, and an increase in DUI arrests. Still, the authors concluded that:

> The Kansas experience supports deterrence theory in that the increase in certainty and severity of punishment provided by the change in the state's Driving Under the Influence law was associated with a reduction in those accidents which are more frequently linked with the combination of drinking and driving. (P. 253)

Another interesting use of a time series design was reported by Ross and White (1987), who explored the effect that seeing one's name in the newspaper had on persons convicted of shoplifting, impaired driving, or failing to take the breathalyzer test. They concluded that publishing the court results of persons arrested for shoplifting in the newspaper resulted in a decrease in the number of shoplifting incidents. However, publishing the names of impaired drivers and persons refusing the breathalyzer did not reduce their numbers.

Multiple Time Series Design

While the Time Series Design seemed to work well tracing the benefits of legislation within Kansas, there is at least one alternative explanation that cannot be ruled out. The number of DUI arrests may be decreasing across the nation not as a result of local legislation but due to such factors as increased awareness of health risks and decreased drinking among Americans. One might argue that the Time Series design suffers from tunnel vision—its scope does not encompass what may be going on in the larger world. The problems with this design are eliminated by adding a control group:

$$O_1 \quad O_3 \quad O_5 \quad X \quad O_7 \quad O_9 \quad O_{11}$$
$$O_2 \quad O_4 \quad O_6 \qquad\quad O_8 \quad O_{10} \quad O_{12}$$

145

where O_1 is the first measurement of the intervention group; O_2 is the first measurement of the control group; O_{11} is the third measurement for the intervention group following the treatment; O_{12} is the sixth measurement of the control group; the broken line between groups indicates non-random assignment.

With this design, an evaluator could identify a control state (in terms of rural-urban mixture, the rate of DUIs per 100,000 population, etc.) or use several states as controls. If there were national trends (such as for a decreased number of arrests for drinking while driving), this should be picked up among the control state(s), and the evaluator would not be so quick to conclude that it was the new legislation that brought about fewer DUIs.

ELIMINATING ALTERNATIVE EXPLANATIONS

The designs that have been presented to this point are subject to problems with internal validity. That is, these designs cannot conclude that it was the intervention alone that accounted for any observed changes. The pre-experimental and quasi-experimental designs cannot rule out many (or most) of the alternative explanations that skeptics of a program's success might be quick to identify. The strongest and most credible information about the effectiveness of an intervention comes from experimental designs. Efforts to eliminate the alternative explanations result in the most rigorous designs but also tend to increase the costs of evaluation.

Before we begin discussing experimental designs, let's look at alternative explanations that sometimes make researchers (or critics) question evaluation results.

THREATS TO THE INTERNAL VALIDITY

History

The role of history can be understood if we consider significant events occurring at the local, state, or national level. For instance, in August of 1987, twenty-seven children were killed outside of Cincinnati when a drunk driver crashed into a bus returning from a weekend outing. Assume that prior to this you had been asked to evaluate a public education program designed to reduce the number of DUIs and planned on using a relatively weak evaluation design (for instance, the One-Group Time Series Design) to monitor the number of arrests for driving under the influence. Some months after the accident, you conclude that the decrease in DUI arrests was due to the intervention, when it probably was the tragedy that resulted in fewer drivers driving while intoxicated.

Without a control group, you might not detect the influence this tragedy had on drivers' attitudes and behavior. Such an event could also be responsible for a greater number of DUI arrests as a consequence of the public becoming less tolerant and more often reporting drunk drivers to law enforcement officials. Law enforcement officials themselves might decide to be more vigilant and to make more arrests for DUI. The comparison between the intervention and the control communities (or states) would help the evaluator to understand any national trends in DUIs.

Within agencies and organizations, changes in policies (e.g., eligibility standards) and procedures can present a historical threat in the sense that the clientele may change over time. Because of scarce resources, an outpatient counseling program may begin to limit itself to only those who are suicidal or who have already been hospitalized on at least one other occasion. How would such a change dilute the power of an intervention to show improvement?

Maturation

Sometimes problems improve as a result of the passage of time. An evaluator might conclude that an intervention was effective when actually the subjects receiving the intervention matured or the passing of time served to make the problem less acute. For instance, persons suffering from the loss of a loved one normally grieve less and are less depressed as time passes. While the program staff may wish to think that it was the support group that made all of the difference, unless there is a control group it is difficult to rule out the role that the passage of time alone may have played.

Testing

If you are using a design (e.g., the Times Series Design) where the same test is administered sequentially a number of times, the persons receiving the intervention may show improvement in their scores as a result of figuring out "correct" responses on the test. On the other hand, their scores could also decrease as a result of becoming careless and bored with repeated use of the same test. Without a comparison group, it is difficult to rule out possible testing effects.

Instrumentation

Just as those enrolled in a program can become bored by taking the same test on numerous occasions, the evaluator or other persons making observations might subtly or unconsciously modify the procedures. Instead of counting every time a hyperactive child got out of his seat in the classroom, the weary observer by the end of the study may be counting only the incidents when the child got out of his seat and was corrected by the teacher. Observations ought to be made in the same way throughout the course of the evaluation. Tests should be administered the same way (e.g., in the same setting, at the same time of day, using the same rules or set of instructions) each time. The effect of this threat to the internal validity of a study can be quickly understood in a situation where, for example, a teacher gave more than the allowed time to a class to finish the posttest and less to the control group. Merely because they had more time, the intervention group might score higher than the control group.

Selection

This alternative explanation plays a potential role whenever control groups are used without random assignment. Suppose you were to start a new intervention and invite former clients (who may still be having problems) to attend. If there is improvement among these clients, will it be due to the recent intervention? Or did the improvement come about because it built upon their prior involvement? Taking another example, suppose you want to start a new support group, and you want to open it up to anyone in the community. To announce the beginning of the support group, you run an invitation in the local newspaper. If this group later shows improvement, it may have been due to the fact that the individuals who participated were unlike others in the community with the same problem. Maybe those who answered the newspaper article were more literate (they read the ad in the newspaper), better educated, more assertive, or more intelligent. One would be left with the nagging thought that maybe the intervention was effective only with the kind of people who would answer an ad. This group may not be representative of the rest of the people in the community with the same problem who failed to respond to the invitation.

Mortality

Mortality refers to the loss of subjects from the evaluation. This threat to the internal validity is a problem for those evaluations that stretch over a long period of time. Professionals in the human services frequently find that their clients move (sometimes without leaving forwarding addresses), drop out of treatment, get locked up, become sick, and sometimes become rehospitalized. For various reasons, it is not at all uncommon to have fewer participants in a program at its conclusion than when it started. A problem exists when too many of the participants drop out. Any commonality among those who drop out could bias the study. For instance, suppose you were running a program for parents of adolescents. Twelve parents sign up to learn how to better communicate with their adolescents. A few parents drop out during the nine week program, but this doesn't concern you because you can objectively show that the program is working—that communication is improving among those parents who remain. However, as you begin to examine your data, you realize that the parents who remained in the program were all college graduates. The parents who dropped out were high school graduates. While the intervention may have worked, it did so only for parents who were college graduates.

PROTECTION AGAINST ALTERNATIVE EXPLANATIONS

The best protection against alternative explanations for the results you note in an evaluation is to control them. Control is made possible by anticipating the kinds of problems that may be encountered. For example, if you expect that you may have mortality problems, build in an incentive. With children, there could be some sort of a party on the last session or after the posttest data have been obtained. With adults, money is an incentive that works reasonably well. But when funds are not available, the evaluator can be creative in other ways, perhaps by issuing "Certificates of Completion" for the intervention group and "Certificates of Appreciation" for the control group. If you expect that repeated testing may present some problems, explore whether there are different or alternate forms of the same test.

If you suspect that critics of the evaluation may say things like, "Well, no wonder! The comparison groups weren't even similar!" then you need to insure that the groups in the study are as similar as possible. Where random assignment isn't possible, you can gain credibility by matching group participants with their controls on important variables (e.g., years of education, income, sex) and then using a statistical test to determine that the groups are comparable. (See chapter 11 for information on the appropriate statistical test to use.) The t-test will tell you whether differences between the two groups are statistically significant.

If there are no significant differences between the control and intervention groups on important variables, then the groups are similar for those variables. However, differences could still exist on variables that are not measured. Showing that groups are similar statistically on certain measures is a help in documenting comparability, but does not provide certainty that they are equivalent. Concern yourself with "plausible" rival hypotheses, and don't worry about every potential variable that could come into play. You need to try to control for as many *plausible* rival hypotheses as possible—not every one that a fertile mind could create.

Another way to produce a credible evaluation is to use a rigorous evaluation design known as an experimental design. These designs eliminate alternative explanations through the use of random selection and assignment; persons are assigned to either the intervention or control groups without any form of bias. Unexpected improvement within a control group developed with randomized procedures allows you to suspect that some alternative explanation (such as history, maturation, or testing) was having an influence.

Before we leave our discussion of alternative explanations, it would be well to note that there are many more threats to the internal validity of a study than have been identified in this brief explanation. As an evaluator, you need to develop a sensitivity or an appreciation for factors that can influence the results of the evaluation. For instance, those involved in an evaluation may be keenly aware that they are being tested and may work harder than they normally would to make a good impression. Any "over-cooperation" will confound the evaluator's data and make it more difficult to understand the true impact of any intervention. If you would like to read more about additional threats to the internal validity of a study, consult Campbell and Stanley (1963), Cook and Campbell (1979), or Mitchell and Jolley (1988).

EXPERIMENTAL DESIGNS

The "classic" experimental design is the standard against which other designs are compared. Experimental research designs are the most rigorous and represent the "ideal" for inferring that an intervention either did or did not have an effect. In an **experimental design**, participants are randomly assigned to either the intervention group or to the control group. The notation for the basic experiment is:

$$R \quad O_1 \quad X \quad O_2$$
$$R \quad O_3 \quad \quad O_4$$

where R stands for subjects who have been randomly assigned to either the intervention or control groups; where O_1 is a pretest or first observation of the intervention group; where O_4 is the posttest or second observation of the control group.

Since the groups are equivalent at the start of the study (this is guaranteed by the random assignment), this design is inoculated against most threats to its internal validity. (Can you see how the evaluator would be able to determine if there were selection bias or effects from maturation or history?) However, random assignment guarantees equivalency between groups only if the Ns are sufficiently large. All too often in small-scale evaluations (e.g., where the Ns are 8 or 9 persons per group), random assignment does not yield equivalent groups. Random assignment is likely to provide equivalency as each of the groups reaches or exceeds 25 to 30 persons in size.

As an example of this design, let's consider the program evaluation of a forty-bed residential treatment program that provides milieu therapy. Velasquez and McCubbin (1980) evaluated such a program using an experimental design where applicants were randomly assigned to either the residential program or informed that they would not be able to enter the program for six months; for the latter group, alternative forms of health services were available (inpatient hospitalization in a different program, day treatment, or another residential facility not providing milieu therapy).

Nine different instruments were used to collect data about potential applicants. There were ratings by the program director for such dimensions as degree of psychiatric impairment and social adjustment. Other measures (the Tennessee Self-Concept Scale and the Problem Solving Scale) were completed by the applicants. Analysis revealed strong evidence that the residential treatment program increased the participants' responsibility for self, social participation, and continuation in employment, improved their self-concept, and reduced the probability of hospitalization six months later. The authors concluded, "The consistency of findings from this experimental investigation present a clear and fairly convincing picture of the effectiveness of this residential program" (p. 357).

Posttest-Only Control Group Design

Another experimental design, the Posttest-Only Control Group Design, is an elegant modification of the basic experimental design. Even without the initial pretests, it is a useful experimental design, ideal for those situations where it was not or is not possible to conduct a pretest or where a pretest could conceivably affect the posttest results. This design is also advantageous on those occasions when matching pretests with posttests is not possible or desired.

Random assignment of subjects establishes equivalence between the control and experimental groups. Measurement of the control group (O_2) serves as a pretest measure for comparison with the experimental group's posttest (O_1). This design can be diagrammed:

$$R \quad X \quad O_1$$
$$R \qquad \quad O_2$$

where R represents subjects who have been randomly assigned to either the control or intervention groups; O_1 is the first measurement (a posttest because it occurs after the intervention); O_2 is the first measurement of the control group.

As an example of this design, imagine that you are a social worker in a forensic program. Your boss, who is the county's prosecuting attorney, asked you to start an intervention program for persons who have been arrested for shoplifting. Careful screening will eliminate any persons who have ever been arrested so that all of your clientele will be first-time offenders. If these first-time offenders complete a four week intervention program on consecutive Saturday mornings, the record of their arrest will be erased. Because the prosecuting attorney will be running for reelection in about two years, she asks that you design a sound evaluation component so that she can point to the program's success in her election campaign.

Assume that there will be more first-time offenders eligible for participation in the intervention program than can be initially served. Given this situation, the only fair procedure would be a random selection where some first-time offenders are chosen to participate in the program and others either are not invited to participate or are informed that they can participate at a later date.

In this example, there is no need to conduct a pretest because all of the persons eligible for participation in the program have already been arrested for shoplifting, and it has been determined that they are first-time offenders. Vitally important is the measure that will be used to gauge the success of the intervention program. Let's say that you and the prosecuting attorney agree that the best indicator of success would be whether the first-time offenders are arrested again for shoplifting.

For simplicity's sake, let's suppose that the posttest data consists of the number of arrests of those who received the intervention during the period beginning one month following their arrest and concluding six months later. The longest wait for the start of the intervention group would be one month; this means that if the intervention is effective, there should be no shoplifting arrests among these program participants in the five month period following the intervention. Similarly, arrest data will be examined for the control group beginning one month from the time of their arrest and will conclude six months later. During this time, they will receive no intervention.

If the shoplifters cannot be randomly assigned to the treatment or to the control conditions, or if the intervention cannot be postponed for those selected to be in the control group, the evaluator could not use this design. The evaluator must rely upon a less rigorous design such as the Nonequivalent Control Group Design. With the quasi-experimental design, there is more flexibility and several options present themselves.

Since not all shoplifters will agree to participating in an intervention program (some will refuse to attend, some will attend once and never return, some would rather pay a fine), those who choose not to participate constitute a "natural" comparison group for the Nonequivalent Control Group Design. If the intervention is successful, fewer of those receiving the intervention should be rearrested than those who were in the comparison group.

Another option would be to use historical or archival data for the comparison. In this instance, the control group would be those first-time shoplifting offenders who received no intervention (simply because it was not available). The evaluator could select a sample of shoplifters who were arrested during some interval of time (e.g., the year prior to the start of the intervention program) and then examine arrest data for each of these first-time offenders for a period of time comparable to that of the intervention group. If the intervention is effective, the intervention group should have fewer repeat shoplifters during a twelve month (or similar) time interval.

Solomon Four-Group Design

The Solomon Four-Group Design is another elaboration of the basic experimental design. As can be seen from the diagram below, this design requires that two groups receive the intervention and that two groups do not. Only two groups are given a pretest, but all four groups are administered the posttest.

This design is very rigorous because it allows the evaluator a great deal of control over testing and concurrent history and thus increases the confidence that can be placed in the findings. However, this design also requires more planning and coordination, and as a result, not many evaluators will have the opportunity to utilize it.

$$R \quad O_1 \quad X \quad O_2$$
$$R \quad O_3 \quad \quad O_4$$
$$R \quad \quad X \quad O_5$$
$$R \quad \quad \quad O_6$$

where R represents random assignment to one of the four conditions (two with treatment); O_1 and O_3 are pretests; O_2, O_4, and O_5 are posttests; O_6 can be considered a pretest.

As an example of this design, imagine you are the director of a summer camp for children who have come from economically deprived homes. Many of the children have been victims of abuse or neglect. You feel that the summer camp experience significantly increases their self-esteem and improves their outlook on life. You know that if you demonstrate such results to funding sources, they will be interested in helping with the expense of the summer camp. You are anxious to conduct an evaluation that is as strong and rigorous as possible. In this example, you would randomly assign eligible children to one of the four conditions specified in the design: two groups would attend summer camp and two groups would not.

While a simple experimental design could be used, you are concerned that the children, being anxious to please and to show that camp was meaningful to them, might infer the nature of the self-esteem instrument and by their responses indicate improved self-esteem, when this may not reflect reality. The more times a test is given to a group, the greater the likelihood that the subjects can understand or anticipate the purpose of the test. One of the advantages of the Solomon Four-Group Design is that any influence of testing can be identified since two of the four groups are tested only once.

A major problem with this design may come from the fact that you may not believe that some children should be denied the experience of summer camp. Depending upon the length of the camp experience and the timing of the posttest, it may be possible for all of the children in the control groups to also participate in summer camp—they attend after they have finished serving in control groups. This would be possible

154

in those situations where the duration of summer camp is only one or two weeks for each group of campers. The issue here is whether a one or two week camp experience increases self-esteem—not whether any improvements to self-esteem are maintained throughout the summer or the subsequent years. If you were concerned about whether the gains in self-esteem were maintained, the posttests would be planned for six months or a year after the completion of the intervention—which would prevent the control group from attending camp in the same summer as those in the intervention group.

CHAPTER RECAP

The aim of this chapter has been to present a range of designs, from the not very rigorous to the experimental. While the "standard" may be the experimental design, it is not always feasible to implement it. This can be seen in the way authors discuss their choice of an evaluation design. Velasquez and Lyle (1985), for instance, wrote, "Although random assignment . . . was technically achievable, strong opposition to this approach from some officials resulted in the selection of a less rigorous design" (p. 148). In another example, Toseland, Kabat, and Kemp (1983) noted, in writing about a smoking-cessation program designed by a clinical social worker,

> The authors used a quasi-experimental, nonequivalent control-group design to evaluate the Breathe Free program. Because of ethical considerations, the American Lung Association of New York State thought it was not appropriate to randomly assign those who wanted to stop smoking to a true experimental treatment-control group design. A control group of persons on a waiting list was also rejected because it was believed that subjects should not have to wait for treatment, that they might lose their motivation to attend a program, and that they might decide to attend other programs if they were placed on a waiting list. (P. 14)

A friend was hired to evaluate a school program one summer, and we talked about the best approach. We decided upon an experimental design, and this is what he recommended to the school. However, the school notified him early in September that they had already launched the program but had not randomly assigned students to control or intervention groups—*all* the students had received the intervention. Since it was no longer possible to use the experimental design he planned, the evaluator had to fall back on the Nonequivalent Control Group Design.

The choice of an evaluation design is often the evaluator's alone, although this is clearly not always the case. The design should follow logically from the questions or hypotheses that need to be explored, the resources you have, the constraints within the agency, as well as what is pragmatically possible.

Evaluation designs are tailored to a specific situation or program. For pedagogic reasons, the choice of a design has been presented here as being selected after an evaluation question has been formulated. But the choice of design and of the evaluation question may not be separate and distinct steps. Cronbach et al. (1980) noted, "We reject the view that 'design' begins *after* a research question is chosen, as a mere techinical process to sharpen the inquiry. Choice of questions and choice of investigative tactics are inseparable" (pp. 213-14). Cronbach also referred to the choice of design as a "spiral process" where the evaluator lays out a rough plan and considers what will be left unsettled. The process may not be straightforward as concerns about information yield, costs, and political importance are considered and balanced (p. 261).

Beginning evaluators are sometimes too critical of their own efforts when they are prevented from using an experimental design. They may think that any design short of the "ideal" experiment will yield worthless data. This simply is not true. Something can be learned from just about any evaluation. Even highly competent evaluators often have to settle for designs much less stringent than the Solomon Four Group Design. Depending upon your audience, nonexperimental designs may, in some instances, be desired as they are less complex and more understandable.

For example, I know of a county prosecutor who was extremely pleased with the results of an evaluation that used the One Group Post-test Only Design. He had been instrumental in getting a drug treatment program started for felons that combined systematic urine sampling and a structured counseling program. At the end of the first nine months, only 12 percent of over 4,500 urine samples from 176 felons indicated alcohol or drug use. Among those with "clean" urine samples, only 22 percent had been rearrested, while 66 percent of those with three or more "dirty" urine samples had been rearrested. Even though 48 percent of those in the program had been rearrested for some offense and there was no randomization or control group, the county attorney was making plans to speak to the state legislature about additional funding so that similar programs could be started in other communities in the state. In this example, the results of the study were perceived as being so powerful that even the relatively weak evaluation design seemed to be inconsequential.

Does the choice of a design make a difference? Yes, it does. It is not often that one can expect the same degree of success as reported in the previous example. I often see frustration and disenchantment with program evaluation when practitioners in the field and students realize much too late how any observed changes in clients after intervention could have been due to alternative explanations.

In our eagerness to evaluate programs, we would do well to remember that there are circumstances that do not warrant evaluation. Carol Weiss (1972), in her now classic book, noted that evaluation is not worth doing in four kinds of circumstances.

1. When there are no questions about the program. . . . Decisions about its future either do not come up or have already been made.
2. When the program has no clear orientation. . . . The program shifts and changes, wanders around and seeks direction.
3. When people who should know cannot agree on what the program is trying to achieve. If there are vast discrepancies in perceived goals, evaluation has no ground to stand on.
4. When there is not enough money or staff sufficiently qualified to conduct the evaluation. Evaluation is a demanding business, calling for time, money, imagination, tenacity, and skill. (Pp. 10–11)

It should also be noted that in any evaluation you may use more than one design. You may use multiple approaches (remember the triangulation discussion in the chapter on needs assessment?), you may use several different instruments, or you may even employ a different design with each instrument.

Suchman (1967) made some important observations regarding the choice of evaluation design. He observed that ultimately the best design is the one most suitable for the purpose of the study, and since designs often reflect compromises dictated by practical considerations, there is no such thing as a single correct design. Questions and hypotheses can be explored using different methods or approaches. This thought was recently expressed by the Ann Hartman (1990), editor-in-chief of *Social Work*: "This editor takes the position that there are many truths and there are many ways of knowing. Each discovery contributes to our knowledge, and each way of knowing deepens our understanding and adds another dimension to our view of the world" (p. 3).

QUESTIONS FOR CLASS DISCUSSION

1. Discuss conducting program evaluations in various community agencies. Do some of the designs in this chapter seem to "fit" some programs better than others? Why?
2. Discuss the advantages and disadvantages of an evaluator monitoring similar programs in different agencies using these four questions:

157

   a. Did this program have objectives derived from the goals for the program?
     __ YES   __ NO   __ Cannot be determined
   b. Did the program serve as many clients as projected?
     __ YES   __ NO   __ Cannot be determined
   c. Did the agency conduct an outcome evaluation of this program?
     __ YES   __ NO   __ Cannot be determined
   d. Did the agency staff seem committed to evaluating the outcome of their program?
     __ YES   __ NO   __ Cannot be determined

3. Discuss the problems of using a self-report questionnaire with smokers in a smoking cessation clinic. What percent might be motivated to indicate that they had stopped when in fact they were still smoking? What would constitute "hard evidence"?

4. Have the class identify a local program that would be interesting to evaluate using one of the designs in this chapter. What evaluation design would be used? What would be the primary outcome variable? What would be the threats to the internal validity? How would you control for these? What would be the data collection procedures? Who would need to assist with the evaluation? Who would be the subjects?

5. Discuss for any specific program the various outcome indicators that might be chosen in a program evaluation. Are some more valuable than others for showing an impact the program is having upon the lives of clients?

MINI-PROJECTS: EXPERIENCING EVALUATION FIRSTHAND

1. Browse through professional journals in a field of your choice to find the report of an evaluation using a nonequivalent control group design. Read the article and critique it.

2. A program has recently been funded to provide intensive services to the homeless. The mission of the program is to identify those who, with the necessary supportive services, can realistically be expected to be employed and self-sustaining within three years. Design a program evaluation for this project. Be sure to identify your evaluation design and other necessary details.

REFERENCES AND RESOURCES

Attkisson, C.C., and Broskowski, A. (1978). Evaluation and the emerging human service concept. In C.C. Attkisson, W.A. Hargreaves, M.J. Horowitz, and

J.E. Sorensen (eds.), *Evaluation of human service programs.* New York: Academic Press.

Campbell, D.T., and Stanley, J.C. (1963). *Experimental and quasi-experimental designs for research.* Chicago, IL: Rand McNally.

Cook, T.D., and Campbell, D.T. (1979). *Quasi-experimentation: Design and analysis issues for field settings.* Chicago, IL: Rand McNally.

Cronbach, L.J., Ambron, S.R., Dornbusch, S.M., Hess, R.D., Hornik, R.C., Phillips, D.C., Walker, D.F., and Weiner, S.S. (1980). *Toward reform of program evaluation.* San Francisco, CA: Jossey-Bass.

Fitz-Gibbon, C.T., and Morris, L.L. (1987) *How to design a program evaluation.* Beverly Hills, CA: Sage.

Grossman, J., and Tierney, J.P. (1993). The fallibility of comparison groups. *Evaluation Review,* 17(5), 556-571.

Hartman, A. (1990). Many ways of knowing. *Social Work,* 35(1), 3-4.

Majchrzak, A. (1986). Keeping marines in the field: Results of a field experiment. *Evaluation and Program Planning,* 9(3), 253-265.

Mitchell, M., and Jolley, J. (1988) *Research design explained.* New York: Holt, Rinehart and Winston.

Patton, M.Q. (1987). *Creative evaluation.* Beverly Hills, CA: Sage.

Radloff, L.S. (1977). The CES-D Scale: A self-report depression scale for research in the general population. *Applied Psychological Measurement,* 3(1), 385-401.

Ross, A.S., and White, S. (1987). Shoplifting, impaired driving, and refusing the breathalyzer. *Evaluation Review,* 11(2), 254-269.

Shipman, S. (1989). General criteria for evaluating social programs. *Evaluation Practice,* 10(1), 20-26.

Shore, E.R., and Maguin, E. (1988). Deterrence of drinking-driving: The effect of changes in the Kansas driving under the influence law. *Evaluation and Program Planning,* 11(3), 245-254.

Suchman, E.A. (1967). *Evaluating research: Principles and practice in public service and social action programs.* New York: Russell Sage Foundation.

Toseland, R.W., Kabat, D., and Kemp, K. (1983). Evaluation of a smoking-cessation group treatment program. *Social Work Research and Abstracts,* 19(1), 12-19.

Velasquez, J.S., and Lyle, C.G. (1985). Day versus residential treatment for juvenile offenders: The impact of program evaluation. *Child Welfare,* 64(2), 145-156.

Velasquez, J.S., and McCubbin, H.I. (1980). Toward establishing the effectiveness of community-based residential treatment: Program evaluation by experimental research. *Journal of Social Service Research,* 3(4), 337-359.

Weiss, C.H. (1972) *Evaluation Research: Methods of assessing program effectiveness.* Englewood Cliffs, NJ: Prentice-Hall.

SEVEN

Cost Effectiveness and Cost Analysis Designs

In the last chapter, we were concerned more with examining a program's effectiveness than with its cost. Realistically, however, we know that most social service agencies have severely restricted budgets. Costs are *always* important considerations—whether or not old programs are on the chopping block and new ones are being planned.

Besides effectiveness, agency directors and managers must also weigh which intervention provides the *most affordable*, favorable outcome. Both costs and program effectiveness ought to be considered before a green light is given for program implementation. We would not want to adopt a program that was inexpensive but had a lower success rate (or higher recidivism rate) than another program of comparable cost.

Would we be quick to adopt a program that was much more expensive than conventional treatment but twice as effective? For example, while the drug clozapine has been shown to improve the quality of life and social functioning for treatment-resistant persons with schizophrenia, there has been considerable controversy about using it because of its cost.

A cost-effectiveness study (Meltzer, et al., 1993) examined the cost of inpatient and outpatient treatment and other costs for patients who remained with clozapine treatment and those who dropped out. By comparing the cost of hospitalization two years before use of clozapine with two years later, the researchers found a cost reduction of 94 percent, or an average of $42,218, for those who remained on the drug. Those who discontinued its use experienced an average cost increase of $6,580 over their prior hospitalization costs ($99,995 compared to $93,415). Even with the expense of the drug, clozapine treatment resulted in a cost savings of $17,404 per patient over a two-year period. The clozapine study is but one illustration of how a "more expensive" intervention can actually save taxpayers more than conventional programs.

Another strong example, this time of how money spent "up front" can be a sound investment, is found with the Special Supplemental Food Program for Women, Infants, and Children (WIC). Although conservative elements in society argue for a reduction in such welfare programs, Buescher, Larson, Nelson, and Lenihan (1993) have shown that for each dollar spent on WIC, the savings to Medicaid were $2.91. Women receiving Medicaid but not WIC benefits were 1.45 times as likely as their WIC counterparts to have a low-weight infant. Costs to Medicaid for newborn services beginning in the first sixty days of life were lower for infants born to women who participated in WIC during their pregnancies. Adequate nutrition reduces infant mortality and reduces Medicaid expenditures.

Policymakers, agency directors, and managers want "efficient" programs. All too often, however, efficiency has meant serving the greatest number of clients with the least cost. Such decisions are based only on the up-front or immediate costs of a program and not on the overall reduction or amelioration of the problem. It's necessary to remember that assumptions about "least costly" must be stated relative to a time frame and a clear outcome objective. Least costly approaches may not always be the most effective.

Because there are a number of ways to attack social problems, there are always options from which to choose. For example, one group of evaluators interested in increasing safety-belt use tested the effectiveness of four different approaches and the corresponding cost. They found that combining persuasive communications and incentives resulted in a 20 percentage point increase in safety-belt use. The total cost of this approach was $770. The cost-effectiveness of this approach could be viewed as $38.50 per percentage point increase ($770/20). Or, it could be computed in terms of the cost it took to convert each driver to a safety-belt user. Twenty-one drivers began using safety belts at a cost of $37 each ($770/21).

An even more effective approach combined persuasive communications, monitoring, prompts, and incentives. While this approach was more effective (a 28 percentage point increase in safety belt use), the costs for this approach were also greater ($5,360). In terms of cost-effectiveness, this was a cost of $191 per percentage point increase, or $97 for each new driver who started wearing a safety belt (Simons-Morton, Brink, and Bates, 1987).

Another set of evaluators compared the cost-effectiveness of alcohol treatment in a partial hospital program and extended inpatient treatment. It was found that the partial hospitalization program (1) cost almost $1,700 less per client and (2) produced more abstinent days per $100 of treatment costs, and that (3) estimates of total treatment costs per abstinent client also favored the partial hospitalization program over the extended inpatient treatment ($18,935 versus $21,637) (McCrady et al., 1986).

Still another group of evaluators found that at the end of six months there was no difference in success rates among patients in a detoxification program who completed either inpatient or outpatient treatment programs. Although inpatient treatment was many times more expensive, the study concluded that the most cost-effective way of treating alcoholism is through outpatient treatment (Hayashida et al., 1989).

Economic factors often are the catalysts for adopting innovative programs. Mor (1987), for example, attributed economic factors as providing the necessary incentive that led to hospice services becoming routinely reimbursed by Medicare. Cost-effectiveness studies are important tools that can be used to help decision-makers allocate scarce resources. Cost accounting is a concept familiar to those in the private sector and the corporate world. It's an approach that has not often been used to evaluate social and human services. Clearly, it is incumbent upon evaluators to examine conventional and alternative ways of providing human services and to use that information to guide interventions tomorrow and thereafter.

EXAMPLE OF A COST-EFFECTIVENESS EVALUATION

Let's compare two programs with the same mission—to assist the "hardcore" unemployed to obtain employment. The first program is called JOB PREP (for Job Preparedness) and the second, WORK NOW. Both are located within large metropolitan areas and were developed to help adults who have never experienced full-time employment. The clientele is composed of about equal proportions of persons who dropped out of school and who are functionally illiterate. Many are recovering drug addicts and persons with criminal records. Both programs begin with

163

Table 7.1
Cost-Effectiveness Comparison of Two Job Training Programs

	WORK NOW, Inc.	JOB PREP, Inc.
Total Program Costs	$275,000	$345,000
Graduation Rate	64%	40%
Persons Employed Full-Time		
One Year	48	73
Cost Per Employed Client	$5,729	$4,726

teaching work preparedness skills (being prompt, proper attitude, appropriate dress) and progress to teaching marketable job skills. As a final step, "interns" are placed with potential employers for actual on-the-job experience. Table 7.1 presents evaluative information on the two programs.

We can tell at a glance that JOB PREP is a more expensive program than WORK NOW. In fact, JOB PREP requires 20 percent more budget than WORK NOW. We also note that the less expensive program has a higher graduation rate than JOB PREP. This is partly explained by the fact that WORK NOW is a less intense program and can be completed a month quicker than JOB PREP. However, JOB PREP is known for doing more screening and more carefully selecting from among its applicants.

If we were to stop at just this point in comparing these two programs, WORK NOW would appear to be the better program. However, if we consider that the mission of the two programs is to help the hard-core unemployed to become *employed,* then we need to go a bit further. Contacting the employers with whom the "interns" of both programs were placed and locating former trainees who were no longer with those employers allows us to establish the number of trainees who are employed in a full-time capacity one year after completion of the program.

By dividing the total program cost by the number of employed graduates of the program, we can develop a cost-effectiveness comparison. We learn that it cost an average of $5,729 to produce an employed graduate of WORK NOW, but only $4,726 to produce a graduate from the JOB PREP program. Even though JOB PREP is a somewhat more expensive program overall, it is more successful than the less expensive program in doing what it was designed to do. The sophisticated comparison looks not only at the budgets and graduation rates, but also at the programs' outcomes in relation to their expenditures.

HOW TO DO A COST-EFFECTIVENESS STUDY

Six basic steps are necessary for a cost-effectiveness study.

Step 1: Define the Program and Its Objectives

It is vitally important that the evaluator fully understand all components and features of the program, what it is designed to produce, and the target population. Accordingly, the evaluator should learn the history of the program, when it began, how it has been modified over time, how the clientele may have changed over the years, and what client data are available. When programs are compared, it is crucial that the same operational definition for successful outcome is used, one that is quantifiable and relatively easy to measure. Decreased recidivism rates, for instance, must be for comparable time periods.

Step 2: Compute Costs

The evaluator must compute the total costs for operating the program. While these will vary from program to program, Levine (1983) suggests that most interventions experience costs in the following areas:

a. **Personnel.** This category includes the salaries and fringe benefits for all program employees. The value of efforts contributed by volunteers should also be included. This can be estimated on the basis of the number of hours worked and the type of assistance being provided. (An hourly wage for someone volunteering to help mail out a newsletter would be estimated at a lower rate than a physician donating free physicals.)

b. **Facilities.** Programs must be housed, and this category includes rent for physical space and related costs of its share of the agency's insurance, electricity, heating, air conditioning, and so on. When these costs are not available by program, they can be crudely estimated by using a proportion derived from a ratio of the program's personnel budget over the agency's budget for all personnel. Where a building is owned by an agency, the cost for similar space can be estimated by contacting a knowledgeable real estate agent or by following a set of procedures outlined by Levine (1983)—which includes such steps as determining the replacement value of the facility, the life of the facility, the cost of depreciation, and the interest on its undepreciated value.

165

d. **Other inputs.** Includes all expenses that do not fit any other category, such as travel and those associated with the administrative structure of the agency (as when an agency director oversees more than one program, but also including those who provided publicity, handle payroll, etc.).

e. **Client inputs.** Includes any contributions required of the clients or their families, such as books and uniforms.

Step 3: Collect Program Outcome Data

Before data are actually collected, a number of practical questions must be considered, such as how many years to include or how much client data to acquire. When programs are relatively new, it may make sense to contact every graduate and dropout. On the other hand, well-established programs with large clientele may require the sampling of clients in the past twelve months.

Step 4: Compute Program Outcomes

In this step, the evaluator must document the program's successes. Examples of indicators of success for various programs are: the number of clients who have not been hospitalized in the past twelve months; the number of clients employed; the number of new foster homes recruited; and the number of clients who complete their GED, the number of first-time DUI offenders who are not re-arrested within twenty-four months. Keep in mind that a program may have more than one indicator of success.

Step 5: Compute the Cost-Effectiveness Ratio

The cost-effectiveness ratio is computed by dividing the total cost of the program by the effectiveness outcome indicator (e.g., the number of successes). This allows decision-makers to see the relationship between costs and outcomes and to choose those programs that have the best cost-effectiveness ratio. Programs with substantial costs but which produce few positive effects can be discontinued and the resulting cost savings applied to more effective interventions.

Step 6: Perform a Sensitivity Analysis

The last step in a cost-effectiveness study is to conduct a sensitivity analysis. This means that recommendations based on the cost-

---

BOX 7.1
Sensitivity Analysis of
The Cost-Effectiveness of Counseling
Smokers to Quit

Overview. Drawing upon published reports of smoking cessation among patients given advice by a physician to quit smoking, this cost-effectiveness study used a hypothetical group of patients who were smokers. The authors estimated that a physician would use four minutes to promote nonsmoking during a routine office visit that cost $30 and would hand out a $2 booklet. Using four separate studies of patients who were given advice by a physician to quit smoking, an average cessation rate at one year was computed to be 2.7 percent.

Sensitivity Analyses. The authors assumed: (1) a 50 percent increase in the cost of an office visit; (2) the cessation rate might drop to 1 percent or rise as high as 4 percent; and (3) although an annual rate of 5 percent was used to discount gains in life expectancy, discount rates of 3 percent and 7 percent were also used in the sensitivity analysis. The authors also examined the effect of a 50 percent relapse rate.

Source: Steven R. Cummings, Susan M. Rubin, and Gerry Oster (1989), *Journal of the American Medical Association*, 261 (1), 75–79.

---

effectiveness data are tested. This step is more important when extensive use of estimation was used in the cost-effectiveness study than when all costs and effects were "real." When estimation was used liberally, the evaluator could go back and make high and low estimates in order to see if a different decision about the program would be justified. If the final decision is not affected by slightly different assumptions, then the evaluator would be more confident in the decision than if the decision were affected by lower or higher estimates.

OTHER METHODS OF COST ANALYSIS

Cost analysis is not limited to cost-effectiveness studies. Levine (1983), for instance, discusses cost-benefit analyses, cost-utility analyses, and cost-feasibility analyses. Of these, cost-feasibility is the simplest and entails estimating expected expenses associated with a program. This is done in order to determine if a given program is affordable. Cost-utility analyses are a little more esoteric and are described as having a major disadvantage—"the results cannot be reproduced on the basis of a standard methodology among different evaluators, since most of the assessments are highly subjective ones that take place in the head of the persons doing the evaluation" (p. 29).

In cost-benefit analysis, effort is made to measure both costs and benefits in monetary units. While it is theoretically possible to enumerate all of the benefits of a given social service program, it is usually difficult to determine a monetary value for these benefits. For example, let's say that you work for an agency that has started a respite program for senior citizens. The program serves people sixty years old and older who live at home and who require constant care. The respite care program provides family members relief from the daily care of a disabled family member. Volunteers are recruited from within the community to provide primary caregivers with time off to take care of personal business, to go shopping, or just to have an afternoon to go to a movie or visit with friends.

The cost of the program can be computed easily enough. (There are the salary and fringe benefits associated with the volunteer coordinator's position, prorated expenses for the volunteer coordinator's share of the receptionist, as well as the prorated facility expenses—rent, insurance, utilities.) However, how do we measure the benefits of this program? What are the benefits of having time away from twenty-four-hour custodial responsibilities? What dollar figure do we place on the pleasure that the caregiver got from enjoying a movie or visiting with some friends? If the disabled senior enjoyed having a volunteer read the newspaper, what was that worth in terms of measuring benefits? Cost-benefit studies require that monetary value of these benefits be estimated or measured. Because of the difficulty in arriving at monetary values of intangible benefits, it may not always make sense to do a cost-benefit analysis. (How does one appraise the value of a new playground for children located within the inner city? How does one value the increase in self-esteem of a fifty-five-year-old migrant laborer who learns to read?)

Since many benefits cannot be easily converted to a dollar figure, evaluators interested in examining a cost-benefit relationship sometimes resort to employing pre/post standardized measurements of such outcome variables as satisfaction with life or satisfaction with services provided. Then, cost of a program or project can be understood relative to an increase in satisfaction.

For instance, the creation of a micro city park on two lots where dilapidated and condemned houses previously existed might raise nearby residents' pride and satisfaction with their neighborhood from a low of 60 percent to 80 percent. If the park was constructed with volunteer help for approximately $250,000, then a cost-benefit analysis could report that the project cost $12,500 for each point of increased satisfaction ($250,000/20 = $12,500). When the benefits are nonmonetary, cost-benefit analyses will be virtually indistinguishable from cost-effectiveness studies.

Because the assessment of a given program's benefits may be somewhat arbitrary, cost-benefit analyses may utilize different perspectives to gauge the benefits. For example, McCaughrin et al. (1993) looked at the costs and benefits of supported employment for clients with developmental disabilities using the perspectives of the supported employee, the taxpayer, and society. They found from the supported employees' perspective that those with moderate or severe mental retardation increased their earnings by $1,027 during the first year, while those with mild mental retardation showed a $4,607 increase. From the taxpayers' perspective, break-even costs could be expected in the fifth year. After four years, eliminated sheltered-employment costs were considered a savings from both the taxpayers' and society's perspective.

In traditional cost-benefit analysis, a ratio is computed by dividing the total benefits by the total costs. If the ratio is larger than 1, then the benefits exceed cost; if the ratio is less than 1, then the costs exceed the benefits. The Buescher et al. (1993) study mentioned earlier showed that for each dollar spent on WIC the benefit (savings to Medicaid) was $2.91. The benefit is clear. Most of us would like to get back almost $3.00 for each $1.00 we spend.

When you are examining costs and program outcomes but your outcome variables are not measured monetarily, call your analysis "cost-effectiveness" instead of "cost-benefit." This simple rule will usually work; however, terminology is not standardized with regard to cost analysis terms. For instance, some prefer the term "benefit-cost analysis," while others will use "cost-benefit analysis." And sometimes the distinction between cost-effectiveness and cost-benefit blurs. An example of this appears in an article addressing the rehabilitation of child molesters (Prentky and Burgess, 1990). Take a look at the first line of the abstract accompanying their report: "This study examined the cost effectiveness of the rehabilitation of child molesters by designing and testing a cost-benefit model" (p. 108).

Examining follow-up data on 129 child molesters who were treated at the Massachusetts Treatment Center, the authors found a 25 percent reoffense rate within five years. They used a 40 percent recidivism rate to estimate costs for those not treated and incarceration costs of $22,662 for seven years per inmate. Including parole supervision for five years, trial costs, and victim-related expenses, Prentky and Burgress estimated that each incarcerated child molester costs $183,333. They computed a savings of $67,989 for each treated offender and concluded by saying, "Hypothetically, then, for every 1,000 child molesters released from prison, the cost to society over a five-year period would be nearly $68 million greater for offenders who received no treatment prior to release" (p. 113).

In terms of a sensitivity analysis, they observed that the recidivism rate for treated child molesters would have to go as high as 62 percent for costs to be comparable; the recidivism rate for untreated molesters would have to drop to 3 percent for costs to be the same.

To the extent that a treatment program lowers recidivism of child molesters from 40% to 25%, it is effective. And clearly, saving taxpayers $68 million would be a large benefit. As this demonstrates, it's possible for evaluators to look at both cost-effectiveness and cost-benefit issues.

FINAL THOUGHTS ON COST ANALYSIS

In an essay on efficiency in the social services, Pruger and Miller (1991) observed:

> Though efficiency never has been treated as a first order concept in the social services, it should be. No other idea on the table or on the horizon cuts so directly to the enterprise. No other has the same potential to revitalize the field as it moves into and through the twenty-first century. (P. 6)

There is no better example of our society's need to find less expensive but more effective solutions to social problems than in the area of corrections. The prison population in the United States is rapidly approaching one million. Another half million are in jails. More than three million are on probation or parole. Additional food for thought: it costs approximately $30,000 to incarcerate an individual for a year.

Now let's dream for a while. What if you could take the same amount of money that it takes to lock up a prisoner for five years and spend that money preventively—on anything that your client would need: clothes, housing, transportation, counseling, job training or additional education. For those with the potential, might it not be cheaper to provide all-expense paid scholarships to public universities than to wait until after a serious offense has been committed and then employ the bludgeon of incarceration?

With a budget of even $100,000 to spend on behalf of each client, how many high-risk individuals could you keep out of prison? Could you demonstrate that there are more effective forms of intervention for reducing crime than incarceration? Given that not all crime can be prevented, are there less expensive but more effective ways to rehabilitate and prevent second offenses?

Despite certain medical ethicists (such as Williams, 1992, and Emery and Schneiderman, 1989) who argue that cost-effectiveness approaches may place some segments of the population at risk for not receiving expensive interventions (e.g., the very old with medical problems), social workers have the burden not only of implementing interventions but also of demonstrating that they are efficient. We have not done nearly enough of this. How many millions of dollars could be saved if we were to systematically examine each of our programs in terms of their cost and effectiveness and then make decisions about which programs to fund?

Important decisions should not be made without data to guide us. It is imperative that we develop the skills necessary to demonstrate the benefit and cost savings when one alternative "treatment" is chosen over another. To the extent that we can successfully identify and adopt the most effective programs, the prestige of the social work profession will be enhanced by a grateful and appreciative society.

QUESTIONS FOR CLASS DISCUSSION

1. Identify local, state, or national programs for which you would like to conduct cost-effectiveness evaluations. Discuss the program outcomes for these. Is there a choice of more than one outcome indicator per program? List all of the relevant indicators.
2. Discuss whether the following desired outcomes are likely to be monetary or nonmonetary. Would your evaluation be a cost-benefit analysis or a cost-effectiveness study?
   a. increased employee morale in a social service agency
   b. improved client satisfaction in an after-school tutoring program
   c. reduced alcohol and drug use within a factory
   d. improved employee health in a state agency
   e. reduced stress for child protection workers
3. An outpatient counseling program has a long waiting list of potential clients. As a new manager, what actions could you take to reduce the waiting list? Make a list of these and discuss each relative to a cost-benefit analysis.
4. Discuss whether is more important to know a program's cost or its effectiveness.

5. During periods of great flux, as when there is a dramatic increase in inflation, sensitivity analyses are important. What are some other situations or factors over which an evaluator has no control and which could change over a two or three year period that could significantly affect the value of "benefits" attributed to a project?

6. Discuss a proposal made to Congress to allow a $3,000 tax deduction for expenses incurred by parents who adopt a handicapped or older child. How would you evaluate such legislation using either a cost-effectiveness or a cost-benefit approach?

MINI PROJECTS: EXPERIENCING EVALUATION FIRSTSHAND

1. For a program of your choosing, outline a cost-benefit analysis. Identify the program, its major objective, monetary benefits and how these would be calculated, and relevant data-collection procedures.

2. For a program of your choosing, outline a cost-effectiveness study. Identify the program, its major objective, outcome indicators, and relevant data-collection procedures.

3. Defend an innovative or unorthodox approach to some social problem with which you are familiar. Justify your proposed program in terms of its relative costs and how it should be evaluated five years after it is implemented.

4. Before reading Shi's (1993) article examining the cost benefit of different health promotion interventions implemented in an industry, make a list of outcome variables you'd use to show savings accruing from the provision of (1) a bimonthly health newsletter and health resource center, (2) classes on stress management, coping with high blood pressure, or smoking cessation, and (3) public health nurses case managing high-risk employees. Compare your choice of variables with those used by Shi.

REFERENCES AND RESOURCES

Buescher, P.A., Larson, L.C., Nelson, M.D., and Lenihan, A.J. (1993). Prenatal WIC participation can reduce low birth weight and newborn medical costs: A cost-benefit analysis of WIC participation in North Carolina. *Journal of the American Dietetic Association*, 93 (2), 163–166.

Emery, D.D., and Schneiderman, L.J. (1989). Cost-effectiveness in health care. *Hastings Center Report*, 19 (4), 8–12.

Greene, V.L., Lovely, M.E., and Ondrich, J.I. (1993). The cost-effectiveness of community services in a frail elderly population. *Gerontologist*, 33 (2), 177–189.

Hatziandreu, E.I., Koplan, J.P., and Weinstein, M.C. (1988). A cost-effectiveness analysis of exercise as a health promotion activity. *American Journal of Public Health*, 78 (11), 1417–1421.

Hayashida, M., et al. (1989). Comparative effectiveness and costs of inpatient and outpatient detoxification of patients with mild-to-moderate alcohol withdrawal syndrome. *New England Journal of Medicine*, 320 (6), 358–365.

Levin, H.M. (1983). *Cost-effectiveness: A primer*. Beverly Hills, CA: Sage.

Lewis, D.R., Johnson, D.R., Chen, T., and Erickson, R.N. (1992). The use and reporting of benefit-cost analyses by state vocational rehabilitation agencies. *Evaluation Review*, 16 (3), 266–287.

McCaughrin, W.B., Ellis, W.K., Rusch, F.R., and Heal, L.W. (1993). Cost-effectiveness of supported employment. *Mental Retardation*, 31 (1), 41–48.

McCrady, B., Longabaugh, R., Fink, E., Stout, R., Beattie, M., and Ruggieri-Authelet, A. (1986). Cost effectiveness of alcoholism treatment in partial hospital versus inpatient settings after brief inpatient treatment: 12-month outcomes. *Journal of Consulting and Clinical Psychology*, 54 (5), 708–713.

Meltzer, H.Y., Cola, P., Way, L., Thompson, P.A., Bastani, B., Davies, M.A., and Snitz, B. (1993). Cost effectiveness of clozapine in neuroleptic-resistant schizophrenia. *American Journal of Psychiatry*, 150 (11), 1630–1638.

Mor, V., Green, D.S., and Kastenbaum, R. (1988). *The hospice experience*. Baltimore, MD: Johns Hopkins University Press.

Pike, C.I., and Piercy, F.P. (1990). Cost effectiveness research in family therapy. *Journal of Marital and Family Therapy*, 16 (4), 375–388.

Prentky, R., and Burgess, W. (1990). Rehabilitation of child molesters: A cost-benefit analysis. *American Journal of Orthopsychiatry*, 60 (1), 108–117.

Pruger, R., and Miller, L. (1991). Efficiency and the social services. *Administration in Social Work*, 15 (1/2), 5–23.

Shi, L. (1993). Health promotion, medical care use, and costs in a sample of worksite employees. *Evaluation Review*, 17 (5), 475–487.

Simons-Morton, B.G., Brink, S., and Bates, D. (1987). Effectiveness and cost-effectiveness of persuasive communications and incentives in increasing safety belt use. *Health Education Quarterly*, 14, 167–179.

Vinokur, A.D., van Ryn, M., Gramlich, E.M., and Price, R.H. (1991). Long-term follow-up and benefit-cost analysis of the JOBS program: A preventive intervention for the unemployed. *Journal of Applied Psychology*, 76 (2), 213–219.

Williams, A. (1992). Cost-effectiveness analysis: Is it ethical? *Journal of Medical Ethics*, 18 (1), 7–11.

Wing, D.M., and Gay, G. (1991). A critical literature review of alcoholism treatment cost-benefit/effectiveness. *Journal of Nursing Quality Assurance*, 5 (4), 28–40.

EIGHT

Measurement Tools and Strategies for Program Evaluation

There once was a primitive culture where counting followed this scheme: one, two, many. If you had more than two of something, you had many. It is clear that our society is much more concerned with counting and measuring things. If we accept a new position paying a salary of $30,000 a year, we certainly don't want to be paid $19,000 or even $29,000. If we buy three-and-a-half pounds of steak at the supermarket, we don't want to be charged for five pounds. Measurement, if not accountability, is fundamental aspect of our society.

We measure almost everything: the speed of computers, the BAUD rate of modems, the horsepower of cars, the calories we burn jogging, the interest rate the bank or credit card company charges. We measure all kinds of things because we want to know if things are changing or improving, because we are hungry for information about the world and our place in it. Progress and our ability to demonstrate and quantify it has become increasingly important to us—whether we are consumers, providers, or program evaluators.

In order to be accountable and show progress, precise measurements must be taken. Evaluators don't just rush out and start gathering data. As we learned earlier, outcome variables must be operationalized. On many occasions, evaluators use "paper-and-pencil" instruments to form the basis for measurements.

We may think of these instruments as questionnaires, although they do not always ask questions of respondents. Some instruments are composed of a number of statements (items) to which the respondent indicates levels of agreement or diagreeement. They can be complex and composed of many scales or as simple as three or four items. Well-developed instruments help us understand why some clients benefitted from an intervention and others did not. They also allow us to examine more closely those whose progress was meager or moderate—interventions don't always have the same effect on every person with the same problem.

Instruments allow us to use quantification to move beyond subjective opinions ("I think these clients have improved") into a domain where we can discuss the amount of change or improvement. ("This group of clients is 37 percent more assertive than they were at the time of pretest." Or, "At the time of the posttest, 55 percent of the intervention group reported no clinically significant symptoms.")

Objective instruments provide evaluators with a certain amount of precision in arriving at the magnitude or intensity of clients' problems and in determining any consequent change in those problems. We are afforded this precision because instruments allow us to quantify abstract or intangible concepts such as self-esteem or assertiveness. These instruments allow us to translate subjective perceptions of problems and concepts into numeric values.

Evaluation instruments are not just plucked from thin air. They must be selected with care. A hastily chosen instrument could provide unreliable or worthless information. It is important to select instruments that not only are psychometrically strong, but also are good indicators of what the programs are attempting to accomplish. Consider the following scenario.

Jim Gradstudent was asked to evaluate a residential treatment center for youth who had experienced some trouble with the juvenile justice system. He had noticed that several of the most successful residents there seemed to have experienced an increase in self-esteem by the time they were released. One afternoon while in the university library he found a self-esteem instrument that looked as if it could be used for the program evaluation. After deciding upon a One Group Pre/Posttest Design, Jim made a number of photocopies of the self-esteem instrument and began administering it to new admissions. Eleven months later he had collected forty-two pre- and posttests from residents who had been discharged from the treatment center. He was surprised to learn that there was very little difference in the pre- and posttest self-esteem scores. Does this mean that the residential treatment program was unsuccessful?

As you think about this scenario, the lack of information in several areas should cause you to raise questions. First of all, is increasing the resident's self-esteem a clearly articulated goal of the residential treatment center? If it is not, would use of a self-esteem inventory to evaluate the whole program be a reasonable measure? Even if it is an important goal of the program, how likely is it that the youth in treatment will actually experience an increase in self-esteem? Is there evidence from the literature to suggest that residential treatment centers for this population commonly increase self-esteem? Could any other variable be used to gauge success of the program?

If it occurred to you that a fair measure of the treatment center's success might be recidivism—subsequent arrests or offenses that would bring these youths to the attention of the juvenile justice system again— you are right. It is not always necessary to use a paper-and-pencil instrument to measure program outcome. Furthermore, the use of an instrument of unknown psychometric qualities should be avoided. Evaluators need to know how "good" instruments are. But more about that later. First, let's examine our alternatives.

WHAT TO MEASURE

We start deciding what to measure when we ask how a program's "success" could best be demonstrated. What is a program trying to accomplish? If it fails, how would that failure be noted? As you can see in Box 8.1, for some programs the criteria are obvious.

Such programs as these do not always require paper-and-pencil instruments to evaluate their outcomes. In some cases, no instrument is required; programs can be evaluated with the data already collected. It is very likely, for instance, that a mental health center will know how many or what percent of its clients in the day treatment program became hospitalized during the course of a year. It should not be difficult for adoption workers to determine the number of or percentage of children for whom a permanent placement was obtained. Forensic programs ought to be able to determine which of their clients are rearrested.

Schools ought to know which of their pregnant students drop out and which ones go on to graduate. Dropping out of school can be viewed as a behavior in much the same way as the logical consequencs of substance abuse (such as arrest or DUI) reflect certain behaviors. So, even though official records are used to gauge the impact of the intervention,

177

programs can be evaluated in terms of *behavioral outcomes* without interviewing, observing, or distributing questionnaires to program recipients.

Many human service agencies are required to annually publish data on the number of clients they serve. Often these data are available on a county basis and may be useful to evaluators trying to determine the impact of broadly focused programs.

The use of official data to measure progress is nothing new. Florence Nightingale is said to have kept statistics on the mortality of British soldiers. She kept track of hospital deaths by diagnostic categories in order to show that improvements in sanitation reduced fatalities. Because of her efforts, the mortality rate dropped from 32 percent to 2 percent within six months (M.A. Nutting and L.L. Dock, 1907, cited in Meisenheimer, 1985).

BOX 8.1
Examples of Behavioral Outcomes for Programs

Program	Success	Failure
Alcohol and drug treatment programs	Days of sobriety	Days drinking, public intoxication, DUIs
Day treatment for the severely mentally ill	Days of independent living in community	Rehospitalizations, number of days in hospital
Juvenile and adult criminal justice diversion programs	Days without arrest; employment or school attendance	Rearrests, days in jail, suspension from school
Employment and training programs	Wages and hours worked	Amount of entitlements received
Adoption programs	Number of permanent placements made	Number of children eligible for adoption still in foster care
Child protection programs	No further reports or evidence of abuse or neglect	Substantiated reports of abuse or neglect

---

Behavioral data can include such specific physiological measurements as those obtained from skinfold calipers, weight gained or lost, biochemical measures such as serum albumin, serum transferrin, and total lymphocyte count. Some drug treatment programs use urine analyses to detect which clients are staying "clean."

Behavioral data can also be obtained through the use of client self-monitoring and seven-day calendar recall methods. Rossiter et al. (1992) found that asking subjects to recall days on which they experienced binge epidsodes and the number of episodes on those days was more likely to illicit accurate information than asking subjects only to recall the number of binge-eating episodes.

Video-and audiotaping clients' interactions with others are additional sources of behavioral data. For instance, to determine if parents interact more appropriately with their young children after a nurturing program, videotaping sessions with parents and their children could be arranged. While there might be some concerns with "staged" behavior, a benefit of videotaping is that facial expressions and general demeanor can be observed. Rating scales can be developed so that there is a quantitative count or rating on the presence or absence of desired behaviors. The tapes can also be used by clients for learning from self-observation, as well as for demonstrating progress.

However, behavioral outcomes are not as easy to measure with every program. For instance, suppose you are the director of a program that provides drug prevention programming for elementary school children. The goal of your program is to prevent these children from becoming addicted as adolescents or adults. Most programs of this type will not have the ability to do any sort of follow-up study three, five, or ten years later to see if the prevention programming resulted in fewer persons with drug dependency problems than in the control group. As a consequence, these and other programs without an ability to measure behavioral outcomes must consider success in terms of clients increasing their *knowledge* about a given problem or in terms of changing clients' *attitudes*.

Sometimes prevention programs measure whether the program recipients have increased their knowledge about a given problem. In AIDS prevention programs, for instance, the goal could be to provide sufficient information about how AIDS is transmitted so that program participants have an increased knowledge about its transmission. One could envision a pretest of twenty items and the typical respondent (before the intervention) getting four or five items correct. After the intervention (assuming that the educational presentation is effective), the typical respondent might answer correctly eighteen or nineteen items on the posttest. This would indicate that respondents' knowledge about AIDS had been increased.

For other programs, the main goal may be to change the participants' attitudes about some behavior or practice. For instance, if you were administering an intervention program for men who batter—the evaluator might use a behavioral measure (arrests, incidents of battering) as an outcome measure, but it would also be possible to determine if program participants had a change in attitudes about battering. The goal of the program might be to help batterers become more empathetic— to put themselves in the place of the victim—and to view battering as unacceptable behavior. In this instance, the evaluator may not want to measure batterers' knowledge about domestic violence but to change attitudes regarding its acceptability. The theory here would be that if attitudes change, so will behavior.

Often, it is much easier to measure attitudes and knowledge than behavior. It is relatively easy to determine if adolescents have become more knowledgeable about drugs or if they have developed attitudes favorable to the use of illicit drugs. It is much more difficult to determine if program recipients sell, buy, or use illegal drugs once they are away from school. Using the men-who-batter example, even after a treatment program has been completed, battering may still occur in the home but go unreported. An evaluator might be tempted to conclude that an intervention program was successful because there were no rearrests among the program participants, when in reality battering was still occurring but perhaps less often or in a somewhat less severe form.

A major advantage of paper-and-pencil measures of knowledge and attitudes is that they can be administered easily in a classroom , waiting room, or office—and outcome data can usually be obtained more quickly than for some behavioral measures (such as clients being rearrested or hospitalized).

A major disadvantage of focusing on knowledge and attitudes is that they may not be directly related to behavior. For example, clients may have knowledge that drug use is bad for them but continue with destructive drug use. (Think of how many persons smoke cigarettes even though the surgeon general's warning is printed on each pack.) Clients can increase their knowledge about alcoholism (or a number of other problems) and yet not change their behavior. We and our clients may have attitudes which are inconsistent with personal behavior. (Some very conservative legislators may favor legalization of illegal drugs not because they use illegal drugs themselves but simply as a way of trying to manage the national problem of drug abuse.) A woman might be in favor of women having a right to an abortion while not viewing that as an acceptable option for herself. The connection between attitudes, knowledge, and behavior is tenuous at best. Probably the "best" measure in any situation would be one closest to the intent of the program intervention. Because it is not always possible to observe behavioral changes or to get reliable measures of specific behaviors, evaluators may opt to use instruments (sometimes called **scales** when they refer to a single concept like hostility or anxiety) to measure changes in attitudes, knowledge, or self-reported behavior. Instruments are evaluated along two primary dimensions: reliability and validity.

RELIABILITY

An instrument or questionnaire is said to be **reliable** when it consistently and dependably measures some concept or phenomenon with accuracy. If an instrument is reliable, then administering it to similar groups yields similar results. A reliable instrument is like a reliable watch—it is not subject to extraneous factors such as temperature, humidity, physical appearance of the person using it, day of the week, cycle of the moon, and so forth.

The reliability of instruments is generally reported in a way that resembles a correlation coefficient—it will be a numerical value between 0 and 1. Nunnally (1978) says that in the early stages of research one can work with instruments having modest reliability (by which he means .70 or higher), that .80 can be used for basic research, and that a reliability of .90 is the minimum where important decisions are going to be made with respect to specific test scores.

What does it mean when an instrument does not have even modest reliability? It means that when the instrument is administered to a group of persons, not all of them will understand or interpret the items in the same way. For instance, suppose I am interested in measuring knowledge about AIDS and I develop the following item: "It is possible to get AIDS from gay employees in restaurants or bars." Six out of ten individuals may interpret this item as asking whether food-handlers can transmit AIDS by handling plates, silverware, or breathing on food. However, if four out of every ten individuals read into the item the question of whether AIDS is transmitted by having sex with the employees of gay restaurants and bars, then this item would detract from rather than contribute to the making of a reliable instrument. While one single item will seldom make a whole scale unreliable, several vague items that can be interpreted differently by various individuals will cause problems with reliability.

When a scale or instrument is used and reported in a professional journal article or evaluation effort, the author should include information about it. If there is no information on instrumentation, there can be no presumption of reliability or validity. This problem commonly arises when the author's instrument or questionnaire is "homemade."

Although there are several ways to demonstrate reliability, most researchers start first with **internal consistency**. With this approach, each of the individual items that make up a scale are examined for how well they correlate with the scale as a whole. The *Statistical Package for the Social Sciences* is one of several computer software programs that can determine a scale's reliability. The reliability procedure provides an item analysis that helps the researcher know which items to drop.

To show you this process, we've incorporated data from a scale currently under development to measure adolescents' attitudes about the value of work (see Box 8.2).

Approximately one-hundred adolescents completed the "My Attitudes about Work" scale. When these data were entered into the computer, the printout in Box 8.3 was obtained.

Look at the column headed "Corrected Item—total Correlation." Q5 and Q8 stand apart from the rest because they are negatively correlated to the scale as a whole. Including these items in my scale has the result of lowering the **alpha** (reliability coefficient). This can be determined by looking at the column on the far right. Dropping Q5 would raise the scale's alpha to .82; deleting Q8 has about the same effect. Because we want the highest internal consistency possible, it would make sense to eliminate both of these items from the scale and use a shorter, revised scale.

However, let's assume that I went back over the scale, reading it closely and checking to see how the items were coded. You'll notice that nine items (Q1, Q2, Q5, Q6, Q7, Q9, Q12, Q13, and Q16) should be coded positively because a "true" response would indicate a favorable view of work. Similarly, "true" responses to items Q3, Q4, Q8, Q10, Q11, Q14, and Q15 should be coded differently (reverse coded) because a "true" response to these items indicates an unfavorable view of work. In reviewing how my items were coded, I realized that I had reversed my instructions to the computer for items Q5 and Q8. Once they were coded correctly, the printout in Box 8.4 resulted.

The alpha obtained the second time is higher than the software program initially estimated. This is because even though Q5 and Q8 were coded erroneously the first time, the computer had no way of knowing this and simply followed instructions—considering them as valuable elements of the scale we wanted to develop. Coded correctly, these items add to, rather than detract from, the scale, resulting in the higher reliability coefficient.

A developer of a scale may compute its internal consistency on multiple occasions, revising the items and trying to find the best combinations of items and the highest alpha that can be obtained with the fewest items. Scale development is somewhat more complex than it is presented here. You may wish to refer to Comrey (1988) or DeVillis (1991) for additional information.

There are several other ways to determine if an instrument has reliability. The *split-half* technique involves deviding a scale in half (using either top and bottom or even and odd items) and examining how well the two halves correlate with each other. Another approach is to devise *parallel* or *alternate* versions of the scale and administer the forms to similar groups. Reliability would be demonstrated when both versions

---

BOX 8.2
My Attitudes about Work

Instructions: For each of the statements below, indicate whether it is True (**T**), or False (**F**) for you. Use a question mark (**?**) if you can't decide.

___ 1. I would like to have a full-time job someday.
___ 2. The idea of working for a living is exciting to me.
___ 3. If I had a job, I would expect it to be boring.
___ 4. Working 40 hours a week in a regular job is a waste of time.
___ 5. I would rather have a job paying minimum wage than no job at all.
___ 6. Earning a paycheck would make me feel important.
___ 7. Holding down a job would give me a good feeling about myself.
___ 8. There are plenty of ways to make money without working.
___ 9. With a job, I would have more repect for myself.
___10. Any job would probably pay less than I deserve.
___11. Only stupid people work for a living.
___12. It is possible to enjoy one's work.
___13. I want to be employed when I grow up.
___14. I would rather be unemployed than have a job that paid only minimum wage.
___15. I would rather be unemployed than have a boss ordering me around.
___16. Working people have more pride than people who don't work.

BOX 8.3
Reliability Analysis—First Effort

Item	Scale Mean if Item Deleted	Scale Variance if Item Deleted	Corrected Item— Total Correlation	Squared Multiple Correlation	Alpha if Item Deleted
Q1	36.8	28.3	.55	.60	.72
Q2	37.4	25.0	.61	.50	.70
Q3	37.2	26.2	.54	.51	.71
Q4	37.1	26.2	.59	.47	.71
Q5	38.3	37.9	−.71	.75	.82
Q6	37.0	28.2	.37	.41	.73
Q7	37.1	26.4	.57	.50	.71
Q8	38.0	35.9	−.46	.29	.81
Q9	37.1	25.8	.64	.56	.70
Q10	37.2	25.5	.61	.50	.70
Q11	36.8	30.3	.24	.42	.74
Q12	36.9	28.4	.47	.42	.73
Q13	36.9	28.6	.41	.50	.73
Q14	37.1	26.3	.55	.68	.71
Q15	37.2	25.3	.64	.59	.70
Q16	37.3	27.2	.42	.36	.73

ALPHA = .77

correlate with each other—the higher the correlation coefficient, the stronger the reliability.

Still another form of reliability (*test-retest*) is demonstrated when the scale holds up well over time with the same group of individuals. Without the benefit of intervention, groups of individuals with any given problem (e.g., low self-esteem) shouldn't experience major increases or decreases. Should an instrument show this over a period of four weeks, for example, then one possible explanation may be that the instrument is not reliable.

Instruments with no or very low reliability are, for all practical purposes, worthless. This is not to say that you can't obtain extremely valuable information from a questionnaire with nothing known about its reliability. The problem is that without evidence that the questions

BOX 8.4
Reliability Analysis—Second Attempt

Item	Scale Mean if Item Deleted	Scale Variance if Item Deleted	Corrected Item— Total Correlation	Squared Multiple Correlation	Alpha if Item Deleted
Q1	38.6	54.1	.52	.60	.89
Q2	39.2	48.8	.65	.50	.88
Q3	38.9	50.4	.60	.51	.88
Q4	38.9	51.1	.58	.47	.89
Q5	38.9	49.5	.72	.75	.88
Q6	38.8	53.4	.41	.41	.89
Q7	38.8	50.8	.61	.50	.88
Q8	39.2	51.0	.47	.29	.89
Q9	38.9	50.2	.66	.56	.88
Q10	39.0	49.9	.62	.50	.88
Q11	38.6	56.4	.25	.42	.89
Q12	38.7	53.9	.48	.42	.89
Q13	38.7	54.0	.44	.50	.89
Q14	38.8	50.0	.66	.68	.88
Q15	39.0	49.3	.68	.59	.88
Q16	39.0	52.0	.45	.36	.89

ALPHA = .89

are reliable, there is no way to guarantee that they would be interpreted the same way if they were administered again.

Survey questionnaires pose a special problem because the reliability of single items cannot be computed. As a rule, adding items to a scale increase its reliability. All else being equal, a longer scale, say twenty-five items, stands a better chance of having acceptable reliability than a scale of two or three items.

Novice evaluators are often tempted to develop scales of their own. However, Thyer (1992) has made this recommendation:

> Avoid this temptation like the plague! The design and validation of a scale or survey is a major project in and of itself, and a program evaluation is NO PLACE to try to develop such a measure. If you ignore this advice and prepare your own scale, your entire study's results may be called into

question because the reader will have no evidence that your new measure is a reliable or valid one. As a social work journal editor, I can attest to the fact that this is a major reason why manuscripts get rejected: a well-meaning practitioner constructs his or her own idiosyncratic scale, obtains interesting results, and tries to publish them. Invariably the reviewers note this fact, reject the study, and sadly suggest that next time the writer should use a previously published scale or outcome measure with well-establised reliability and validity. (Pp. 139–140)

Without doubt, instances may arise when you will have to develop your own scale because no instrument exists to measure the dimension you need to quantify. Or, because you find an instrument that has some problem associated with it, such as requiring a reading comprehension level that is too high, containing too many items for children or adolescents with short attention spans, or having weak or unknown reliability and validity.

Reliability is a concern not only if you revise or devise an instrument to use in your evaluation, but also if you rely upon secondary data like rearrests, suicides, and subsequent reports of abuse and neglect. The concern is not with the form or questionnaire used to create the data as much as it is with the reliability of the data-gathering and reporting procedures.

Siefert, Schwartz, and Ortega (1994), for example, investigated the infant mortality rates in Michigan's child welfare system and found a higher postneonatal death rate among those infants in foster care placement than was occurring statewide. However, when the authors sought to verify information held by the Michigan Department of Social Services, they found that five of the sixty-six infants initially identified as having died during the study period were actually alive. The management information system used by the Department of Social Services to report administrative data was unable to supply information about the physical handicap status of infants in the study because of coding errors and omissions. Further, a 30 percent error rate in recording entry and exit dates from specific types of placements was also noted (Lerman, 1990, cited in Siefert, Schwartz, Ortega, 1994).

Most, if not all, social indicators vastly underestimate the true incidence of social problems in our country. We know, for example, that the incidence of domestic violence, child abuse, date rape, and so forth is much greater than the recorded arrests. Sometimes clients cross state lines and commit offenses that evaluators may not know about. And, there can be indications of problems (e.g., suicide attempts) that never come to the attention of authorities.

This is *not* to suggest that you should refrain from using official reports to judge the success of the programs you are evaluating. In some agencies, hospitals and health care settings in particular, records may be excellent and very useful to the evaluator. For instance, Sundel, Garrett, and Horn (1994) have reported on a restraint reduction program in a nursing home that showed that the number of residents on restraints was reduced significantly.

If your measurement strategy is to use existing records for the evaluation, you need to be familiar with the procedures that generated the data. You may find problems of over or under reporting, that the staff on one shift are more conscientious or more lax than another, that there were policy or procedural changes in reporting that no one remembered to tell you. Understand that any official records are somewhat limited in their ability to describe what's "really" going on, but they often constitute the best information available. In some instances, this type of data is superior to asking clients or their partners about subsequents acts of violence or participation in other illegal activities (such as those that would constitute parole violations). However, the literature in your field may be able to guide you in determining whether self-reported data from clients will provide more reliable estimates of the behavior than official records.

If the data you are collecting for your program evaluation comes from judgments, observations, or interviews of two or more persons who are rating the behavior independently, then you must be concerned with *inter-rater reliability*. Suppose you are screening persons with chronic mental illness for entry into a new program that will provide them with guaranteed employment, an apartment, and intensive case management. The program is designed for only the most functional of all those who have been hospitalized for mental illness. When you meet with Jill, the fourth person referred, you immediately notice that she doesn't make eye contact with you and seems to be staring into space a good deal of the time. Jill appears to be distracted, preoccupied with her own inner world, and you decide she would not be a good candidate for the program.

However, your colleague, Dr. Perceptive, is not troubled by Jill's lack of eye contact, viewing this as only shyness or fear of rejection. Based on Jill's well-reasoned responses, Dr. Perceptive gives Jill a high rating and recommends that she be selected for the program. If you and Dr. Perceptive don't agree at least 70 percent of the time or your scores don't correlate at least at .80 on a large sample, then you don't have adequate inter-rater reliability. The major way to improve inter-rater reliability is through training and role-playing so that the raters begin to adopt a more uniform perspective and recognize the same criteria.

187

VALIDITY

An instrument is said to be **valid** when it closely corresponds to the concept it was designed to measure. Let's say that you are developing a self-esteem inventory and in a sudden flash of inspiration it occurs to you that a high level of self-esteem would be indicated if respondents could identify the twenty-seventh president of the United States. If you incorporate a number of similar items into your self-esteem inventory, you probably would not create a self-esteem scale but rather a scale that measures knowledge of American history. This scale would very likely not be valid for measuring self-esteem.

There are various ways to go about demonstrating that an instrument has validity. Sometimes experts are asked to review it to see if the entire range of the concept is represented in the sample of items selected for the scale. This is known as **content validity**. For instance, if you were developing a scale to measure progress in the treatment of bulimia and did not include the behaviors of eating uncontrollably, binge eating, or intentionally vomiting, then you would not have covered the entire range of behaviors that ought to go into a scale designed to measure progress in treating bulimia. Sometimes the term **face validity** is used when one's colleagues look over an instrument and agree that it appears to measure the concept. Neither content nor face validity is sufficient for establishing that the scale has "true" validity.

Concurrent validity is demonstrated by administering to the same subjects the new scale and another scale that has previously been determined (proven) to have validity. If the two scales correlate well, then the scale is said to have concurrent validity.

Predictive validity is demonstrated when scores on the new scale predict future behavior or attitudes. If you have developed an instrument to predict which parents are likely to abuse their children and three years later you find that a high percentage of these parents did abuse their children, then your instrument would have predictive validity.

Construct validity is concerned with the theoretical relationship of the scale to other variables. Does the scale perform as hypothesized? Does it differentiate along expected lines and between known groups? For instance, suppose you develop an instrument to measure attitudes about drug usage. You would have evidence of construct validity if it showed that college students attending Baptist colleges held antidrug attitudes and that known drug abusers in a court-ordered treatment program had prodrug attitudes. Such findings would show that the instrument could discriminate between those who had positive and those who had negative attitudes about drugs. An instrument that cannot make these kinds of discriminations would be of no use to program evaluators.

For that reason, we were very interested in whether a sample of adolescents judged to have "good" attitudes about work would have higher scores than adolescents judged to have "poor" attitudes when tested on the "My Attitudes about Work" scale discussed earlier in the chapter. Fortunately, we found statistically significant differences—those in the "good" attitudes group had higher scores on the scale than those judged to have "poor" attitudes about work. Thus, there is some beginning evidence of the scale's validity.

Like reliability, there are many forms and approaches to estblishing validity. Factor analysis may sometimes be used to understand the structure of a scaled construct. For example, Russell, Kao, and Cutrona (1987, cited in Shaver and Brennan, 1991) conducted confirmatory factor analysis in order to determine that measures of loneliness and social support defined distinct factors. This was consistent with their expectation that loneliness is unidimensional and more strongly related to mood and personality than to absence of social support. To understand this, think about how you would go about constructing a scale to measure loneliness. A validity issue is the distinction between loneliness and depression. To what extent do they overlap and how are they different? Is loneliness a transient emotion (a state) or a character trait?

To further complicate the problem of understanding validity, there is no standardized taxonomy of validation terms. As Koeske (1994) observes:

> After nearly four decades of methodological scholarship on measurement validation and its applications in research contexts, there exists no fully comprehensive language system for identifying and differentiating types of validity and procedures for their assessment. (P. 45)

Think of the problem of establishing validity as a gradual, ongoing, confirmatory process that builds upon each study. However, if you are reviewing scales for potential use in a program evaluation, you can afford to be a little more critical. Choose those that have the most extensive evidence of validity—whether criterion, structural, construct, convergent, discriminant, predictive, or concurrent.

While reliability and validity have been presented as separate concepts, they are interrelated in a complex fashion. If an instrument can be empirically demonstrated to have validity (and we're not talking about just face or content validity), then it can generally be assumed to have adequate reliability. However, a reliable instrument may not be valid for the purpose we want to use it. That is, an instrument may provide dependable measurements, but of some concept unrelated to what we thought we were measuring. However, both reliability and validity ought to be demonstrated as evidence that an instrument is psychometrically strong. This is not an either/or choice. The evaluator should try to obtain information about the instrument's reliability and validity before adopting it. If you know nothing about the reliability and validity of an instrument, it is important to realize that the results obtained from its use will have very little meaning. One obvious way of avoiding having to establish that your new scale has reliability and validity is to use instruments that already have been demonstrated to have sufficient reliability and validity.

Although our focus has been chiefly on reliability and validity, there are a number of other characteristics of instruments to consider when choosing among several for use in a program evaluation. These considerations have been summarized in Box 8.5.

LOCATING APPROPRIATE INSTRUMENTS

You have been asked to conduct a program evaluation, and the committee you are working with wants you to find a self-esteem instrument. Where do you start? *Measures for Clinical Practice* by Joel Fischer and Kevin Corcoran (1994) is first place you might want to look. These two authors have compiled a large number of brief assessment instruments to measure everything from anxiety to satisfaction with treatment.

Another useful source is Nurius and Hudson (1993). All of their scales are twenty-five items in length, and individuals with scores above 30 are usually found to have a "clinically significant problem." Their scales are copyrighted but can be purchased in blocks of fifty or on a computer diskette. Scales include:

Clinical Anxiety Scale
Global Screening Inventory
Generalized Contentment Scale
Index of Self-Esteem
Index of Peer Relations
Index of Alcohol Involvement
Index of Marital Satisfaction
Index of Sexual Satisfaction
Index of Family Relations
Index of Parental Attitudes

A third useful reference is *Measures of Personality and Social Psychological Attitudes* (1991) by Robinson, Shaver, and Wrightsman. Their sourcebook provides 150 examples of instruments organized in chapters on subjective well-being, self-esteem, social anxiety and shyness, depression and loneliness, alienation and anomie, interpersonal trust, locus of control, authoritarianism, sex roles, and values.

The advantage of browsing through these publications is that they afford you an opportunity to visualize the scales. However, it is not always possible to see examples of instruments without purchasing them. Useful reference guides exist to help you locate instruments, but these generally do not contain test specimens. For instance, Touliatos, Perlmutter, and

---

BOX 8.5
Considerations for Selecting Outcomes Measures

Instruments should be:

- *Relevant and appropriate to the client group.* Instruments may be inappropriate in terms of clients' primary symptoms or problems, attention span, reading level, and may not correspond well with the purpose of intervention.
- *Easy to administer.* Overly complex instruments or those with complicated instructions may not get administered uniformly across various sites—particularly if you are dependent upon others to collect your data. Will it be a burden upon clients and interfere with treatment?
- *Useful and easy to interpret.* The scores you obtain should be clear and understandable—unambiguous for the majority of clients. Will the scores assist with diagnosis or treatment planning? Interpretation is often facilitated if there is a single outcome score and if norms are available on similar treatment groups and nonclients.
- *Reliable and vaild.* Additionally, is it easy to "fake" desirable scores?
- *Sensitive to change.* If clients get better or worse, is the instrument capable of showing small gradations of improvement or deterioration? Scales with too few items may have a difficult time showing change in small increments. At the same time, you don't want a scale so senstitive that you are led to erroneous conclusions by a client having a bad day or if the client completes the scale at home rather than in the agency.
- *Relatively inexpensive.* Cost considerations include purchase of the instrument, scoring it, and training staff in its use.

Straus (1990) have abstracted close to a thousand instruments. However, they don't provide examples of these scales. To see one you would have to write the original author or track down the journal article that contained it. Conoley and Kramer, editors of the *Tenth Mental Measurements Yearbook* (1989), have assembled reviews of close to four hundred commercially available tests. The publication is organized like an encyclopedia—reviews of tests are found alphabetically by test title. The classified subject guide lists a number of tests under "personality" that may be of interest to social workers.

Resources that also may be of use to you are:

Brodsky, S.L. and Smitherman, H.O. (1983). *Handbook of Scales for Research in Crime and Delinquency*. New York: Plenum Press.

Fredman, N. and Sherman, R. (1987). *Handbook of Measurements for Marriage and Family Therapy*. New York: Brunner/Mazel.

McDowell, I. and Newell, C. (1987). *Measuring Health: A Guide to Rating Scales and Questionnaires*. London: Oxford University Press.

Miller, D.C. (1991). *Handbook of Research Design and Social Measurement*. Newbury Park, CA: Sage.

Nurius, P.S., and Hudson, W.W. (1993). *Human Services Practice, Evaluation, and Computers*. Pacific Grove, CA: Brooks/Cole.

Robinson, J.P., Shaver, P., and Wrightsman, L.S. (1991). *Measures of Personality and Social Psychological Attitudes*. San Diego, CA: Academic Press.

Touliatos, J., Perlmutter, B.F., and Straus, M.A. (1990). *Handbook of Family Measurement Techniques*. Newbury Park, CA: Sage.

Other references, although somewhat dated, may help you to locate a specific test or instrument:

Chun, Ki-Taek, Cobb, S., and French, J.R., Jr. (1975). *Measures for Psychological Assessment: A Guide to 3000 Original Sources and Their Applications*. Ann Arbor, MI: Institute for Social Research.

Educational Testing Service. (1988). *The ETS Test Collection Catalog. Vol. 2, Vocational Tests and Measurement Devices*. New York: Oryx Press.

Educational Testing Service. (1989). *The ETS Test Collection Catalog. Vol. 3, Tests for Special Populations*. New York: Oryx Press.

Fredman, N., and Sherman, R. (1987). *Handbook of Measurements for Marriage and Family Therapy*. New York: Brunner/Mazel.

Goldman, B.A. and Busch, J.C. (1982). *Directory of Unpublished Experimental Mental Measures.* New York: Human Sciences Press.

Hamill, D.D. (1989). *A Consumer's Guide to Tests in Print.* Austin, TX: Pro-ED.

Keyser, D.J. and Sweetland, R.C. (1984). *Test Critiques.* Kansas City, MO: Test Corporation of America.

Keyser, D.J. and Sweetland, R.C. (1987). *Test Critques Compendium: Reviews of Major Tests from the Test Critiques Series.* Kansas City, MO: Test Corporation of America.

Lake, D.G., Miles, M.B., and Earle, R.B., Jr. (1973). *Measuring Human Behavior: Tools for the Assessment of Social Functioning.* New York: Teachers College Press.

McDowell, I., and Newell, C. (1987). *Measuring Health: A Guide to Rating Scales and Questionnaires.* New York: Oxford University Press.

McCubbin, H., and Thompson, C. (1987). *Family Assessment Inventories for Research and Practice.* Madison: University of Wisconsin.

Robinson, J.P., Athanasiou, R., and Head, K.B. (1969). *Measures of Occupational Attitudes and Occupational Characteristics.* Ann Arbor, MI: Institute for Social Research.

Sweetland, R.C., and Keyser, D.J. (1986). *Tests: A Comprehensive Reference for Assessments in Psychology, Education, and Business.* Kansas City, MO: Test Corporation of America.

WHEN REFERENCE BOOKS DON'T PROVIDE THE INSTRUMENT YOU WANT

If you don't find the instrument you need by looking through one of the reference books, don't despair. The next step is to conduct a thorough search of the literature. You have to do this anyway, even if you have an instrument, because you need to know what others have learned when they evaluate programs similar to the one you wish to evaluate. They may have discovered that the instrument did not provide the kind of information they had hoped for, or that some other problem developed with its use. There is no need to repeat their mistakes, particularly if they tell you how to avoid them.

Search such abstracting services as *Psychological Abstracts, Social Work Abstracts, Index Medicus (Medline),* and ERIC for the topic that is closest to the clients' problem or focus of the intervention. These may be searched manually or via a computer. For instance, PsycLIT is available in a CD-ROM format; PsycINFO is an on-line database that can be accessed through such services as BRS, DIALOG, OCLC, and FirstSearch (although there it is called PsycFIRST and carries the most recent three years). Be prepared for hundreds of citations if you search for the subject "self-esteem." You'll quickly learn to skim past those studies based on populations very different from your own. Evaluations of other programs using the instrument you have in mind will provide useful data for comparison—particularly if your design doesn't employ a control group.

You may want to consult a reference librarian before you begin your literature searches. Since librarians do this much more often than you, they are likely to know ways to keep you from being inundated with references. For instance, I searched Medline for the key words "patient satisfaction" and found almost 2,400 citations. Next, I tried "consumer satisfaction" and discovered 689 citations. But when I tried "client satisfaction," there were only 35 references.

Those studies that have used an instrument to measure some dimension of interest to you (whether self-esteem, client satisfaction, or something else) may reproduce the scale in the journal article. However, don't bet on it. Because of space limitations, few instruments are printed in articles. Commonly what is found are examples of items from the scale and information about the scale's reliability and validity. You may have to look up the article and consult its bibliography—perhaps searching through several other articles in order to find the instrument. In some instances, you will need to write to the author to obtain a copy of the instrument and permission to use it. This can be problematic when the article is not recent and the author cannot be located. When this obstacle is encountered, it may be possible to find more recent articles by the same author or even to identify others who have cited the original author in their bibliographies by looking in the *Social Sciences Citation Index*.

Sometimes students make statements like, "I want to start a new group in the nursing home, but I don't know which instrument to use." A series of questions about the goals of the group or program—what it was designed to accomplish—usually helps to clarify things. Then we can discuss what data may be available readily and what is feasible to measure. On occasion, students need to do some library research before they can settle on a particular instrument. Suppose the new group in the nursing home is designed to help members adjust to being away from loved ones or their homes. The intent of the group is to help group members become less lonely.

Once in the library, the student might look under such headings as "loneliness," "depression," "nursing homes," "adjustment to nursing homes," "elderly," "aged," or even "geriatric patients." With a little searching, articles describing evaluation plans, instruments, and results of other evaluation efforts will likely be found. Additionally, becoming familiar with the literature helps the evaluator ground the evaluation effort in terms of theoretial models and expectaions for the program's potential success rate. This is particularly important in those instances where programs have been rapidly implemented with little prior planning or design.

Still another approach to locating instruments is to write publishing companies that specialize in selling research instruments. Fisher and Corcoran (1994) have listed over thirty such firms. Not to be overlooked are individual investigators who develop instruments and then form or link up with publishing companies to sell and market them. The evaluator finds references to these instruments in journal articles and then may purchase the authors' manuals that discuss reliability and validity, interpretation, characteristics of the normative samples, and other references on the instrument.

A final approach is to contact a faculty member at a university who is known to engage in research. They may know of useful instruments. Even if they don't personally have the instrument you need, they may be able to refer you to other faculty or sources.

When every effort has been made to locate appropriate instruments and none have been found, then it may be time to consider developing your own instrument.

CONSTRUCTING "GOOD" EVALUATION INSTRUMENTS

A student recently asked me to assist her in getting some reliability data on an instrument she had developed. As a serious and conscientious student she had conducted a thorough literature search and could find no instrument to measure the concept in which she was interested. She talked with knowledgeable persons in the field, developed a list of questions, and reviewed and revised them. In short, she did about everything she could have been expected to do. When we computed the alpha coefficient (reliability) for her ten-item scale with some initial data, it turned out to be a puny .35—not good enough to use with her project. Consequently, the project soon stalled.

Developing good instruments requires much more explanation than an introductory evaluation text can provide. However, it is possible to point out some errors commonly made when constructing instruments or developing questionnaires.

Look at the examples of the questions in Box 8.6. Can you identify anything wrong with these questions?

In the first question, you should notice that there are two positive evaluation choices ("excellent" and "good"), but only one negative possibility. Respondents have two opportunities to say something good about the program but only one to indicate dissatisfaction. This response scale is biased towards (more likely to get) positive feedback about the program than negative feedback. It is not balanced. A better way to handle this

---

BOX 8.6
Examples of Poorly Constructed Questions

1. Please rate the quality of our services:
   a. excellent   b. good   c. poor

2. Do you come here often for help?
   a. yes   b. no   c. don't know

3. What is your marital status?
   a. single   b. married   c. divorced

4. How long have you been a client with us?
   a. six months or less
   b. under a year
   c. one year or longer

5. What is your income?
   a. $10,000 to $20,000
   b. $20,000 to $30,000
   c. $30,000 or more

6. Do you not make a practice of shopping only on weekends?
   a. yes   b. no   c. undecided

7. Do you have a male relative and a female relative over fifty-five years of age living at home with you?
   a. yes   b. no   c. undecided

8. Approximately how many minutes do you dream each evening?
   a. under 15   b. 16 to 30   c. more than 31 minutes

9. Wouldn't you agree that clients should keep their accounts current with the agency?
   a. yes   b. no   c. undecided

10. Do you drink enough to be an alcoholic?
    a. yes   b. no   c. undecided

---

would be to provide the response categories of "excellent," "good," "undecided," "fair," and "poor."

The problem with the second question is that "often" is not defined. What does often mean to you? Once a week? Once a month? Daily? The same difficulty would exist if the term "regular" were used (e.g., "Do you attend A.A. meetings regularly?).

The third question doesn't get specific responses. One could be single because one had never married, because one was a widow or widower, or because one had been married and was in the process of legally dissolving it. On some occasions, it may be important to list as a separate response those who are "separated."

In the fourth question, there is a problem with the response set. Note that the response categories are not mutually exclusive. If one had been a client for exactly six months, both "a. six months or less" and "b. under a year" would be correct. There is also a problem with overlapping response categories in item five. A client with a $20,000 income might select a. because it was the first category he or she read, or b. because it suggests a desired income category. An additional problem with the income question is that "income" is a vague term. Is the intent of the question to identify the principal wage earner's annual salary? Or, does the question seek to know the total family income from all sources? Confusion about whether the question is asking for take-home (net) or gross pay is also likely.

Question six creates problems because the word "not" makes the question more complex than it needs to be. Many people will have to read the question a second time. Some individuals will inadvertently fail to see "not." Also, note that "shopping" is not defined. Does shopping refer to all shopping—shopping for essentials as well as nonessentials? What if one runs out of milk and stops to pick up a quart on the way home from work Thursday evening? Is stopping to buy a newspaper or a magazine considered to be shopping?

Item seven is called a "double-barreled" question. It asks two things in one sentence. It is entirely possible to have a male relative over the age of fifty-five living at home without having a female relative over fifty-five residing there—and vice versa. How would you respond to this question if you had only the male relative fifty-five or older but not the female living at home?

Item eight asks for information that the respondent cannot be reasonably expected to have. Most of us do not know how long we dream each evening. This question asks for information that can only be conjecture. Absurd questions and those which ask for information that respondents don't have not only may yield worthless data but on occasion may provoke an angry response resulting in respondents refusing to continue any further with the interview or the questionnaire.

When constructing questionnaires and developing items for instruments, one must be careful to use vocabulary that will be understood by the potential respondents. Avoid jargon and technical talk.

Item nine is an example of a leading question. Few people tend to disagree with a question that suggests the answer. Further, there is an issue here of social desirability. Most people do not disagree with normal social conventions (e.g., cleanliness, being sober on the job). We all want to be liked by other people, and there is a tendency to give responses that are "acceptable" even if that is not what we really believe or how we really act.

It may not be easy for clients whose behavior is excessive or outside of "normal" social behavior to admit the true extent of their problem. For example, few active alcoholics will admit to being an alcoholic—yet they might admit to "occasionally drinking more than they should." Terms such as "alcoholic," "junkie," "addict," and "delinquent" are stigmatizing to respondents, and most individuals will not deliberately choose a response that characterizes them as being flawed, deviant, or markedly different from the rest of humanity.

Additionally, question 10 assumes that the respondent has knowledge that he or she may not have. When asking questions that have the potential for forcing negative labels on respondents, it is almost always better to rephrase and ask more neutrally about the behavior itself. In this case, improved questions might be:

> In the past four weeks, how many days have you had any alcohol to drink?
> On the days you drank, how much did you usually drink?
> Have you tried to quit drinking but were unable to do so?
> Once you started drinking, how often has it been difficult to stop before you became completely intoxicated?
> In the past four weeks, how often have you taken a drink first thing in the morning?

Finally, there are important considerations in terms of what questions are asked first. As a general rule, it is better to ask sensitive questions (such as those about income, age, sexual practices) toward the end of the questionnaire. The theory is that individuals are more likely to respond to these items once they have become involved in the process of completing the questionnaire (or in the case of interviews, established rapport with the interviewer). For further assistance in the development of questionnaires, refer to Dillman (1991), Bradburn and Sudman (1979), Schuman and Presser (1981), Sudman and Bradburn (1982), and Alreck and Settle (1985).

Example 1: But It's So Easy to Design a Questionnaire

Susie Caseworker was employed as a hospital social worker in a rural community. She was one of two social workers responsible for patients in a rural hospital. While Susie liked her job, one annoying problem was that the Emergency Room staff could page her and she would have to drop what she was doing and race to the Emergency Room. She was constantly being interrupted and taken away from her patients in order to be of assistance in the Emergency Room. In her opinion, this happened with enough frequency to justify the hospital hiring another social worker solely for assignment in the Emergency Room. She discussed this with the hospital administrator, who said that he would make a decision once she had documented the need for an Emergency Room social worker. The five questions in Box 8.7 are those that Susie prepared as part of that effort. Her intention was to give the survey to each nurse and physician who worked in the Emergency Room. Let's evaluate the questions Susie was going to ask.

Box 8.7 shows how difficult preparing an instrument can be. Consider the information which these five questions will produce. Will these questions provide the kind of evidence that will convince the hospital administrator of the need for an Emergency Room social worker? How can these questions be interpreted or misconstrued? What additional questions would you want to ask?

A potential problem with the first question is that it assumes that physicians and nurses know how and on which occasions a social worker could be utilized. If physicians and nurses don't know exactly what it is that a social worker does, then it is entirely possible that they would under- or overestimate the number of occasions when a social worker could be appropriately employed. These Emergency Room workers may not know when a social worker "ought" to be utilized. Do they think social workers are to be used to hold the hand of a person in pain? Or to provide grief counseling only when the chaplain isn't around? Are social workers to empty bedpans or watch small children when there is no one else to supervise them? Better information might be obtained if the Emergency Room staff were asked to identify the needed activities to be performed by social workers or the occasions when a social worker could be used.

A related but missing question could be developed to identify times that a social worker was most needed. There may be shifts (such as between 11:00 P.M. and 7:00 A.M. on weekends when there are more emergencies requiring assistance from a social worker. It may be that the existing hospital social workers can adequately cover the Emergency Room during weekdays, but that the greatest need for a social worker is on the weekends and evenings.

It might be helpful to ask the Emergency Room staff respondents to enumerate the number of times during an average day, weekend, and evening shift when the services of a social worker would be beneficial. Here, too, the response set is important. Knowing that respondents indicated that a social worker could have been used an average of twenty-five times per shift is a lot more powerful information than knowing the most frequent response was "occasionally" or "frequently."

The second question inappropriately attempts to assess the profes-

---

BOX 8.7
Emergency Room Survey

Place an "x" by the answer that best corresponds to your thinking.

1. There are times when a social worker could be utilized in the Emergency Room.
   ( ) never   ( ) seldom   ( ) occasionally
   ( ) frequently   ( ) always

2. When I worked with a social worker, he/she acted in a professional manner.
   ( ) never   ( ) seldom   ( ) occasionally
   ( ) frequently   ( ) always

3. When I needed a social worker, one was readily available.
   ( ) never   ( ) seldom   ( ) occasionally
   ( ) frequently   ( ) always

4. I see cases where family members are not coping well with a relative's illness or injury.
   ( ) never   ( ) seldom   ( ) occasionally
   ( ) frequently   ( ) always

5. I have seen situations in the Emergency Room where social workers could have done counseling.
   ( ) never   ( ) seldom   ( ) occasionally
   ( ) frequently   ( ) always

---

sionalism of the existing social work staff. Professionalism is not the issue at hand. The inclusion of this question does not help to assess the need for a social worker in the Emergency Room.

The problem with the third question is that there is no way to know how many occasions the respondent might have had a need for a social worker. The emphasis appears to be on availability. If a social worker was needed five times last week and was readily available all five times, would the respondent check "frequently" or "always"? Although it is not clear, perhaps the author of this question was trying to explore the time lag between the request for the social worker and the amount of time it took the social worker to disengage from other duties and to appear in the Emergency Room. If the social workers can always respond within a five or ten minute period, perhaps there is no need to add another social worker just for the Emergency Room. If this is the case, the evaluator might want to ask the question, "What is the longest you have had to wait for the social worker to disengage from other responsibilities and to travel to the Emergency Room?" This question could be followed by another: "About how often does this occur?"

Question four is vague and could be improved by asking how often (in terms of times per shift, week, or month) are cases observed where family members need brief counseling or referral from a social worker.

Question five seems to repeat the first question. It could be improved by listing a number of situations in which it is likely that Emergency Room staff would want to have a social worker available to assist. Once again, a frequency count of the times a social worker was needed (during a standard time period) would supply better information than the vague "occasionally" or "frequently."

Example 2: Evaluating Inservice Training

John Practitioner had responsibility for training social workers in a large state agency. John wanted to evaluate a major new training program for supervisors that he firmly believed would make them more effective managers. Knowing how participants at professional training sessions and workshops typically give positive feedback (remember our discussion about client satisfaction studies?), John was determined to go beyond asking "Did the presenter do a good job?" "Was the presentation clear and well organized?" or, "What is your overall rating of this workshop?" Instead, John wanted to know how the week-long workshop would impact trainees' as they performed their jobs. He developed the instrument in Box 8.8. Will this instrument help him to know the impact the workshop had on the trainees?

201

BOX 8.8
Evaluation of the Supervision Workshop

1. Will this training help you reduce absenteeism among your staff?
   ( ) very little   ( ) moderately   ( ) very much

2. Will this training help you with the operating costs of your office?
   ( ) very little   ( ) moderately   ( ) very much

3. Will this training help you deal with staff's documentation of records?
   ( ) very little   ( ) moderately   ( ) very much

4. Will this training help you reduce accident rates among your staff?
   ( ) very little   ( ) moderately   ( ) very much

5. Will this training help you to increase the productivity of your employees?
   ( ) very little   ( ) moderately   ( ) very much

6. Will this training help you to get improved ratings from your district manager?
   ( ) very little   ( ) moderately   ( ) very much

These questions, drawn from a longer instrument, are straightforward and easy to understand. They do not seem to be vague, double-barreled, stigmatizing, and so forth, problems we discussed earlier. There is only one major problem with this collection of items—they measure the respondents' *attitudes* about whether the training has assisted them. John Practitioner has missed the mark if he is truly interested in the "effect" of the intervention. Despite his best intentions, John has prepared a questionnaire that essentially is just another version of other consumer satisfaction efforts.

There is nothing wrong with this if that is what the evaluator wanted to accomplish. But in John's case, he wanted to measure the effect or outcomes of the workshop—the transferability to solving problems on the job. What John really wanted to measure are such things as:

1. absenteeism (is there less absenteeism after the workshop than before?)

2. operating costs (are costs lower?)
3. documentation of records (are a greater percentage of records in compliance with quality assurance standards?)
4. accident rates (are there fewer accidents?)
5. productivity (does productivity increase?)
6. performance ratings (do performance ratings of supervisors improve?)

In devising this instrument, John decided not to examine the increase in knowledge or applied skills that could be measured with a paper and pencil test. Without recognizing it, John had developed a consumer satisfaction instrument that examined participants' opinions or attitudes about the workshop. Given his concerns and interests, John would have been better advised to obtain behavioral data such as absenteeism, operating costs, and accident, performance, and productivity rates for the preceding quarter or year for the departmental supervisors' use and to compare those rates with the data after training. John need not worry about what the participants *thought* about the training as long as it produced demonstrable results.

If you find it necessary to develop your own instrument and borrow items from already established scales, you will still need to show that your new instrument has reliability and validity. Reliability and validity can be affected by the new items that precede or follow any borrowed items in your modified scale.

QUESTIONS FOR CLASS DISCUSSION

1. What is wrong with the following questionnaire items?
   a. Describe your mother's condition during pregnancy.
   b. Yes or No: Have you ever been involved in any accidents?
   c. Have you been called names and had your life threatened?
2. Barbara Daydreamer designed a three item questionnaire to be used as a pre- and posttest instrument to measure adolescents' knowledge of alcoholism as a disease. Later she was surprised to find that there were no significant differences between pre- and posttest scores. How would you explain this?
3. Discuss the following item taken from the evaluation instrument Barbara designed for adolescents:
   When you are an adult, what are the chances that you will be a drinker?
   _____ I am certain I will never drink
   _____ I don't think I will drink

_____ I am not sure
_____ I think I will drink
_____ I am sure I will drink

4. If you were asked to evaluate an instrument measuring hyperactivity described in a journal, what information about the instrument would you want to find in the article?

MINI-PROJECTS:
EXPERIENCING RESEARCH FIRSTHAND

1. Skim one of the books containing rapid assessment instruments noted in this chapter. Make a list of at least five scales that you might be able to use in your future practice. Explain how each might be used.
2. Read one of the articles on the development and validation of a scale referenced at the end of this chapter. Summarize, in a short paper, all the steps the author went through.
3. Draft a set of ten or so items for a potential scale you would like to see developed. Then outline a plan to test the scales's reliability and validity. What would you need to do?
4. Develop a needs assessment instrument or client satisfaction questionnaire for a program with which you are familiar. Present it to the class for constructive criticism.

REFERENCES AND RESOURCES

Alreck, P.L., and Settle, R.B. (1985). *The survey research handbook*. Homewood, IL: Irwin.

Bradburn, N., and Sudman, S. (1979) *Improving interview method and questionnaire design*. San Francisco, CA: Jossey-Bass.

Comrey, A.L. (1988). Factor-analytic methods of scale development in personality and clinical psychology. *Journal of Consulting and Clinical Psychology*, 56 (5), 754–761.

DeVillis, R.F. (1991). *Scale development: Theory and applications*. Newbury Park, CA: Sage.

Dillman, D.A. (1991). The design and administration of mail surveys. In W. Richard Scott and Judith Blake (eds.), *Annual reviews of sociology*. (pp. 225–249). Palo Alto, CA: Annual Reviews, Inc.

Fischer, J., and Corcoran, K. (1994). *Measures for clinical practice*. New York: Free Press.

Koeske, G.F. (1994). Some recommendations for improving measurement validation in social work research. *Journal of Social Service Research*, 18 (3/4), 43–72.

Meisenheimer, C.G. (1985). *Quality assurance: A complete guide to effective programs*. Rockville, MD: Aspen Systems Corp.

Nunnally, J.C. (1978). *Psychometric theory*. New York: McGraw-Hill.

Randall, E.J., and Thyer, B.A. (1994). A preliminary test of the validity of the LCSW examination. *Clinical Social Work Journal*, 22 (2), 223–227.

Rossiter, E.M., Agras, W.S., Telch, C.F. and Bruce, B. (1992). The eating pattens of non-purging bulimic subjects. *International Journal of Eating Disorders*, 11 (2), 111–20.

Schuman, H., and Presser, S. (1981). *Questions and answers in attitude surveys*. New York: Academic Press.

Seifert, K., Schwartz, I.M., and Ortega, R.M. (1994). Infant mortality in Michigan's child welfare system. *Social Work*, 39 (5), 574–579.

Shaver, P.R., and Brennan, K.A. (1991) Measures of depression and loneliness. In John P. Robinson, Philip R. Shaver, and Lawrence S. Wrightsman (eds.), *Measures of personality and social psychological attitudes*. New York: Academic Press.

Sudman, S., and Bradburn, N.M. (1982). *Asking questions: A practical guide to questionnaire design*. San Francisco, CA: Jossey-Bass.

Sundel, M., Garrett, R.M., and Horn, R.D. (1994). Restraint reduction in a nursing home and its impact on employee attitudes. *Journal of American Geriatric Society*, 42 (4), 381-387.

Thyer, B.A. (1992). Promoting evaluation research in the field of family preservation. In E.S. Morton and R.K. Grigsby (eds.), *Advancing family preservation practice* (pp. 131–149). Newbury Park, CA: Sage.

Tripodi, T. (1983). *Evaluative research for social workers*. Englewood Cliffs, NJ: Prentice-Hall.

READINGS ON INSTRUMENT CONSTRUCTION

Abell, Neil. (1991). The index of Clinical Stress: A brief measure of subjective stress for practice and research. *Social Work Research and Abstracts*, 27(2), 12-15.

Camasso, M.J., and Geismar, L.L. (1992). A multivariate approach to construct reliability and validity assessment: The case of family functioning. *Social Work Research and Abstracts*, 28(4), 16-26.

Combs-Orme, T.D., Orme, J.G., and Guidry, C.J. (1991). Reliability and validity of the Protective Services Questionnaire (PSQ). *Journal of Social Service Research*, 14(1/2), 1-20.

Comrey, A.L. (1988). Factor analytic methods in scale development in personality and clinical psychology. *Journal of Consulting and Clinical Psychology*, 56, 754-761.

Hudson, W.W., Nurius, P.S., Daley, J.G., and Newsome, R.D. (1990). A short-form scale to measure peer relations dysfunction. *Journal of Social Service Research*, 13(4), 57-69.

Klein, W.C. (1992). Measuring caregiver attitude toward the provision of long-term care. *Journal of Social Service Research*, 16(3/4), 147-161.

Koeske, G.F., and Koeske, R.D. (1992). Parenting Locus of Control: Measurement, construct validation, and a proposed conceptual model. *Social Work Research and Abstracts*, 28(3), 37-46.

MacNeil, G. (1991). A short-form scale to measure alcohol abuse. *Research on Social Work Practice*, 1(1), 68-75.

Mischke, H.D., and Venneri, R.L. (1987). Reliability and validity of the MAST. *Journal of Studies in Alcohol*, 48(5), 492-501.

Nasuti, J.P., and Pecora, P.J. (1993). Risk assessment scales in child protection: A test of the internal consistency and interrater reliability of one statewide system. *Social Work Research and Abstracts*, 29(2), 28-33.

Nugent, W.R., and Thomas, J.W. (1993). Validation of a clinical measure of self-esteem. *Research on Social Work Practice*, 3(2), 191-207.

Poertner, J. (1985). A scale for measuring clients' satisfaction with parent education. *Social Work Research and Abstracts*, 21(3), 23-28.

Polansky, N.A., Gaudin, J.M., and Kilpatrick, A.C. (1992). The Maternal Characteristics Scale: A cross validation. *Child Welfare*, 71(3), 271-282.

Schondel, C., Shields, G., and Orel, N. (1992). Development of an instument to measure volunteers' motivation in working with people with AIDS. *Social Work in Health Care*. 17(2), 53-71.

Shields, J.J. (1992). Evaluating community organization Projects: The development of an empirically based measure. *Social Work Research and Abstracts*, 28(2), 15-20.

Smith, M.K., and Ford, J. (1990). A client-developed functional level scale: The community Living Skills Scale (CLSS). *Journal of Social Service Research*, 13(3), 61-84.

Thyer, B.A., and Westhuis, D. (1989). Test-retest reliability of the Clinical Anxiety Scale. *Phobia Practice and Research Journal*, 2(2), 113-115.

NINE

Illustrations of Instruments

It's one thing to talk about reliability and validity on a theoretical level, but theory takes on much more meaning when you have real instruments to inspect. With some scales we get a sense of face validity almost immediately. Seeing the actual wording used by the scale developers assists us in thinking about how our clientele or study population might respond. Will it be over their heads? Will there be too many items for their level of attention? Are the questions too obvious or too subtle? For those who are not familiar with testing and what paper and pencil instruments actually look like, we have secured the permission of several authors to reproduce all or portions of their instruments.

As you review this small sampling of instruments, you'll realize that when items are well chosen, acceptable internal consistency can be obtained with very few items. Some scales are elegant in their simplicity. You'll probably also note that some scales look as if they could be improved upon. You may even wonder why some items were included and others left out. Measuring intangible concepts is not an easy task—it's a challenge even for the most experienced and capable researcher.

However, we also hope you come to a personal realization that a number of fine scales have been developed that you may want to use in your practice or agency—scales like the Child Abuse Potential Inventory that social workers and other practitioners *ought* to use much more often before placing children in foster care, adoptive care, or returning them to their parents.

There is nothing cryptic or obscure about the many wonderful instruments that are our tireless servants, constantly at our beck and call. They can be used to assess clients, to conduct basic research, and even to evaluate programs. They perform their tasks dependably time and time again—or else they wouldn't have the reliability they are reported to have.

If nothing else, explore the use of any instrument that is relevant for an actual client or group. See if the instrument doesn't give some new insight or provide you with objective data to help confirm your professional judgment.

Though a small sample, the following instruments demonstrate the great variety of those available. Because some of these instruments are protected by copyright, you should not reproduce them without permission. Read the section on "Availability" in order to know whether you must purchase the scale or request permission to use it.

As you review these instruments, ask yourself how they might be used in a program evaluation effort. What hypotheses or questions would they help you explore? What programs or special populations could they be used with?

CHILD ABUSE POTENTIAL INVENTORY
Description

The CAP Inventory is a 160-item self-report questionnaire with a primary clinical scale, the physical child abuse scale, and six factor scales measuring distress, rigidity, unhappiness, problems with child and self, problems with family, and problems with others. Additionally, it contains three validity scales: the lie scale, the random response scale, and the inconsistency scale to check for "faking good," "faking bad," or randomly responding. An ego strength scale has recently been developed from items in the CAP Inventory. The CAP Inventory has been used successfully to evaluate a variety of secondary and tertiary prevention programs. The scale is currently being used worldwide by the U.S. Air Force to evaluate interventions with physical child abusers. Preliminary analyses indicate a significant decrease in posttreatment abuse scores that was maintained at a six-month follow-up (Milner, 1994).

Psychometric Data

There is an extensive body of research on the CAP Inventory. Internal consistency estimates for the abuse scale range from .91 to .96. Test-retest

Figure 9.1
Child Abuse Potential Inventory

CAP INVENTORY FORM VI

Joel S. Milner, Ph.D
Copyright 1977, 1982, 1984, Revised Edition 1986
Printed in the United States of America

Name: _____ Date: _____ ID#: _____

Age: _____ Gender: Male _____ Female _____ Marital Status: Sin___ Mar___ Sep___ Div___ Wid___

Race: Black __ White __ Hispanic __ Am. Indian __ Number of children in home _____

Other (specify) _____ Highest grade completed _____

INSTRUCTIONS: The following questionnaire includes a series of statements which may be applied to yourself. Read each of the statements and determine if you **AGREE** or **DISAGREE** with the statement. If you agree with a statement, circle **A** for agree. If you disagree with a statement, circle **DA** for disagree. Be honest when giving your answers. Remember to read each statement; it is important not to skip any statement.

●OOO

1.	I never feel sorry for others	A	DA
2.	I enjoy having pets	A	DA
3.	I have always been strong and healthy	A	DA
4.	I like most people	A	DA
5.	I am a confused person	A	DA
6.	I do not trust most people	A	DA
7.	People expect too much from me	A	DA
8.	Children should never be bad	A	DA
9.	I am often mixed up	A	DA
10.	Spanking that only bruises a child is okay	A	DA
11.	I always try to check on my child when it's crying	A	DA
12.	I sometimes act without thinking	A	DA
13.	You cannot depend on others	A	DA
14.	I am a happy person	A	DA
15.	I like to do things with my family	A	DA
16.	Teenage girls need to be protected	A	DA
17.	I am often angry inside	A	DA
18.	Sometimes I feel all alone in the world	A	DA
19.	Everything in a home should always be in its place	A	DA
20.	I sometimes worry that I cannot meet the needs of a child	A	DA
21.	Knives are dangerous for children	A	DA
22.	I often feel rejected	A	DA
23.	I am often lonely inside	A	DA
24.	Little boys should never learn sissy games	A	DA
25.	I often feel very frustrated	A	DA

●OOO

reliabilities for the abuse scale are also strong. A number of cross-validation studies indicate the abuse scale has overall classification rates in the low 80 percent to low 90 percent range. Predictive validity has been demonstrated in a longitudinal study showing a significant relationship between elevated CAP abuse scores and subsequent confirmed physical child abuse. Construct validity has similarly been reported by a number of investigators.

Availability

This instrument is copyrighted. You will need to purchase the manual and copies of the instrument from PSYTEC, Inc., P.O. Box 564, DeKalb, Illinois 60115 (815-758-1415).

Scoring

Scoring templates, scoring sheets, and computer scoring programs can be purchased along with the instrument from PSYTEC.

For Further Reference

Milner, J.S. (1986). *The Child Abuse Potential Inventory: Manual*, 2d ed. Webster, NC: Psytec Corp.

Milner, J.S. (1989a). Additional cross-validation of the Child Abuse Potential Inventory. *Psychological Assessment: A Journal of Consulting and Clinical Psychology*, 1, 219–223.

Milner, J.S. (1989b). Applications and limitations of the Child Abuse Potential Inventory. *Early Child Development and Care*, 42, 85–97.

Milner, J.S. (1990). *An interpretive manual for the Child Abuse Potential Inventory*. Webster, NC: Psytec.

Milner, J.S. (1991). Medical conditions and the Child Abuse Potential Inventory specificity. *Psychological Assessment: A Journal of Consulting and Clinical Psychology*, 3, 208–212.

Milner, J.S. (1994). Assessing physical child abuse risk: The Child Abuse Potential Inventory. *Clinical Psychology Review*, 14 (6), 547–583.

Milner, J.S., Charlesworth, J.R., Gold, R.G., Gold, S.R., and Friesen, M.R. (1988). Convergent validity of the Child Abuse Potential Inventory. *Journal of Clinical Psychology*, 44 (2), 281–285.

Milner, J.S., Gold, R.G., and Wimberley, R.C. (1986). Prediction and explanation of child abuse: Cross-validation of the Child Abuse

Potential Inventory. *Journal of Consulting and Clinical Psychology,* 54 (6), 865–866.

Milner, J.S., and Robertson, K.R. (1989). Inconsistent response patterns and the prediction of child maltreatment. *Child Abuse and Neglect,* 13 (1), 59–64.

Wolfe, D.A., Edwards, B., Manion, I., and Koverola, C. (1988). Early intervention for parents at risk of child abuse and neglect: A preliminary investigation. *Journal of Consulting and Clinical Psychology,* 56, 40–47.

CLINICAL ANXIETY SCALE

Description

The Clinical Anxiety Scale is a twenty-five-item instrument designed to measure problems individuals have with anxiety and to have a clinical cutting score of 30. The scale can be used to measure a client's anxiety level before, during, and after a treatment program. The authors advocate its use as a self-report outcome measure for single-system research designs (Westhuis and Thyer, 1989).

Psychometric Data

The Clinical Anxiety Scale has a coefficient alpha of .94 and two week test-retest correlations that range from .64 to .74. Validity has been demonstrated in the scale's ability to discriminate well between groups known to be suffering from anxiety and low-anxiety control groups. A discriminant validity coefficient of .77 and a phi coefficient of .81 have been reported when two criterion groups were dichotomized around the cutting score of 30.

Availability

The Clinical Anxiety Scale is available in pads of fifty or with other rapid assessment instruments on computer diskette from WALMYR Publishing Co., P.O. Box 24779, Tempe, AZ 85285-4779.

Scoring

Seven items on the CAS are first reverse scored (these are indicated on the bottom of the scale), then summed along with the remaining scores.

Figure 9.2
The Clinical Anxiety Scale

```
┌────────────────────────────────────────────────────────────────────┐
│  ┌──┐                                                                │
│  │█ █│   CLINICAL ANXIETY SCALE (CAS)                                │
│  └──┘                                                                │
│                                                                      │
│  Name: _____  Today's Date: _____  │
│                                                                      │
│  This questionnaire is designed to measure how much anxiety you are  │
│  currently feeling. It is not a test, so there are no right or wrong │
│  answers. Answer each item as carefully and as accurately as you can │
│  by placing a number beside each one as follows.                     │
│                                                                      │
│          1  Rarely or none of the time                               │
│          2  A little of the time                                     │
│          3  Some of the time                                         │
│          4  A good part of the time                                  │
│          5  Most or all of the time                                  │
└────────────────────────────────────────────────────────────────────┘
```

1. ____ I feel calm.
2. ____ I feel tense.
3. ____ I feel suddenly scared for no reason.
4. ____ I feel nervous.
5. ____ I use tranquilizers or antidepressants to cope with my anxiety.
6. ____ I feel confident about the future.
7. ____ I am free from senseless or unpleasant thoughts.
8. ____ I feel afraid to go out of my house alone.
9. ____ I feel relaxed and in control of myself.
10. ____ I have spells of terror or panic.
11. ____ I feel afraid in open spaces or in the streets.
12. ____ I feel afraid I will faint in public.
13. ____ I am comfortable traveling on buses, subways or trains.
14. ____ I feel nervousness or shakiness inside.
15. ____ I feel comfortable in crowds, such as shopping or at a movie.
16. ____ I feel comfortable when I am left alone.
17. ____ I feel afraid without good reason.
18. ____ Due to my fears, I unreasonably avoid certain animals, objects or situations.
19. ____ I get upset easily or feel panicky unexpectedly.
20. ____ My hands, arms or legs shake or tremble.
21. ____ Due to my fears, I avoid social situations, whenever possible.
22. ____ I experience sudden attacks of panic which catch me by surprise.
23. ____ I feel generally anxious.
24. ____ I am bothered by dizzy spells.
25. ____ Due to my fears, I avoid being alone, whenever possible.

1,6,7,9,13,15,16

The number of completed items are subtracted, the remainder is multiplied by 100, and that value is divided by the product of the number of items completed times 4. A range of scores from 0 to 100 is produced. Higher scores indicate more severe problems with anxiety. Computer software is available for scoring the scales.

For Further Reference

Thyer, B.A., and Westhuis, D. (1989). Test-retest reliability of the Clinical Anxiety Scale. *Phobia Practice and Research Journal*, 2 (2), 113–115.
Westhuis, D., and Thyer, B.A. (1989). Development and validation of the Clinical Anxiety Scale: A rapid assessment instrument for clinical practice. *Educational and Psychological Measurement*, 49, 153–163.

CES-D SCALE

Description

Developed by the staff at the Center for Epidemiologic Studies, National Institute of Mental Health, the CES-D is a brief self-report scale designed to measure depressive symptomatology in the general population (Radloff, 1977). It was developed from previously existing scales and was designed not to distinguish primary depressive disorders from secondary depression or subtypes of depression but to identify the presence and severity of depressive symptomatology for epidemiologic research, needs assessment, and screening (Radloff and Locke, 1986).

Psychometric Data

This depression scale has been found to have high internal consistency (.85 in the general population and .90 in the patient sample) and acceptable test-retest stability. The CES-D scores discriminate well between psychiatric inpatient and general population samples and moderately well among patient groups with varying levels of severity. The scale has excellent concurrent validity, and substantial evidence exists of its construct validity (Radloff, 1977).

Availability

The CES-D Scale is in the public domain and may be used without copyright permission. The Epidemiology and Psychopathology Research Branch is interested, however, in receiving copies of research reports that have utilized the instrument.

Scoring

Because the CES-D is a twenty-item scale, it is easily scored. Responses are weighted 0 for "Rarely or none of the time" to 3 for "Most of the time." Items 4, 8, 12, and 16 are reverse-scored (given a 3 for "Rarely"

Figure 9.3
CES-D Scale

```
                                          CES-D Scale

            Circle the number for each statement which best describes how often you felt
                            or behaved this way-during the past week

                                      Rarely or      Some or a     Occasionally    Most or
                                      None of        Little of     or a            All of
                                      the Time       the Time      Moderate        the Time
                                                                   Amount of
                                                                   Time
                                      (Less than     (1-2 Days)    (3-4 Days)      (5-7 Days)
                                      1 Day)

         DURING THE PAST WEEK:

1.  I was bothered by things that  usually
    don't bother me                        ____          ____          ____          ____

2.  I  did  not  feel  like  eating;   my
    appetite was poor                      ____          ____          ____          ____

3.  I felt that I could not shake off  the
    blues even with help from my family or ____          ____          ____          ____
    friends

4.  I  felt that I was just  as  good  as
    other people                           ____          ____          ____          ____

5.  I had trouble keeping my mind on  what
    I was doing                            ____          ____          ____          ____

6.  I felt depressed                       ____          ____          ____          ____

7.  I  felt that everything I did was  an
    effort                                 ____          ____          ____          ____

8.  I felt hopeful about the future        ____          ____          ____          ____

9.  I thought my life had been failure     ____          ____          ____          ____

10. I felt fearful                         ____          ____          ____          ____

11. My sleep was restless                  ____          ____          ____          ____

12. I was happy                            ____          ____          ____          ____

13. I talked less than usually             ____          ____          ____          ____

14. I felt lonely                          ____          ____          ____          ____

15. People were unfriendly                 ____          ____          ____          ____

16. I enjoyed life                         ____          ____          ____          ____

17. I had crying spells                    ____          ____          ____          ____

18. I felt sad                             ____          ____          ____          ____

19. I felt that people disliked me         ____          ____          ____          ____

20. I could not get "going"                ____          ____          ____          ____
```

Courtesy Department of Health and Human Services.

214

and 0 for "Most"). The range of possible scores is 0 to 60. High scores indicate the presence and persistence of depressive symptoms.

For Further Reference

Comstock, G.W. and Helsing, K.J. (1976). Symptoms of depression in two communities. *Psychological Medicine*, 6, 551–563.

Radloff, L.S. (1977). The CES-D Scale: A self-report depression scale for research in the general population. *Applied Psychological Measurement*, 3 (1), 385–401.

Radloff, L.S. and Locke, B.Z. (1986). The Community Mental Heath Assessment Survey and the CES-D Scale. In Weissman, M.M., Myers, J.K., and Ross, C.E., (Eds.), *Community Surveys of Psychiatric Disorders*. New Brunswick, NJ: Rutgers.

Weissman, M.M., Sholomskas, D., Pottenger, M., Prusoff, B.A., and Locke, B.Z. (1977). Assessing depressive symptoms in five psychiatric populations: A validation study. *American Journal of Epidemiology*, 6 (3), 203–214.

THE UCLA LONELINESS SCALE (VERSION 3)

Description

A great deal of the research on loneliness has been conducted with an earlier version of this instrument (Russell, Peplau, and Cutrona, 1980; Russell, Peplau, and Ferguson, 1978), which consisted of twenty statements that reflected how lonely individuals described their experience. However, all of the items were worded in a negative or lonely direction, and high correlations were found with depression scores, suggesting a potential problem with discriminant validity.

Version 3 of the loneliness scale eliminates double negatives and complex wording and assesses loneliness again with twenty items; eleven are negatively worded (in a lonely direction) and nine are positively worded (nonlonely). The latest version has been used with college students, nurses, teachers, and elderly individuals.

Psychometric Data

The reliability of this latest version ranged from .89 to .94 across different samples. In the elderly sample, the loneliness scores did not change significantly over a one year period. Factor analysis provides support for view-

215

Figure 9.4
UCLA Loneliness Scale (Version 3)

UCLA Loneliness Scale (Version 3)

Instructions:
The following statements describe how people sometimes feel. For each statement, please indicate how often you feel the way described by writing a number in the space provided. Here is an example:

How often do you feel happy?

If you never felt happy, you would respond "never"; if you always feel happy, you would respond "always."

NEVER	RARELY	SOMETIMES	ALWAYS
1	2	3	4

*1. How often do you feel that you are "in tune" with the people around you? _____

2. How often do you feel that you lack companionship? _____

3. How often do you feel that there is no one you can turn to? _____

4. How often do you feel alone? _____

*5. How often do you feel part of a group of friends? _____

*6. How often do you feel that you have a lot in common with the people around you? _____

7. How often do you feel that you are no longer close to anyone? _____

8. How often do you feel that your interests and ideas are not shared by those around you? _____

*9. How often do you feel outgoing and friendly? _____

*10. How often do you feel close to people? _____

11. How often do you feel left out? _____

12. How often do you feel that your relationships with others are not meaningful? _____

13. How often do you feel that no one really knows you well? _____

14. How often do you feel isolated from others? _____

*15. How often do you feel you can find companionship when you want it? _____

*16. How often do you feel that there are people who really understand you? _____

17. How often do you feel shy? _____

18. How often do you feel that people are around you but not with you? _____

*19. How often do you feel that there are people you can talk to? _____

*20. How often do you feel that there are people you can turn to? _____

Courtesy Dr. Daniel Russell.

ing the UCLA Loneliness Scale as a unidimensional measure. Correlational analyses reveal the scale to be negatively associated with measures of social support and positively correlated with other measures of loneliness. Loneliness was found to be significantly related to neuroticism and introversion-extraversion. Version 3 is a reliable and valid assessment of loneliness that should be applicable in a wide variety of populations.

Availability

Dr. Russell encourages researchers to use this instrument and to keep him informed of findings with it. His address is: Daniel W. Russell, Department of Psychology, W112 Lagomarcino Hall, Iowa State University, Ames, IA 50011-3180.

Scoring

Asterisked items should be reverse scored (i.e., 1 = 4, 2 = 3, 3 = 2, 4 = 1). The scores for each item are then summed together and higher scores indicate greater degrees of loneliness. In two large samples of college students and nurses, the means were 40 and the standard deviation 9.5 (Russell, 1995).

For Further Reference

Constable, J.F., and Russell, D. (1986). Effect of social support and the work environment upon burnout among nurses. *Journal of Human Stress,* 12, 20–26.

Russell, D.W. (1995). The UCLA Loneliness Scale (Version 3): Reliability and validity evidence. Unpublished manuscript.

Russell, D., Altmaier, E., and Van Velzen, D. (1987). Job-related stress, social support, and burnout among classroom teachers. *Journal of Applied Psychology,* 72, 269–274.

Russell, D., and Cutrona, C.E. (1991). Social support, stress, and depressive symptoms among the elderly: Test of a process model. *Psychology and Aging,* 6, 190–201.

Russell, D., Peplau, L.A., and Cutrona, C.E. (1980). The revised UCLA Loneliness Scale: Concurrent and discriminant validity evidence. *Journal of Personality and Social Psychology,* 39, 472–480.

Russell, D., Peplau, L.A., and Ferguson, M.L. (1978). Developing a measure of loneliness. *Journal of Personality Assessment,* 42, 290–294.

ROSENBERG SELF-ESTEEM SCALE

Description

The Rosenberg Self-Esteem Scale was originally developed on a sample of over five thousand high school juniors and seniors from ten randomly selected schools in New York state. A recent query in *Social Science Citation Index* produced close to 1,300 citations for Rosenberg's instrument—making it the most popular measure of global self-esteem and prompting Blascovich and Tomaka (1991) to observe that "it is the standard with which developers of other measures usually seek convergence" (p. 120).

Psychometric data

Fleming and Courtney (1984) have reported a Cronbach alpha of .88 and test-retest correlations of .82 with a one-week interval. Rosenberg (1965) presented a great deal of data on the construct validity of this measure. Demo (1985) reported self-esteem scores correlating .55 with the Coopersmith SEI.

Availability

This scale is in the public domain and may be used without securing permission.

Scoring

Using the Likert procedure, responses are assigned a score ranging from 1 to 4. Items 1, 3, 4, 7, and 10 are reverse scored. (For example, item 1, "On the whole I am satisfied with myself," the "strongly agree" response is assigned a score of 4 and "Strongly disagree" is assigned a score of 1.) This procedure yields possible total scores ranging from 10 to 40. The higher the score, the higher the self-esteem.

For Further Reference

Blascovich, J. and Tomaka, J. (1991). Measures of self-esteem. In John P. Robinson, Phillip Shaver, and Lawrence Wrightsman (Eds.), *Measures of personality and social psychological attitudes*. New York: Academic Press.

Demo, D.H. (1985). The measurement of self-esteem: Refining our methods. *Journal of Personality and Social Psychology*, 48, 1490–1502.

Figure 9.5
Rosenburg Self-Esteem Scale

Rosenburg Self-Esteem Scale

Instructions:

BELOW IS A LIST OF STATEMENTS DEALING WITH YOUR GENERAL FEELINGS ABOUT YOURSELF.
IF YOU AGREE WITH THE STATEMENT, CIRCLE A. IF YOU STRONGLY AGREE, CIRCLE SA.
IF YOU DISAGREE, CIRCLE D. IF YOU STRONGLY DISAGREE, CIRCLE SD.

		Strongly Agree	Agree	Dis- agree	Strongly Disagree
(1)	On the whole, I am satisfied with myself.	SA	A	D	SD
(2)	At times I think I am no good at all.	SA	A	D	SD
(3)	I feel that I have a number of good qualities.	SA	A	D	SD
(4)	I am able to do things as well as most other people.	SA	A	D	SD
(5)	I feel I do not have much to be proud of.	SA	A	D	SD
(6)	I certainly feel useless at times.	SA	A	D	SD
(7)	I feel that I'm a person of worth, at least on an equal plane with others.	SA	A	D	SD
(8)	I wish I could have more respect for myself.	SA	A	D	SD
(9)	All in all, I am inclined to feel that I am a failure.	SA	A	D	SD
(10)	I take a positive attitude toward myself.	SA	A	D	SD

Courtesy Morris Rosenberg.

Dobson, C., Goudy, W., Keith, P., and Powers, E. (1979). Further analysis of the Rosenberg Self-Esteem Scale. *Psychological Reports*, 44, 639–641.

Fleming, J.S., and Courtney, B.E. (1984). The dimensionality of self-esteem. II. Hierarchical facet model for revised measurement scales. *Journal of Personality and Social Psychology*, 46, 404–421.

Hensley, W.E., and Roberts, M.K. (1976). Dimensions of Rosenberg's Self-Esteem Scale. *Psychological Reports*, 38, 583–584.

Rosenberg, M. (1965). *Society and the Adolescent Self-Image*. Princeton, NJ: Princeton University Press.

Wylie, Ruth C. (1989). *Measures of Self-Concept*. Lincoln: University of Nebraska Press.

ADULT-ADOLESCENT PARENTING INVENTORY

Description

The Adult-Adolescent Parenting Inventory (AAPI) is designed to provide an index of risk for abusive and neglecting parenting and child-rearing behaviors. Items were developed from four constructs about abusive and neglecting parenting: inappropriate parental expectations of the child, lack of empathy toward the child's needs, parental value of physical punishment, and parent-child role reversal. The AAPI consists of thirty-two items and takes about twenty minutes to complete. It is written at the fifth-grade reading level and can be administered orally to nonreaders.

Psychometric Data

Approximately three thousand adolescents have participated in the field testing of the inventory. Items in each of the four constructs produced an internal reliability equal to or greater than .70. The total test-retest reliability of all items was .76. In terms of diagnostic and discriminatory validity, research with the AAPI has shown that abused adolescents express significantly more abusive attitudes than their nonabused peers. Abusive adults express significantly more abusive attitudes than nonabusive adults. Standardized norms for the AAPI have been based on samples of over one thousand nonabusive adults, 780 abusive adults, 300 abused adolescents, and 6,480 nonabused adolescents. Bavolek (1984) has reported that parents completing a comprehensive parenting and nurturing program significantly increased their parenting attitudes upon completion of the program.

Figure 9.6
Adult-Adolescent Parenting Inventory

Adult-Adolescent Parenting Inventory
AAPI

	Strongly Agree	Agree	Uncertain	Disagree	Strongly Disagree
1. Young children should be expected to comfort their mother when she is feeling blue.	SA	A	U	D	SD
2. Parents should teach their children right from wrong by sometimes using physical punishment.	SA	A	U	D	SD
3. Children should be the main source of comfort and care for their parents.	SA	A	U	D	SD
4. Young children should be expected to hug their mother when she is sad.	SA	A	U	D	SD
5. Parents will spoil their children by picking them up and comforting them when they cry.	SA	A	U	D	SD
6. Children should be expected to verbally express themselves before the age of one year.	SA	A	U	D	SD
7. A good child will comfort both of his/her parents after the parents have argued.	SA	A	U	D	SD
8. Children learn good behavior through the use of physical punishment.	SA	A	U	D	SD
9. Children develop good, strong characters through very strict discipline.	SA	A	U	D	SD
10. Parents should expect their children who are under three years to begin taking care of themselves.	SA	A	U	D	SD
11. Young children should be aware of ways to comfort their parents after a hard day's work.	SA	A	U	D	SD
12. Parents should slap their child when s/he has done something wrong.	SA	A	U	D	SD
13. Children should always be spanked when they misbehave.	SA	A	U	D	SD
14. Young children should be responsible for much of the happiness of their parents.	SA	A	U	D	SD
15. Parents have a responsibility to spank their children when they misbehave.	SA	A	U	D	SD

Please go to next page.

Availability

The AAPI is protected by copyright. You will need to purchase the manual, copies of the instrument, and other supplies from Family Development Resources, Inc., 3160 Pinebrook Rd., Park City, UT 84060.

Scoring

The AAPI is available in two forms, A and B. Scoring stencils are used with AAPI profile worksheets in order to plot the standard scores. A computerized version of the AAPI is also available with reusable diskettes.

For Further Reference

Bavolek, S.J. (1984). An innovative program for reducing abusive parent-child interactions. *Child Resource World Review*, 2, 6–24.

Bavolek, S.J. (1989a). Assessing and teaching high-risk parenting attitudes. *Early Child Development and Care*, 42, 99–112.

Bavolek, S.J. (1989b). *Research and validation report of the Adult-Adolescent Parenting Inventory (AAPI)*. Eau Claire, WI: Family Development Resources, Inc.

Bavolek, S.J., and Bavolek, J.D. (1985). *Nurturing Program for Parents and Children Birth to Five Years*. Eau Claire, WI: Family Development Resources, Inc.

Bavolek, S.J., Kline, D.F., and McLaughlin, J.A. (1979). Primary prevention of child abuse: Identification of high risk adolescents. *Child Abuse and Neglect: The International Journal*, 3, 1071–1080.

Fox, R.A., Baisch, M.J., Goldberg, B.D., and Hochmuth, M.C. (1987). Parenting attitudes of pregnant adolescents. *Psychological Reports*, 61, 403–406.

THE HOPE SCALE

Description

In the last thirty years most scholars have conceptualized hope as a unidimensional construct that centers on an overall perception that goals can be met (Snyder et al., 1991). Many writers have used the concept of hope and its absence in individuals to explain diverse behavior, including physical health and psychopathology. The Hope Scale is based on the idea that hope is not dichotomous (present or absent). Rather, individuals should have varying degrees of hope. Snyder et al. view hope as composed

Figure 9.7
The Hope Scale

```
                      The Hope Scale
Directions: Read each item carefully. Using the scale shown below, please
select the number that best describes YOU and put that number in the blank
provided.

   1 = Definitely false          3 = Mostly true
   2 = Mostly false              4 = Definitely true

_____  1.  I can think of many ways to get out of a jam.
_____  2.  I energetically pursue my goals.
_____  3.  I feel tired most of the time.
_____  4.  There are lots of ways around any problem.
_____  5.  I am easily downed in an argument.
_____  6.  I can think of many ways to get the things in life that are
                 most important to me.
_____  7.  I worry about my health.
_____  8.  Even when others get discouraged, I know I can find a way
                 to solve the problem.
_____  9.  My past experiences have prepared me well for my future.
_____ 10.  I've been pretty successful in life.
_____ 11.  I usually find myself worrying abut something.
_____ 12.  I meet the goals that I set for myself.
```

Snyder et al. (1991).

of two goal-appraisal components—agency and pathways. The agency component is characterized by a willful sense of determination and energy to meet goals. The pathways component reflects an individual's perception of available routes by which a goal might be attained. Twelve items make up the Hope scale; four items deal with the agency component, four with pathways, and four are constructed to be distractive—to make the overall intent of the scale less obvious.

Psychometric Data

Cronbach's alphas ranged from .74 to .84 on the total scale. For the Agency subscale, alphas ranged from .71 to .76, and from .63 to .80 on the Pathways subscale. Test-retest reliability has been shown to be .73 over an eight-week interval and .76 and .82 over ten-week intervals in two samples. In terms of convergent validity, the Hope Scale correlated .60 and .50 with optimism as measured by the Life Orientation Test

(LOT); .55 and .54 with the Generalized Expectancy for Success Scale; −.51 with the Hopelessness Scale; and −.42 with the Beck Depression Inventory. Factor analyses revealed that the theory-based components of agency and pathways were distinguishable. Persons in psychological treatment had lower scores than college students. Men and women tend to have virtually identical scores across various samples.

Availability

This instrument has been reproduced in Snyder et al. (1991) and Babyak, Snyder, and Yoshinobu (1993). Correspondence should be sent to C.R. Snyder, Department of Psychology, 305 Fraser Hall, University of Kansas, Lawrence, KS 66045.

Scoring

Responses to the distracter items 3, 5, 7, and 11 are ignored. Items 1, 4, 6, and 8 compose the Pathways subscale; the Agency subscale is composed of items 2, 9, 10, and 12. There are no reverse scored items on the two subscales.

For Further Reference

Babyak, M.A., Snyder, C.R., and Yoshinobu, L. (1993). Psychometric properties of the Hope Scale: A confirmatory factory analysis. *Journal of Research in Personality*, 27, 154–169.

Snyder, C.R., Harris, C., Anderson, J.R., Holleran, S.A., Irving, L.M., Sigmon, S.T., Yoshinobu, L., Gibb, J., Langelle, C., and Harney, P. (1991). The will and the ways: Development and validation of an individual-differences measure of hope. *Journal of Personality and Social Psychology*, 60 (4), 570–585.

CHILD SEXUAL BEHAVIOR INVENTORY

Description

Sexually abused children exhibit more sexual behavior than do non-abused children, but most standardized questionnaires only minimally assess this behavior. Friedrich et al. (1992) have demonstrated the benefits of group treatment with nineteen sexually abused boys on a thirty-five item rating form. The instrument has gone through several revisions, and research with it is ongoing. The version printed in this chapter is the one that appears in Friedrich et al. (1991).

Figure 9.8
Child Sexual Behavior Inventory

Child Sexual Behavior Inventory

Please circle the number that tells how often your child has shown the following behaviors recently or in the last six months:

Never	Less than 1/month	1–3 times/month	At least 1/week
0	1	2	3

1. 0 1 2 3 Dresses like the opposite sex.
2. 0 1 2 3 Talks about wanting to be the opposite sex.
3. 0 1 2 3 Touches sex (private) parts when in public places.
4. 0 1 2 3 Masturbates with hand.
5. 0 1 2 3 Scratches anal and/or crotch area.
6. 0 1 2 3 Touches or tries to touch their mother's or other women's breasts.
7. 0 1 2 3 Masturbates with object.
8. 0 1 2 3 Touches other peolple's sex (private) parts.
9. 0 1 2 3 Imitates the act of sexual intercourse.
10. 0 1 2 3 Puts mouth on another child/adult's sex parts.
11. 0 1 2 3 Touches sex (private) parts when at home.
12. 0 1 2 3 Uses words that describe sex acts.
13. 0 1 2 3 Pretends to be the opposite sex when playing.
14. 0 1 2 3 Makes sexual sounds (sighing, moaning, heavy breathing, etc.).
15. 0 1 2 3 Asks others to engage in sexual acts with him or her.
16. 0 1 2 3 Rubs body against people or furniture.
17. 0 1 2 3 Inserts or tries to insert objects in vagina/anus.
18. 0 1 2 3 Tries to look at people when they are nude or undressing.
19. 0 1 2 3 Imitates sexual behavior with dolls or stuffed animals.
20. 0 1 2 3 Shows sex (private) parts to adults.
21. 0 1 2 3 Tries to view pictures of nude or partially dressed people (may include catalogs).
22. 0 1 2 3 Talks about sexual acts.
23. 0 1 2 3 Kisses adults not in the family.
24. 0 1 2 3 Undresses self in front of others.
25. 0 1 2 3 Sits with crotch or underwear exposed.
26. 0 1 2 3 Kisses other children not in the family.
27. 0 1 2 3 Talks in a flirtatious manner.
28. 0 1 2 3 Tries to undress other children or adults against their will (opening pants, shirt, etc.).
29. 0 1 2 3 Asks to view nude or sexually explicit television shows (may include video movies or home box office type shows).
30. 0 1 2 3 When kissing, tries to put tongue in other person's mouth.
31. 0 1 2 3 Hugs adults he or she does not know well.
32. 0 1 2 3 Shows sex (private) parts to children.
33. 0 1 2 3 If a girl, overly aggressive; if a boy, overly passive.
34. 0 1 2 3 Seems very interested in the opposite sex.
35. 0 1 2 3 If a boy, plays with girl's toys; if a girl, plays with boy's toys.
36. 0 1 2 3 Stands too close to people.
37. 0 1 2 3 Tries to put mouth on mother's or other women's breasts.
38. 0 1 2 3 Likes to walk around in underclothes.
39. 0 1 2 3 Shy with men they don't know.
40. 0 1 2 3 Overly friendly with men they don't know.
41. 0 1 2 3 Shy about undressing.
42. 0 1 2 3 Touches animals' sexual parts.
43. 0 1 2 3 Walks around house without clothes.
44. 0 1 2 3 Other sexual behaviors (please describe).

Reproduced by permission of *Pediatrics*.

Psychometric Data

Internal consistency was found to be .82 for a normative sample and .93 for a clinical sample. Two ratings by seventy mothers four weeks later produced a Pearson correlation of .85, which suggests stability in sexual behavior. Factor analysis revealed one large factor accounting for 40 percent to 53 percent of the variance in the normative and clinical samples. Analysis of covariance found twenty-seven of thirty-five behaviors to differ significantly among the groups. In terms of cross-validation, a sample of children two to five years of age suspected to be sexually abused differed significantly on the CSBI from children not identified as sexually abused.

Availability

For the latest version of the instrument, contact Dr. William Friedrich, Department of Psychiatry and Psychology, Mayo Clinic, Rochester, MN 55905.

Scoring

Parents rate their children's behavior on a scale that ranges from "never" to "at least once a week." These values (ranging from 0 to 3) are then summed.

For Further Reference

Friedrich, W.N., Grambsch, P., Broughton, D., Kuiper, J., and Beilke, R.L. (1991). Normative sexual behavior in children. *Pediatrics*, 88 (3) 456–464.
Friedrich, W.N., Grambsch, P., Koverola, C., Lang, R.A., Wolfe, V., and Broughton, D. (1992). Child Sexual Behavior Inventory: Normative and clinical comparisons. *Psychological Assessment*, 4 (3), 303–311.
Friedrich, W.N., Luecke, W.J., and Place, V. (1992). Psychotherapy outcome of sexually abused boys. *Journal of Interpersonal Violence*, 7 (3), 396–409.

BRIEF SYMPTOM INVENTORY™

Description

The Brief Symptom Inventory™ (BSI®) is a fifty-three item self-report inventory designed to identify psychological symptom patterns of psychi-

Figure 9.9
Brief Symptom Inventory

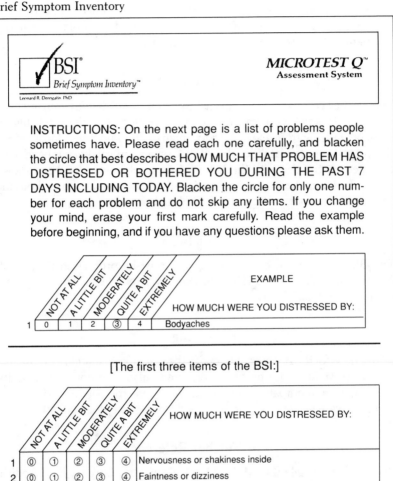

atric, medical, and normal populations in about ten minutes. A condensed version of the Symptom Checklist 90-R, the BSI is scored in terms of nine primary symptom dimensions—somatization, obsessive-compulsive, interpersonal sensitivity, depression, anxiety, hostility, phobic anxiety, paranoid ideation, psychoticism—and three global indices.

The General Severity Index is a summary measure of the general level of pathology and is the most important of these indices. The BSI has been widely used, and norms are available for adolescents, psychiatric inpatients and outpatients, and nonpatients.

Psychometric Data

The BSI has very acceptable internal consistency reliabilities, ranging from .71 on the Psychoticism scale to .85 on Depression. Test-retest reliabilities are good, ranging from a low of .68 to a high of .91. The three global indices all have test-retest reliabilities above .80. Convergent validity has been demonstrated for the BSI with the MMPI. Construct validity has been shown when a factor analysis on a psychiatric outpatient sample of one thousand confirmed the construction of the symptom dimensions.

Availability

The BSI is protected by copyright and must be purchased from NCS Assessments, P.O. Box 1416, Minneapolis, MN 55440. The telephone number is 800-627-7271.

Scoring

Instructions for the BSI are contained in the *BSI Administration, Scoring, and Procedures Manual*. BSI profile reports are available for nonpatient adults, adolescents, and outpatient and inpatient psychiatric patients. Microcomputer software can also be purchased for scoring and progress reports.

For Further Reference

Beutler, L.E., Engle, D., Mohr, D., Daldrup, R.J., Bergen, J., Meredith, K., and Merry, W. (1991). Predictors of differential response to cognitive, experiential, and self-directed psychotherapeutic procedures. *Journal of Consulting and Clinical Psychology*, 59, 333–340.

Derogatis, L.R., and Melisaratos, N. (1983). The Brief Symptom Inventory: An introductory report. *Psychological Medicine*, 13, 595–605.

Katon, W., Van Korff, M., Lin, E., Lipscomb, P., Russo, J., Wagner, E., and Polk, E. (1990). Distressed high utilizers of medical care: DSM-III-R diagnoses and treatment needs. *General Hospital Psychiatry*, 12, 355–362.

Northouse, L.L. (1988). Social support in patients' and husbands' adjustment to breast cancer. *Nursing Research*, 37 (2), 91–95.

Verinis, J.S., Wetzel, L., Vanderporten, A., and Lewis, D. (1986). Improvement in men inpatients in an alcoholism rehabilitation unit: A week-by-week comparison. *Journal of Studies on Alcohol*, 47, 85–88.

Williams, J.B., Rabkin, J.G., Remien, R.H., Gorman, J.M., and Ehrhardt, A.A. (1991). Multidisciplinary baseline assessment of homosexual men with and without human immunodeficiency virus infection. *Archives of General Psychiatry*, 48, 124–130.

Zabora, J.R., Smith-Wilson, R., Fetting, J.H., and Enterline, J.P. (1990). An efficient method for psychosocial screening of cancer patients. *Psychosomatics*, 31 (2), 192–196.

QUESTIONS FOR CLASS DISCUSSION

1. Think about the instruments contained in this chapter. Brainstorm possible new uses for each of them. For example, could the Child Abuse Potential Inventory be used in conjunction with a parent education intervention geared towards teen mothers? Could it be used as a screening mechanism when hiring new child-care workers in residential agencies and group homes? What uses might the Clinical Anxiety Scale have?

2. Discuss the advantages and disadvantages of developing a new instrument versus spending effort to search for one that may not even exist. What would be the major determinants affecting your decision?

MINI-PROJECTS:
EXPERIENCING RESEARCH FIRSTHAND

1. From the articles on scale development and validation listed in the "For Further Reference" sections, summarize, in a short paper, all of the steps the authors went through.

2. With a partner, attempt to create a scale measuring some concept of your choice. Present the scale to the class for a discussion of its face and content validity.

3. Using either a scale that you've developed or one with known psychometrics, collect a small sample of data from your classmates or others. Enter the data into a computer with statistical analysis software so that you can compute the scale's internal consistency. Discuss what you found and possible explanations for the results.

TEN

Pragmatic and Political Considerations

Ideally, program evaluations are conducted because of a commitment to providing the best possible services. But there can be other motives as well. For instance, an evaluation of an agency may be used to get rid of an administrator when the board of directors wants to hire a new person. Whether we like it or not, evaluations can be used as bludgeons to bring about changes in programs and personnel. The novice evaluator is well advised to remember that any evaluation may be perceived as a political activity by those being evaluated. Those not involved in the planning of the evaluation are often suspicious of some "hidden agenda." Evaluation is intrinsically threatening to those being evaluated.

In agencies where staff morale is already poor, where there is a widespread feeling that the program is not working the way it should, or where there is inadequate supervision and incompetent leadership, evaluation is even more threatening because staff fear a "house-cleaning" that will take away their jobs. On the other hand, an administrator may request a program evaluation to show that the criticism he or she has been receiving is unwarranted. The results of a program evaluation could be used to fend off critics of a program rumored to be unpopular or extremely expensive, or even because the director is attempting to secure funding for new staff positions.

Within any organization, there are likely to be as many opinions as to the "real" purpose and value of an evaluation as there are reasons for conducting the evaluation. As a result, some staff will be supportive and helpful, others will be threatened because the evaluation was "imposed." Staff who feel under attack may attempt to undermine the evaluation effort. The evaluator may be seen as an investigative reporter, a critic, a "spy," a benevolent consultant, or some combination of these. Kennedy (1983) noted that:

> Evaluation is an inherently contradictory activity. . . . Evaluators are expected to help organizations achieve their goals, yet because organizations may consist of parts whose goals are incompatible, helping one group may entail hindering another. . . . Evaluators are often expected to observe organizational activities from an objective position, yet their credibility may depend on being perceived as sympathetic friends. Most of these tensions are inherent in the task of evaluation. (P. 519)

The program evaluation literature contains many references to the political nature of program evaluation. Coffee (1989), in discussing opinions toward evaluators, noted that some individuals view evaluators as "mean-spirited, politically motivated, rewarded only for finding out what is wrong. . ." (p. 59). Chelimsky (1987) in an article entitled "What Have We Learned about the Politics of Program Evaluation?" noted that "the choice of the program to evaluate emerges in *real terms* from the political process, with the determination of the types of policy questions to be asked being a function of the decision makers" (p. 10). Cronbach et al. (1980) in *Toward Reform of Program Evaluation* summarized major points in a number of theses. Several of these speak to the political arena in which evaluators must operate. For instance, "the evaluator has political influence even when he does not aspire to it"; "evaluators' professional conclusions cannot substitute for the political process"; and, "a theory of evaluation must be as much a theory of political interaction as it is a theory of how to determine facts" (p. 3).

Evaluators should not be naive in believing that program evaluation efforts are somehow immune to political processes and pressures. Muscatello (1989), in writing about his experience as manager of an evaluation team within a large public organization, observed that evaluators are sometimes asked by decision makers to develop data to verify or legitimize decisions that have already been made—an activity, he said, to which purists in the evaluation field may take exception. Other political implications for the evaluator are also apparent in that the "good evaluator" will work with the "good manager" to "ensure that the conclusions and recommendations reached during the study are overlaid first with relevant policy considerations, and then with the realities of organizational politics, organizational environment, and future business strategies" (p. 17). Muscaletto further cautions:

> If this overlay process does not take place, implementation becomes far less practical and the effectiveness of the evaluation function is diminished, along with its value to the organization. For any segment of his or her business, the chief executive officer has the right to ask, "Why do I need this function and/or these people?" Certainly it is a healthy company whose officers ask each segment of the business, "What have you done for me lately?" If the manager of a program evaluation unit cannot demonstrate impact for the evaluation function, then the logical business decision is to eliminate the unit itself. (P. 17)

This theme has also been discussed by Chelimsky (1987) who has written, "We must be useful to others if we are to be successful. That means understanding the political system in which evaluation operates, and understanding the information needs of those policy actors who use evaluation" (p. 17).

At the same time, the evaluator may be pressured by the administrator or administration to show that a program is successful—whether it is or not. Because of the potential for losing funds, administrators may be anxious that even negative findings be worded in such a way as to present the program in the best possible light. They may ask the evaluator to emphasize the positive points (see Kytle and Millman, 1986, for instance), to include anecdotal accounts from satisfied clients or favorable remarks of influential persons in the community (even though these individuals may know little about the program). Similarly, administrators may be concerned with the order in which the findings are presented. They may want the favorable points made early in the evaluation report and the negative points buried deep in the report. House (1986) has cautioned **internal evaluators** (staff evaluators employed full-time by an organization) against confusing the interests of the organizations with those of individual administrators with whom they identify personally.

The political realities are such that administrators don't always want the "truth" but may be looking for an evaluator to prepare an innocuous final report that will minimize any identified problems. Failing to get a "sugar coated" version, these administrators may secretly hope that any document containing bad news will be so difficult to understand that even interested persons won't be able to wade in very far. We sound a bit cynical here, but decisions are not always made impartially; objective information is not always desired.

Evaluation activities always pose a potential threat to someone or some group. Any time we are evaluated, whether as students or faculty or employees, we fear negative evaluation—being labeled or identified as inadequate or incompetent. Staying in touch with how we feel when we are evaluated makes us sensitive to the feelings of others when we plan to evaluate their activities.

If the staff feel that they are being scrutinized in a situation where there is no examination of the administrative hierarchy, they will feel threatened. On the other hand, if the staff feel that the problems lie not with their functioning but at the administrative level and the evaluation will detect this, they will be less threatened. Evaluators must be mindful that anyone fearing loss of job or other negative repercussions from an evaluation will feel threatened. Even if staff do not fear loss of job but feel that the program has been unjustly singled out, they will feel threatened.

If staff feel threatened, they are likely to be less cooperative than the evaluator would desire. While they may not be as vicious as to slash the tires on the evaluator's car, they may quite pleasantly refuse to complete questionnaires or forms that are needed by the evaluator. They may be "too busy" to review their closed client records or to contact active clients for evaluation purposes. They may "forget" to return questionnaires on the date requested, or they may have "lost" the evaluator's instructions. If the evaluation requires ongoing data collection and the evaluator is not in the agency on a regular basis and has not designed adequate data collection mechanisms, the resulting data may be collected sporadically, only when it was convenient, or perhaps not at all. Passive-aggressive staff may argue, "We are here to help clients . . . not to use them as guinea pigs. We are too busy helping—we don't have the luxury of time to conduct research!"

Evaluators should not underestimate the amount of power that they are perceived to have by persons within the organization being evaluated. Thompson (1989) has described the evaluator as a "power broker." Part of the reasoning for this is that the evaluator can speak and act for others in positions of authority. Evaluators can stimulate action and change by speaking for and acting as agents for those who are reluctant to do so on their own. By gathering information and focusing on the important issues, the evaluator assists the decision makers in becoming more knowledgeable (and therefore more powerful).

The evaluator will be viewed by some agency staff as a "hired gun" who has come into the agency to do away with certain staff by documenting their inefficiency or ineffectiveness. According to this line

234

of thinking, the hired gun takes orders from those who did the hiring. The evaluator will not be seen as objective or even as interested in hearing the "truth" because of ties to those who are paying the consulting fees.

Regardless of whether you are an internal evaluator or an **external** (contract) **evaluator,** you will find that program evaluation is almost always conducted in a political arena. A finding that pleases one group may make another group unhappy. It can be expected that political pressures will vary in strength depending on what is at stake. The wise evaluator will be sensitive to any factors (political or otherwise) that can affect his or her judgment. Because it is not easy to know if you are being too accommodating or too intractable, you may find it useful to share your preliminary ideas or even a rough draft of a final report with a trusted friend or colleague who would be in a position to detect any lack of fairness or balance. When a program has serious problems, it is quite easy to focus on the negatives and fail to see the positives. Both need to be reported.

Agency directors often argue that anecdotal accounts of successes obtained by selected clients ought to be included. It makes a director feel better to report some success even though the program didn't accomplish all that was intended. There's no harm in reporting such accounts, particularly when these anecdotal reports of individual cases are used to corroborate the findings of quantitative data. However, anecdotal data alone, in the absence of quantitative evaluation, is selective reporting and cannot constitute a credible evaluation.

Program evaluation *does not* consist of picking out anecdotal reports to illustrate particular outcomes and conveying the impression that this material is somehow "representative" of program outcomes. Such a practice would be deceptive at best and should be discouraged. On the other hand, employing anecdotal reports or selected quotes to illustrate various service outcomes, to "flesh out" the bare bones of reported quantitative outcomes, is a useful practice.

GUIDELINES FOR EVALUATION IN POLITICALLY CHARGED ARENAS

To help you stay as impartial and fair as possible, the following guidelines may be of use in managing political pressures:

1. Maintain your independence. There may be some pressure from within the organization to present the results in a favorable light. This problem is reported quite often in evaluation literature (see Worthen and White, 1987, and Kytle and Millman, 1986, for example). Prepare

235

for such pressures. Suggest ahead of time that some of the findings may be positive and some may be negative. Let it be known that information from a variety of perspectives will be gathered and examined.

The evaluator's autonomy is less likely to be compromised when there is a clear notion of the purpose of the evaluation and what the evaluator's role will be. As an evaluator, will you be a consultant making suggestions to help a program grow and improve? Or will you be a "fact finder" who uncovers and diagnoses unhealthy programs so that the administration can perform "surgery"? Insist upon a contract that states explicitly the evaluation sponsors' expectations of you and the evaluation product.

Your independence is safeguarded when, in the process of negotiating a contract, you insist upon editorial authority in writing the evaluation report. Do not allow the evaluation sponsor to have final authority for writing or revising your evaluation report. (However, it is often a good idea to brief key personnel once you have a draft copy of the report ready. Sometimes such briefings can provide the evaluator with a different perspective or new way of interpreting the data. Briefings may also serve the useful purpose of keeping the administration from being totally surprised by negative findings. The little bit of additional time this may require is well worth its expenditure in a politically charged arena—a director will have time to prepare a response or implement corrective actions even before the report becomes "official.")

2. Negotiate a contract. One way to reduce confusion about the evaluator's role and the purpose of the evaluation is to draft an agreement or contract. These contracts can be complex or simple and will vary widely depending upon the amount of time and remuneration involved, the intricacy of the evaluation, and the amount of trust between the evaluation sponsor and the evaluator. (Worthen and White, 1987, and Herman, Morris, and Fitz-Gibbon, 1987, can be consulted for additional information on negotiating a contract.) Essentially, these agreements should cover:

a. The purpose or focus of the evaluation. (Incorporate a list of the questions that the evaluation sponsor wants answered or hypotheses that will be investigated.)

b. The beginning and ending dates of the evaluation. (At a minimum, it is important to specify deadlines when the evaluation products must be finished.) On some occasions, it may also be advisable to describe the sponsor's expectations of a final product—in terms of appearance, the amount of detail it will contain, and so forth.

c. The evaluation methodology; data, staff, and facilities needed. (Will the evaluation design necessitate the use of control groups?

236

Will random assignment of clients be necessary? Will it be necessary to obtain sensitive information from clients? What other data will be necessary to access? How many and what employees will need to assist?)

d. The budget needed. (Not only is agreement important on the consultant's fee, but also there should be a definite budget for such items as travel, supplies, printing, secretarial services, and so on. It is also important to specify the payment schedule—when the evaluator can be expected to be paid.)

e. Ownership of the data and editorial authority. (At the end of the evaluation, who keeps the computer printouts, completed questionnaires, and other data? You may need the data, or at least access to it, should you decide to write an article for a professional journal. Further, it should be clear who will write and have editorial authority over the final evaluation report, and to whom it will and can be disseminated.)

In some instances, it is necessary for the evaluator to gather some information about the program or agency before an evaluation design and data collection procedures can be recommended. This design phase (sometimes called a feasibility study) may be negotiated separately so that the evaluator can later submit a realistic estimate for conducting the actual evaluation.

3. **Attempt to obtain evaluative information from as many sources as you can.** Be inclusive rather than exclusive. Talk to clients, staff, board members, citizens in the community—in short, talk to anyone who may have an opinion about the program. Use more than one evaluation design if time and resources allow. Consider the worst case scenario—what would you be able to conclude if the evaluation model you have planned does not work as it was intended? What other sources of data would be available for evaluation? Along this line Michael Quinn Patton (1982) has written, "In my judgment it is not practical to base one's entire practice on a single model in the hope (or expectation) that said model will always work" (p. 43).

4. **Explain and communicate the purpose of the evaluation and its methodology to staff and other interested parties.** Schedule a staff meeting and allow the staff to raise questions and interact with you. You may even want to use a committee of practitioners for advisory purposes. They can provide you with feedback with regard to the evaluation procedures. They will know the educational level and abilities of the clients and, if they want to help you, may be able to point out ways to get around certain organizational obstacles or barriers. At a minimum, allowing staff

to raise questions will help reduce the level of anxiety they have about the evaluation. Providing staff with information will help suppress some of the rumors that may surface about the "real" purpose of the evaluation. We find that the involvement of staff provides a richer and more comprehensive evaluation than can be obtained when they are not involved. Since they are likely to know the serious problems with the program, it is good evaluation practice to keep staff both informed and involved. Staff and administrators are also more likely to use the results of the evaluation if they participated in the process and their interest was kept at a high level.

While it may seem like just common sense, it is vitally important that any instructions or directions be communicated clearly. Staff and clients will not be as familiar with the evaluation methodology or the instruments as the evaluator. They may require detailed instructions, special training, or additional preparation. (We once heard of an evaluation where the staff were given a rather lengthy questionnaire with practically no instructions at all. In the absence of guidelines, the staff improvised. Some requested additional instructions, others "guessed" at what the evaluator wanted.) On the other hand, we can also overdo the instructions. They can be too complex for busy people to quickly comprehend. If instructions are not readily understood, they are not likely to be followed. There should be virtually no confusion due to the complexity of evaluation procedures or feelings of frustration as a result of the "burden" that is imposed upon clients, staff, or members of boards of directors.

OTHER PRAGMATIC PROBLEMS

While navigating the shoals of agency politics, the evaluator must be alert to day-to-day problems that arise when he or she is not able to personally supervise the evaluation. An evaluator once told us of her frustration when staff affiliated with a special project kept broadening the eligibility criteria in order to provide services to a greater number of needy persons. The evaluator discovered this much later when she followed-up on service recipients and found out that they did not meet the criteria of persons for whom the project had been designed to help. Many of the service recipients could not be included in the evaluation. Much too late to do anything about it, the evaluator had a much smaller group of service recipients to evaluate than had been planned. To make matters worse, somewhere along the line the staff had quit trying to randomly assign clients to the "regular" or the "intensive" intervention programs. They had begun using their own criteria to decide who could best benefit from the programs.

"War stories" of this type abound. Most evaluators have vivid memories of evaluations gone awry. While it would be rare for an evaluation to experience no problems at all, the experienced evaluator learns to anticipate problems before they occur and plan for them. For instance, in planning for a large scale survey to be mailed, the evaluator needs not only to calculate the amount of time required to type the questionnaires, stuff and address the envelopes, and sort the mail by zip codes in time for the post office to deliver them but also to allow for an extra day or two for secretaries to get sick, computers to break down, and holidays and vacation days. Things that have never happened before may occur at a critical time. For this reason, many evaluators estimate the amount of time taken for certain tasks beyond their control (e.g., the delivery of the mail) and then double their estimates to give a comfortable "cushion" in case unanticipated problems arise. Even for those activities that are within your control, the unexpected can happen and can result in missing a deadline if the planning does not allow for some "slippage."

Most nonpolitical problems that occur during a program evaluation are due to events and slippages beyond the evaluator's control. For instance, the director of data processing informs you that it will take three weeks longer than promised to get around to your request to pull five-hundred random client addresses. Questionnaires don't get administered because the evaluator depended upon someone else in the agency to oversee the effort, and that individual got caught up in some more pressing problems. Clients' problems almost always have a higher priority than program evaluation.

To have fewer problems, assume as much responsibility as possible. Don't rely upon others to select the clients, design your forms, collect your data. Control as much of the process as you can manage. What you can't do, hire your own staff to do. If there is no other alternative but to rely upon agency staff who have competing interests and responsibilities, stay in close contact with them. Don't call once at the beginning of the project and then again six months later when you need the data. Visit the agency or site often, let them know you, train and prepare those who will be collecting the data, and get them some reduction in their other responsibilities if possible. Involve staff in the process, keep them informed, and be considerate of the other demands upon their time.

DETERMINING SAMPLE SIZE

Another pragmatic concern is, "How many clients do I sample?" or, "How many interviews (questionnaires) do I need for a good evaluation?" There is no single or quick response to questions about how large the

239

sample should be. Before discussing sample size, let's talk a bit about concerns that follow from *how* a sample is selected.

In the simplest of designs, for example, a one-group pretest-posttest, sampling may not be an issue. If twenty-one clients are involved in a new support group for care-givers of persons with Alzheimer's disease, there is no need to randomly select clients. The evaluation should involve all of those who are attending the support group. However, if the support group has been going on for a long time—say, the past ten years—then the evaluator has some decisions to make. By contacting only the currently active consumers of a program, the evaluator might not be able to identify problems that caused members to drop out or to become inactive. In other words, there is the strong possibility of biased findings. This is always a problem when evaluators rely upon **convenience samples**.

Samples of convenience are just what they sound like—a group of persons easily obtained because they are close at hand and accessible. An example of a sample of convenience would be interviewing the first fifteen clients who walked past your office on a Monday morning, the first day of the month. Such a procedure might appear on the surface to generate a random sample, but it is possible that all fifteen were returning from a special program or field trip. Or, they might all have been new clients who got lost while looking for the exit.

Since a convenience sample of clients is not randomly selected from a larger population, it is impossible to know how well they represent the "true" population. For that reason, convenience samples are known as nonprobability samples and are generally viewed as not being rigorous or scientific. Nonprobability samples do not allow you to discuss margin of error or confidence level. Does that mean you can't learn from them? No, but the results are likely to be regarded as more preliminary or exploratory than definitive.

Think for a moment what might result if you offer a new, experimental intervention for a certain problem, and you advertise in the newspaper for volunteers. Those who contact you are likely to be more severely affected by the problem (they're highly motivated) than those who also have the problem but who *don't* contact you. What might you conclude about the intervention? If it works with volunteers, who are highly motivated, there is no guarantee it will work with those who are less motivated, perhaps more shy. If it doesn't work, there's the possibility that it may be beneficial to those who didn't volunteer and whose problem is less chronic or milder in some way. A strong selection bias prevents you from knowing as much as you might know if a random sample of all those with the problem had been selected.

Let's return to the example of the Alzheimer's support group. Given a choice of contacting the most recent program dropouts or a random sampling of *all* the dropouts, you obtain a stronger evaluation from a random sampling of *all* those who dropped out. Practically speaking, though, going back to the start of the program may not be desirable or necessary—particularly if the program has undergone a major change. You could begin at that point and randomly select clients.

In a situation where a program is relatively new—let's say, one hundred clients have completed the program—gather evaluation data from all of the clients. You will never obtain a 100 percent response rate. Clients move and don't leave forwarding addresses, they may choose not to respond, they are hospitalized or locked up, and they die. Even if you get addresses and/or phone numbers for all one hundred clients, it is very likely that less than half of them will respond to your survey. So, had you randomly drawn fifty names, as few as fifteen and maybe no more than twenty-five may respond. The number of respondents you are likely to obtain is a major consideration when deciding upon a sampling strategy. As a rule, the more recent a client's involvement and the more favorable his or her experience, the more likely the client will respond.

A common assumption when trying to decide how many persons to sample is that 10 percent of a client population makes an adequate sample. Yet, this rule of thumb could provide too small a sample (in the case of small populations) or too large a sample (when there is a large population). To understand what size sample is appropriate, we need to consider margin of error and confidence intervals. **Margin of error** refers to the precision of our findings. A margin of error of 5 percent means that the actual findings could vary by as much as 5 points either positively or negatively. A consumer satisfaction survey, for instance, with a 5 percent margin of error associated with a finding of 65 percent of clients "highly satisfied" with services would mean that the true value in the population could be as low as 60 percent ($65 - 5 = 60$) or as high as 70 percent ($65 + 5 = 70$). This 5 percent margin of error is pretty standard. If, however, you require greater precision, (e.g., plus or minus 2 points), then you will need to increase your sample size.

The other term that is important to understand is confidence interval. The **confidence interval** is a statement of how often you could expect to find similar results if the survey were to be repeated. Since every survey varies slightly (depending upon who is selected to be in the sample), the confidence interval informs about how often the findings will fall outside the margin of error. For instance, in a sample developed to have a 95 percent confidence interval with a 5 percent margin of error, the results would miss the actual values in the population by more than 5 percent only one time in twenty samples. In ninety-five out of one hundred samples, the results would fall within the 5 percent margin of error.

There are two ways to determine the appropriate sample size for your evaluation effort. One approach is to find reference books or texts that contain tables to aid in determining necessary sample sizes. An example is Chester McCall's (1980) *Sampling and Statistics Handbook for Research in Education: A Technical Reference for Members of the Research Staff of the National Education Association and Its State and Local Affiliated Association.* McCall has prepared tables that allow you to determine sample size based on levels of confidence (99 to 90 percent), and margins of error (1 to 5 percent) when the absolute proportion of the trait, characteristics, or attitude in the population is not known. (When the level of the expected attitude, trait, or characteristic is unknown, a conservative estimate of 50 percent is used. Somewhat smaller samples can be developed when the known proportion in the population is less than 50 percent.)

A second approach is to actually calculate the sample size and adjust for the desired margin of error, confidence interval, and population proportion. The following formula (found in Krejcie and Morgan, 1970) can be used:

Sample Size $= X^2 NP(1-P) \div d^2(N-1) + X^2 P(1-P).$

Where: $X^2 = 3.841$ (the table value of chi-square for 1 degree of freedom at the 95% confidence level)

$N =$ the population size

$P =$ the population proportion (without other evidence, this is assumed to be .50)

$d =$ the margin of error or degree of accuracy needed (e.g., .05)

From this formula, sample sizes for the populations in table 10.1 have been calculated. Note that when the population is small, sample sizes constitute a larger proportion than when the population is very large. For example, 24 would be needed to make the necessary sample when the client population is 25 (a proportion of 96 percent) where only 357 would be needed when the population was 5,000 (a proportion of 7 percent). As the population size increases, the sample size increases

Table 10.1

Appropriate Sizes of Simple Random Samples with a 5% Margin of Error
and 95% Confidence Level, Assuming a Population Proportion of 50%

Population Size	Sample Size
25	24
50	44
75	63
100	80
150	108
200	132
250	152
300	169
400	196
500	217
750	254
1,000	278
2,000	322
4,000	351
5,000	357
10,000	370
15,000	375
20,000	377
25,000	378
50,000	381
100,000	384
1,000,000	384

at a slower or diminishing rate. Sample size remains relatively constant
as it approaches 380, so that a sample of 384 is needed whether the
population is 100,000 or 1,000,000 (given a 5 percent margin of error
and 95 percent confidence).

The 5 percent margin of error and 95 percent confidence are regarded as providing all the precision needed for most research and evaluation purposes in the social sciences. However, there may be occasions
when greater or less precision is required. If, for instance, you would be
comfortable with a 90 percent confidence level and a 5 percent margin
of error, smaller samples could be used. By substituting 2.71 for the
chi-square value of 3.841, you can determine that for a population of
500, the 90 percent confidence level requires a sample size of 176, and
with a population of 1,000 a sample of 213 is needed. Compare these
with the sample sizes in table 10.1.

Although it is seldom necessary to have more confidence than 95
percent or to decrease the margin of error below 5 percent, when greater
precision and confidence is necessary, the formula can similarly be ad-

243

justed. To compute a sample size that would provide a 99 percent level of confidence and a margin of error of 3 percent, you would substitute 6.64 for the chi-square value of 3.841 in the above formula and .03 for d (the margin of error). For populations of 500 and 1,000, this would result in samples of 394 and 649, respectively.

Either table 10.1 or the formula provides the evaluator with a means for determining the necessary sample size to obtain accurate estimates. In both instances, it is understood that a random selection process will be used to select the sample. (Consult a text on basic research methodologies if you don't know how to draw a random sample.)

It doesn't make sense to worry about random selection when the population is very small. For instance, although table 10.1 indicates that with a population of twenty-five you need to contact only twenty-four, we'd probably interview all twenty-five anyway. If these twenty-five individuals were staff of some agency being asked about their job satisfaction, it's easy to imagine how the one who didn't get asked for his or her opinions could feel devalued, angry, or even paranoid. Besides, by the time you figure out a fair and equitable random assignment process, you could have interviewed or contacted the individual.

Also, keep in mind that 20 to 30 percent response rates are not uncommon with mail surveys. If you had a thousand clients in your program and if you randomly selected 278 to receive a questionnaire, you might plan on getting fifty to eighty responses. It is also possible that you might receive as few as twenty-five. What problems would there be if you evaluated a program using a small minority of clients? You cannot assume that a minority of responders have the same experiences, opinions, or behaviors as those who did not respond. Because you have less than a majority of the sample responding, you have a self-selected group that is very likely biased. You would have lost the advantage of drawing the initial sample randomly. To give your evaluation credibility, one of the most important things you can do, besides drawing an adequately sized random sample, is to get a response rate greater than 50 percent. There are several ways to go about this—sending postcard reminders, mailing a second questionnaire, and so forth. For additional information on how to improve your response rates, refer to Dillman (1991), Alreck and Settle (1985), or Fink and Kosecoff (1985).

Response rates are important to the evaluator, and low response rates are always suspect. However, the sheer number of people who go to the trouble to express their opinions about a matter can also be persuasive. A conservative U.S. Congressman changed his stance on legislation to ban the manufacture of semiautomatic weapons based on the number of responses received from a congressional mailing. Representative Hubbard noted that he mails out 230,000 newsletters and gets back responses from 37,000 (a 16 percent response rate). When asked if he was concerned about relying on unscientific results, Hubbard said, "Unscientific? It's convincing at times. It tells me the same things I'm hearing in town meetings . . . in my district" (*Lexington Herald-Leader*, Oct. 13, 1989).

ETHICAL CONSIDERATIONS

Due to past abuses of human subjects by researchers (see, for instance, Jones, 1981; Conot, 1983; Faden and Beauchamp, 1986; Grundner, 1986; Lifton, 1986; Annas and Grodin, 1992; and Edgar, 1992), federal law requires primary investigators who are affiliated with organizations receiving federal funds (universities, hospitals, and other large public service organizations) to contact an Institutional Review Board (IRB) to determine if their proposed research and evaluation activities protect the dignity and rights of participating subjects.

Review boards have been established in research-conducting institutions, although they are not often found in smaller social service agencies, and have the authority to approve, disapprove, or modify proposed research activities. Further, they periodically review ongoing research and may suspend or terminate research previously approved that deviates from the original prospectus.

IRBs are *not* interested in reviewing routine evaluations to determine if a client's condition has improved; they would not want to review single-system designs, as a general rule. If, however, an evaluation is being planned that would aggregate data from multiple clients who received the same intervention, IRB approval may be required—particularly if the evaluator makes use of "identifiable private information" (Grigsby and Roof, 1993).

IRBs often require that clients consent to involvement in a research or evaluation activity. Because of the logistical problem of tracking down clients to get their approval when a retrospective review of records is desired, many agencies have adopted the practice of notifying their clients at the point of intake that their records may be used for research purposes at some future time. A right-of-notice form attempts to obtain written consent from clients and advises them of their power to refuse.

Reviewing historical or archival data when consent of subjects has not been obtained is often possible when there is a legitimate research interest. IRBs exist to protect American citizens from harm, not to prevent research. If confidentiality of records is carefully observed (and there is very seldom any need for evaluators to record individual names, addresses, or personally identifying information in their databases), the risk of harm to former clients or patients is virtually zero.

IRBs perform several levels of review. The most cursory of these (when the investigator asks for an exemption) requires only that a small summary of the proposed research or evaluation be written specifying the objectives, the subject population, how the subjects will be recruited, the research procedures, and any potential physical, psychological, social, or legal risks to subjects. A full review requires a lengthier application and sometimes a personal appearance before the IRB to explain or defend the proposal.

Exemptions are usually routine when such activities as those listed below are planned:

1. Research conducted in established or commonly accepted educational settings, involving normal educational practices such as instructional strategies or the effectiveness of instructional techniques, curricula, or classroom management methods.
2. Research involving the use of educational tests (e.g., aptitude, achievement, or diagnostic) if information taken from these sources is recorded in such a manner that subjects cannot be identified directly or through identifiers linked to the subjects and if any disclosure of the subjects' responses outside the research would not place the subjects at risk of criminal or civil liability or be damaging to the subjects' financial standing, employability, or reputation.
3. Research involving survey or interview procedures and observation of public behavior when it meets the conditions specified above.
4. Research involving the collection or study of existing data, documents, or records if these sources are publicly available or if the information is recorded by the investigator in such a manner that subjects cannot be identified directly or through identifiers linked to the subjects.
5. Research and demonstration projects conducted by or subject to the approval of federal department or agency heads which examine or evaluate public benefit or service programs or procedures for obtaining benefits or services under those programs, including possible changes to programs or procedures.
6. Research involving survey or interview procedures and educational tests when the respondents are elected or appointed public officials or candidates for public office or where federal statutes require the confidentiality of the personally identifiable information will be maintained through the research and thereafter.

However, exemptions generally are *not* available when certain vulnerable populations are to be used in the study (e.g., children, prisoners, and the mentally disabled), or when there is deception of subjects, or techniques that expose the subject to discomfort or harassment beyond levels normally encountered in daily life. Further, exemption is not available when the information obtained from medical or agency records is recorded in such a way that subjects can be identified directly or through identifiers linked to the subjects.

If you are employed by a small social service agency that receives no direct federal funding, your agency is not likely to have an IRB to review your evaluation proposal. In situations where the evaluation involves determining if clients improved during the course of the agency's regular programs, and there is no deprivation of services to those in a control group, there is probably no need to create or consult an IRB at a university or larger agency.

However, if experimental or unorthodox interventions are proposed that may pose some degree of risk to clients, if vulnerable populations are involved, if deception of clients is planned, or if there are strong incentives or penalties to keep clients involved—then it would be wise to have an impartial human subjects committee review plans for the evaluation.

Even if there is absolutely nothing controversial about a program, it is a good idea to discuss your proposed evaluation methodology with others. For example, suppose you are evaluating a shelter for battered women and propose to contact the women six months after they left the shelter. Although a phone call is harmless enough in ordinary circumstances, if these women are still involved in physically abusive relationships, knowledge that they received services from such a agency (and by implication may still be receiving services) could trigger new abuse from their violent partners.

When recipients of some service (e.g., food stamps) are asked to fill out questionnaires, they may feel coerced to respond. They may fear loss of benefits if they don't comply. This is why IRBs often require that research subjects sign consent forms that advise them of their right to refuse without any penalty.

Although policies vary somewhat from institution to institution, many IRBs expect to be consulted whenever faculty or students collect data from human subjects with the goal of publishing the results. (This would include dissertations.) On the other hand, permission usually is not needed for students to interview or contact clients as part of a college course.

Whether you are affiliated with a university or agency with its own IRB, or just attempting to do your best without the advice and consultation of an IRB, several guidelines should be kept in mind for conducting ethical research with human subjects.

ETHICAL GUIDELINES

Guideline 1: Research subjects must be volunteers

All of those participating in a research or evaluation effort should freely decide to participate. No coercion of any kind can be used to secure participants for a study. Subjects must also be competent to understand their choices. If they are not able to fully comprehend (e.g., individuals under the age of majority), then their legal caretakers must give permission, and the subjects still must assent. This means that even if parents have given permission for their children to participate in a research project, these children may still refuse to participate. The subject's right to self-determination must be respected, and the research participant is free to withdraw from the study at any time. In many instances, IRBs *require* that written permission be obtained from subjects of the research. Consent forms usually provide general but brief information on the nature of the project and indicate that the subject is free to withdraw consent and to discontinue participation in the project at any time without any penalty or loss of benefits. When evaluating a social service program, it is vitally important that recipients of services fully understand their right to refuse participation in a study and that this will in no way affect delivery of services to them in the present or any future time.

Guideline 2: Potential subjects should be given sufficient information about the study to determine any possible risks or discomforts as well as benefits.

Sufficient information includes an explanation of the purpose of the research, the expected duration of the subject's participation, the procedures to be followed, and the identification of any of those that might be experimental. The evaluator must be specific about any procedures that will involve the research subjects. If there are potential risks, these must be identified. Subjects should be given the opportunity to raise and have answered any questions about the study or any procedures that will be used. Subjects must also be allowed to inquire at any time (and have their questions answered) about procedures that are used. Consent forms should be written at a level of readability that the program participants can understand.

Guideline 3: No harm shall result as a consequence of participation in the evaluation.

While there is much less possibility of harm resulting from an intervention in the social or human services than from biomedical research, this guideline suggests that *no* harm should result. This guideline would be violated, for instance, if an evaluator contacted battered women some months after they had returned to an abusive situation and if there was a risk that talking to the evaluators might trigger another episode of violent assault.

More intangible, although no less important, clients can suffer emotional or psychological harm—as when their reputations are injured. For example, suppose a questionnaire is mailed to clients of a drug treatment or sexual offenders' program and one is accidentally sent to a client's work address and inadvertently opened by a secretary or is delivered to a neighbor and opened by mistake. This could result in the loss of a job or in the client's reputation being irreparably damaged. The potential for inadvertent harm of this type should concern every evaluator.

Guideline 4: Protection of sensitive information.
The privacy of human subjects is protected by:
a. allowing subjects to respond anonymously, if at all possible. If the research design cannot accommodate anonymity, protection is provided by:
b. separating any personally identifying information from the research data through the use of numeric or other special codes. Where complete anonymity is not possible (e.g., because pretest and posttest scores have to be matched for each subject), it may be possible to use Social Security numbers or specially created codes (such as the first four letters of a client's mother's maiden name and the last four digits of the client's own Social Security number) to help guard against unauthorized persons accidentally recognizing or identifying program participants.

The privacy of human subjects is further protected by not capturing or reporting any personal information (names, addresses, phone numbers, or personal descriptors such as Mayor, Eminence, Kentucky) that would result in research subjects being identified by persons other than the project's evaluators. When sensitive data must be obtained, it should be kept in locked cabinets or files until no longer needed and then destroyed (material to be protected includes master lists of codes, lists of respondents, mailing lists, completed questionnaires, and transcripts of interviews).

LOCATING CONTROL GROUPS

Students and practitioners often have negative opinions about evaluation because they assume that the use of evaluation designs and randomization necessitates that some clients will be denied services. However, denying services to a group of clients solely for the purpose of creating a control group would not be approved by many institutional review boards. Fortunately, seldom would such a situation be required for an evaluation. There are less problematic ways to obtain control groups without running the risk of litigation or possible violation of professional ethics by denying services.

For instance, instead of an experiment, the evaluator may want to conduct a comparative study. With a quasi-experimental nonequivalent control group design, the evaluator does not deny the control subjects the intervention received by the experimental subjects but finds a control group in a different geographical area where the intervention may not be available. Or, the evaluator may decide to compare the experimental subjects with the service recipients of another, similar agency. In this scenario, the evaluator could compare clients receiving an intervention from Agency A with clients receiving the same intervention but from Agency B. While there are obvious limitations to this design (a possible selection bias, for example) there is a control group for comparison. However, there is no requirement that you go outside your agency for a comparison group. Sometimes different approaches have evolved over time and are favored by some portion of the staff but certainly not all of the staff.

Another possible source of nonintervention-group subjects is those who start a program and then drop out. Of course, the longer they remain in the program before leaving, the more likely they are to be similar to those who complete the program. While it may not be a fair comparison to equate those who drop out of an intervention after one session with those who complete it, at least it would provide a best-case, worst-case scenario. If the intervention has any effect at all, it should be demonstrated in such a comparison.

Not only do clients drop out of treatment, but they also don't show up—even when attendance is mandated by child protective service or an officer of the court. A few individuals may even decide to go to jail, pay a stiff fine, or perform community service instead of attending a treatment program. Such clusters of referred or potential clients provide natural comparison groups that allow the evaluator to show the power of the intervention.

Long waiting lists are another source of control subjects. If there is a lengthy list of clients waiting for services, it might be possible to consider these as a control group (providing, of course, that the intervention is short enough that it would be concluded before those on the waiting list began receiving services). Clients on a waiting list might appreciate a periodic contact with an agency representative (even if it

BOX 10.1

Use of Multiple Control Groups

Evaluating a Diversion Program for First-Time Shoplifters

David Royse and Steven A. Buck

It's possible to employ more than one control group in an evaluation. In a diversion program for first-time shoplifters, we compared the group who completed intervention against three other groups: those who started the diversion program but dropped out (n = 42), those who were arrested for shoplifting in a two year period prior to the start of the program (n = 87), and those who were not admitted to the program (n = 87) largely because they failed to keep appointments to arrange for diversion or elected to go to a hearing on the charge.

We found a recidivism rate of 4 percent for the ninety-nine persons who completed the diversion program and re-arrest rates about six times as large (25 percent) for those in the three comparison groups. Since the re-arrest rate in the group of individuals who were arrested prior to the start of the diversion program had a much longer period of time during which they could have been re-arrested, these findings suggest that the recidivism rate among shoplifters who do not receive intervention is probably no greater than 25 percent.

One obvious reason why the diversion program was successful is because those who were likely to be recidivists may have screened themselves out of the program by not keeping appointments or dropping out.

Source: *Journal of Offender Rehabilitation*, 17 (112) (1991), 147–158.

is limited to the administration of a pretest and posttest) because it would constitute evidence that they had not been forgotten by the agency and that they are still queued for services.

A fourth possibility is to continue the usual or regular services with some clients (this would be the control group) and provide another group with the standard intervention *plus* a new and more intensive (experimental) intervention. For example, in an agency providing assistance to dysfunctional families, the control group would be assigned a caseworker as usual. The intervention group would receive a caseworker and twelve to twenty hours of home-based counseling each week for twelve weeks. To address any ethical concerns about which families receive the intensive services, a lottery (another way of saying random assignment) could be held.

In programs for clients that have very similar problems, it may be possible to evaluate different modalities or ways of delivering the intervention without denying services. One group of clients might receive individual counseling, another could receive group counseling, and a third group might receive educational information through seminar type lectures with audiovisual aids. Of course, such decisions depend greatly on the type of problem, its severity, the population being served, as well as the agency itself. Many alternatives are available, and evaluators merely need to keep in mind that denial or withholding of treatment is seldom needed in order to obtain control groups.

ETHICAL DILEMMAS

Most evaluators of social service programs are not likely to be involved in research where physical harm may occur to the subjects in the study. Often, program evaluations rely upon data already available in the public or agency records. Unless there is some indication of coercion or the respondent is from a vulnerable population (children, persons with mental illness, prisoners), anyone who responds to a mailed questionnaire or to a telephone/personal interview is usually understood to have consented to do so.

Adverse consequences are much more likely to derive not from an intervention but from unethical use of confidential information gathered as part of the evaluation effort—for instance, if a faculty member hired to be an evaluator for a substance abuse treatment agency discovered that the dean of his college was in a treatment group for cocaine addicts and revealed this information to his or her colleagues. Irreparable harm to reputations or careers could come from disclosing information about illegal or immoral acts, mental illness, contagious diseases, and so forth. It is the evaluator's responsibility to safeguard information entrusted to him or her by subjects who volunteer it in good faith so that no harm will result.

Even though we may think of ourselves as being ethical individuals, we may not be. Would it, for example, be all right to throw out data that doesn't conform to expectations about the way a program *really* performs? There are times, however, when an evaluator should toss out information from a respondent or several respondents during a data collection effort. For instance, you are examining the effect of

BOX 10.2

Unethical Behavior?

The topic of ethical behavior is always fascinating. We were discussing it one evening in class, and a student who had been a church secretary told how her boss, a minister, kept a suggestion box. Every so often he would encourage his parishioners to contribute ideas to it. He wanted to know who was making the recommendations, however, and asked that all suggestions be signed.

When he emptied the box, the secretary said that he "analyzed" the suggestions based on whether the parishioner tithed regularly and attended regularly. The suggestions of those who didn't meet this criteria were unceremoniously thrown away. Even worse, the secretary said, the minister added his own suggestions to the box and presented them as from an anonymous member of the congregation.

group psychotherapy on persons on dialysis, and you find that one person in the control group has been on dialysis many months longer than anyone else in the study. Statistically speaking, that person might be called an **outlier** (a data point that stands apart from the rest) and may be discarded, because data on that individual deviates too greatly from the others and skews the average for the group as a whole. There's nothing unethical about removing an extreme case that causes distortion of the data.

If you encounter an ethical dilemma, you probably need to talk with someone else about how to proceed. If there is no institutional review board within your agency, an IRB at the university nearest to you may be able to provide some aid.

Many organizations have developed codes of ethics or professional standards. While these tend to be fairly general, in some instances they may help an evaluator decide the right course of action. Some are rather specific in addressing the protection of confidential information, protecting anonymity, lying, obtaining consent, and so forth. Organizations with codes of ethics include:

American Association for Public Opinion Research
American Educational Research Association

American Evaluation Association
American Psychological Association
American Political Science Association
American Sociological Association
National Association of Social Workers

CHAPTER RECAP

This chapter described some of the ways evaluation may be viewed. The evaluator needs to be sensitive to "hidden agendas" and perceptions about his or her role that may indicate a misunderstanding of actual purpose. It is important to discuss with all involved parties the planned evaluation and to address fears, concerns, and questions. One way to make the evaluation somewhat less burdensome on clients is to make use of scientifically selected random samples of clients. Procedures for determining appropriate sample sizes were explained. Finally, Institutional Review Boards were discussed as well as the evaluator's responsibility for insuring that any evaluation meets ethical guidelines.

While we are aware that information gleaned from clients benefits the evaluator and agency, it also benefits clients. Clients may directly benefit from improvements made to a program as a result of an evaluation. Positive arguments can be made for clients' participation in evaluation and research projects. Korchin and Cowan (1982) have noted that subjects may gain from some new therapeutic procedure. Even if that doesn't occur, participants may feel that the study was important and that they have made a contribution that will be of help to others. Participants may also feel honored to have been selected, or may have experienced an increase in self-worth as a result of receiving attention associated with being a participant in an evaluation. People are often flattered when asked to share their opinions or insights. Finally, research and evaluation projects can be interesting and may challenge the participant to think or grow in new or different ways.

Even when a new or experimental program is being compared with the regular or standard treatment, it would be hard to make the case that it is unethical to expose participants to the new program (where the traditional program was thought to be superior) or to argue that all the clients should receive the experimental intervention because it is not known which of the treatments is superior. As Moore (1985) notes, "No one is deliberately deprived of the best therapy, even though because of our ignorance one group will receive an inferior treatment. . . . Controlled and randomized experiments are the only method for discovering which therapy is superior" (p. 93). Our practice knowledge increases with each solid evaluation effort. Evaluation allows us to continually improve the services provided to our clients and, as a consequence, to improve the quality of their lives.

Will you be confronted with ethical challenges in your practice as an evaluator? Morris and Cohn (1993) recently surveyed over four hundred members of the American Evaluation Association. Two-thirds (65 percent) of the respondents said they had encountered ethical problems. Surprisingly, three of the four most frequently reported conflicts arose *after* the data had been collected. Clients (stakeholders) were reported to pressure evaluators much more about what was reported and what happened to the report than about the process of conducting the evaluation.

As an internal evaluator you may feel loyalty to your employer, which may compromise your scientific objectivity and place you at risk for experiencing ethical conflicts. Persons hired as internal evaluators should read Mathison's (1991) article on role conflicts. External evaluators might want to read Fetterman's (1992) account of sponsor-evaluator relationships gone sour and the use of legal intervention when the sponsor attempted to change the structure, scope, content, and purpose of the evaluation after the planning phase was completed.

Finally, we have noted the importance of obtaining representative samples of subjects and have raised red flags about convenience samples. But it is extremely difficult to find outcome evaluations where clients were truly chosen randomly from a larger population of interest. Is it possible to become *too* concerned with issues of external validity? The answer is *yes*. Thyer (1992) observes:

> The actual practice is almost always to employ a convenience sample selected on the basis of availability (such as clients seen at your agency). One may not generalize the findings from such studies to other clients with similar problems, no matter how large the sample size. A study done on one hundred families selected on the basis of convenience in the town of Roosterpoop, Georgia, does not yield findings that can be extrapolated to all families in Roosterpoop, in Georgia, or anywhere else. All evaluations of practice are likely to be seriously compromised by problems with external validity. However, every evaluator hopes that independent replications will eventually demonstrate external validity.

QUESTIONS FOR CLASS DISCUSSION

1. From your knowledge of local agencies (but without disclosing the names of these agencies), discuss political pressures or agendas

which might influence (either positively or negatively) any evaluation efforts.

2. Discuss ways in which the political pressures identified in answers to question 1 might be neutralized or negated.

3. Discuss the external evaluator's responsibility upon concluding that objectivity had been lost or that a program evaluation cannot be done well. Discuss whether the responsibilities would be any different if an internal evaluator were involved.

4. Suppose that a thorough evaluation concludes that a program in an agency is not effective or is not cost-effective. Discuss how the results might be alternatively used or misused by persons with different political aspirations.

5. Give estimates of the number of service recipients in programs with which you are familiar. Then, assume a survey must be made of this population. Using the table provided in this book, determine the sample sizes needed for a confidence interval of 95 percent with a 5 percent margin of error.

6. With the same client population groups in mind, discuss the advantages and disadvantages associated with using nonprobability samples of fifteen, fifty, and seventy-five clients.

7. What are the various ways people react when they learn there is going to be an evaluation of their program or agency? What is the most common response?

8. Discuss, without naming any names or providing too much identifying information, instances where you have observed or *think* you have observed unethical behavior.

MINI-PROJECTS:
EXPERIENCING EVALUATION FIRSTHAND

1. Envision a scenario where an agency asks you to conduct a program evaluation. Prepare a contract that could result from the negotiations. Provide as many details as possible.

2. Obtain a copy of the exemption certification form used by an institutional review board at a nearby university. Complete the form as if you were proposing a program evaluation at a local social service agency.

3. Draft a consent form to be signed by clients who need to release personal information for a planned program evaluation. Briefly explain the nature of the project and what the clients are expected to provide, and include a statement informing clients that they

have the right to refuse to participate without any penalty or loss of benefits. Compare your product with a model or copy obtained from the institutional review board at a nearby university.

4. How have human subjects been abused in the name of research? Using the resources of your library, write a small paper which highlights unethical or inhumane research projects from prior years. You might want to start by looking at some of the experimentation conducted by Nazi doctors on human subjects. Relative to the United States, see Jones (1981) or learn more about the controversy that has swirled around Laud Humphreys or Stanley Milgram.

REFERENCES AND RESOURCES

Alreck, P.L., and Settle, R.B. (1985). *The survey research handbook.* Homewood, IL: Richard D. Irwin.

Altschuld, J.W., Thomas, P.M., McColskey, W.H., Smith, D.W., Wiesmann, W.W., and Lower, M.A. (1992). Mailed evaluation questionnaires: Replications of a 96 percent return rate procedure. *Evaluation and Program Planning,* 15, 239–246.

American Psychological Association. (1985). *Standards for educational and psychological testing.* Washington, DC: APA.

Annas, G.J., and Grodin, M.A. (1992). *The Nazi doctors and the Nuremberg Code: Human rights in human experimentation.* New York: Oxford University Press.

Baumrind, D. (1985). Research using intentional deception: Ethical issues revisited. *American Psychologist,* 40 (2), 165–174.

Boruch, R.F. (1987). Conducting social experiments. *Evaluation practice in review.* New Directions for Program Evaluation, no. 34. San Francisco, CA: Jossey–Bass.

Chelimsky, E. (1987). What have we learned about the politics of program evaluation? *Evaluation Practice,* 8 (1), 5–21.

Church, A.H. (1993). Estimating the effectiveness of incentives on mail survey response rates: A meta-analysis. *Public Opinion Quarterly,* 57 (1), 62–79.

Coffee, J.N. (1989). Advice for the evaluated. *Evaluation and the federal decision maker.* New Directions for Program Evaluation, no. 41. San Francisco, CA: Jossey–Bass.

Conot, R.E. (1983) *Justice at Nuremberg.* New York: Harper & Row.

Cronbach, L.J., Ambron, S.R., Dornbusch, S.M., Hess, R.D., Hornik, R.C., Phillips, D.C., Walker, D.F., and Weiner, S.S. (1980) *Toward reform of program evaluation.* San Francisco, CA: Jossey–Bass.

Dillman, D.A. (1991). The design and administration of mail surveys. In W. Richard Scott and Judith Blanke (eds.), *Annual reviews of sociology.* Palo Alto, CA: Annual Reviews, Inc.

Edgar, H. (1992). Twenty years after the legacy of the Tuskegee syphilis study: Outside the community. *Hastings Center Report,* 22 (6), 32–35.

Faden, R.R., and Beauchamp, T.L. (1986). *A history and theory of informed consent*. New York: Oxford University Press.

Fetterman, D.M. (1992). Investigative evaluation and litigation. *New Directions for Program Evaluation*, 56, 15–28.

Fink, A., and Kosecoff, J. (1985). *How to conduct surveys: A step-by-step guide*. Beverly Hills, CA: Sage.

Grigsby, R.K., and Roof, H.L. (1993). Federal policy for the protection of human subjects: Applications to research on social work practice. *Research on Social Work Practice*, 3 (4), 448–461.

Grundner, T.M. (1986). *Informed consent: A tutorial*. Owings Mill, MD: Rynd Communications.

Herman, J.L., Morris, L.L., and Fitz-Gibbon, C.T. (1987). *Evaluator's handbook*. Newbury Park, CA: Sage.

House, E.R. (1986). Internal evaluation. *Evaluation Practice*, 7 (1), 63–64.

Jones, J.H. (1981). *Bad blood: The Tuskegee syphilis experiment*. New York: Free Press.

Kennedy, M.M. (1983). The role of the in-house evaluator. *Evaluation Review*, 7 (4), 519–541.

Kimmel, A.J. (1988) *Ethics and values in applied social research*. Beverly Hills, CA: Sage.

Korchin, S.J., and Cowan, P.A. (1982). Ethical perspectives in clinical research. In P.C. Kendall and J.N. Butcher (eds.), *Handbook of research methods in clinical psychology*. New York: Wiley.

Krejcie, R.V., and Morgan, D.W. (1970). Determining sample size for research activities. *Educational and Psychological Measurement*, 30, 607–610.

Kytle, J., and Millman, E.J. (1986). Confessions of two applied researchers in search of principles. *Evaluation and Program Planning*, 9, 167–177.

Lifton, R.J. (1986). *The Nazi doctors: Medical killing and the psychology of genocide*. New York: Basic Books.

Mathison, S. (1991). Role conflicts for internal evaluators. *Evaluation and Program Planning*, 14, 173–179.

McCall, C. (1980). *Sampling and statistics handbook for research in education: A technical reference for members of the research staff of the National Education Association and its state and local Affiliated Association*. Washington, DC: National Educational Association.

McLemore, J.R., and Neumann, J.E. (1987). The inherently political nature of program evaluators and evaluation research. *Evaluation and Program Planning*, 10 (1), 83–94.

Moore, D. (1985). *Statistics: concepts and controversies*. New York: Freeman.

Monahan, J. (1980). *Who is the client? The ethics of psychological intervention in the criminal justice system*. Washington, DC: American Psychological Association.

Morris, M., and Cohn, R. (1993). Program evaluators and ethical challenges. *Evaluation Review*, 17 (6), 621–642.

Muscatello, D.B. (1989). Evaluation and the management process. *Evaluation Practice*, 10 (3), 12–17.

Patton, M.Q. (1982). *Practical evaluation.* Beverly Hills, CA: Sage.

Siebert, J.E., and Stanley, B. (1988). Ethical and professional dimensions of socially sensitive research. *American Psychologist, 43* (1), 49–55.

Sonnichsen, R.C. (1989). Program managers: Victims or victors in the evaluation process. *Evaluation and the federal decision maker.* New Directions for Program Evaluation, no. 41. San Francisco, CA: Jossey–Bass.

Thompson, R.J. (1989). Evaluator as power broker: Issues in the Maghreb. *International innovations in evaluation methodology.* New Directions for Program Evaluation. San Francisco, CA: Jossey–Bass.

Thyer, B.A. (1992). Promoting evaluation research in the field of family preservation. In E.S. Morton and R.K. Grigsby (eds.), *Advancing family preservation practice* (pp. 131–149). Newbury Park, CA: Sage.

Wise, R.I. (1980). *The evaluator as educator.* New Directions for Program Evaluation, no. 5. San Francisco, CA: Jossey–Bass.

Worthen, B., and White, K. (1987). *Evaluating educational and social programs: Guidelines for proposal review, onsite evaluation, evaluation contracts, and technical assistance.* Boston, MA: Kluwer–Nijhoff.

ELEVEN

Making Sense of
Evaluation Data

We are an intelligent species, and the use of our intelligence quite properly gives us pleasure. In this respect the brain is like a muscle. When it is in use we feel very good. Understanding is joyous.

— Carl Sagan, *Broca's Brain* (1979)

Once you have gathered all the information that you intend to collect, the next step is to examine it. This phase of the evaluation process is not unlike the experience of a paleontologist who walks along a dry riverbed and detects a small, oddly shaped fragment. As the loose sand is brushed away, more and more of the object is revealed until it is no longer a tiny fragment of fossil, but the fossilized femur of a dinosaur. A little more excavation and another piece is found and then another, until the whole skeleton is uncovered.

What evaluators seek is very similar—we want to be able to assemble bits of data into a logical structure, a meaningful pattern that gives us insight into the workings of a program that previously may never have been exposed to scientific scrutiny.

Just as paleontologists do not usually find a complete skeleton, evaluators must often be content with data that is incomplete. Sometimes we must take surrogate and even tangential bits of data and construct information from them.

The purpose of data analysis is to answer the questions that were the catalyst for the program evaluation. If there were hypotheses to be tested, analysis of data informs as to whether the hypotheses are supported by the data. We condense information (sometimes massive amounts of data) until meaningful patterns, trends, or relationships emerge.

Regardless of the program you are evaluating, it is very likely that at some point you will need to use one or more statistical procedures. There will be times when you will want to conclude there were statistically significant differences between pre- and posttests or between the control and intervention groups. If the differences between groups are markedly different (say 45 percent of those in the control group are successful compared to 83 percent of those in the intervention group), it may be possible to conclude that the intervention was an unqualified success, and perhaps no one will challenge it. However, what if the intervention group had only five participants and the control group was based on scores from two hundred different individuals? Would you still feel secure about concluding that the intervention was an unqualified success? In computing a probability level, statistical procedures take into account the number of individuals and the variation in their scores. Most evaluators cannot determine if observed differences between groups are statistically significant by visual observation and mental calculations.

The argument for using statistical procedures in analyzing data is that the data coupled with appropriate research designs provide objective evidence that the program was or wasn't successful—information not dependent upon the evaluators' whims or judgment. Avoiding the use of statistical procedures when they are needed not only is amateurish but also suggests incompetence. Statistical procedures lend credibility and professionalism to your final report. Even though your audience may not understand what a t-test is or how to compute a chi square, your usage of these statistical procedures helps you to determine if differences are "real" and helps your audience to have faith in your ability and expertise. In some instances, the use of statistical procedures may help defuse hostility by removing an element of subjectivity.

If large amounts of data are collected and need to be analyzed, you may want to use a computer to help with management and analysis of the data. Preparing data to be entered into the computer is not difficult and can be easily learned. Descriptive terms (like *male* or *female*) are converted to numerical values (0, 1) for computer processing. (For a lengthier explanation of how to code data for machine processing, refer to chapter 9 in Royse, 1995.)

While there are many statistical software programs to choose from, the *Statistical Package for the Social Sciences* (SPSS) is one found on most large computers used by universities. (It can also be purchased for personal computers.) But before you can begin discussing how to analyze data on the computer, you need to know how to make sense of data. This is explained in the following sections.

UNIVARIATE ANALYSIS

Univariate analysis looks at one variable at a time. There are several reasons for doing this. First, you might want to know how many respondents with a certain characteristic have been obtained. (If you were concerned with the variable of marital status, you may want to know how many questionnaires have been completed by divorced respondents. If the sample is too small, the evaluator may decide to increase it.) The examination of the variables one at a time can sometimes indicate that a certain group of individuals was inadvertently missed or that the range of responses was compressed (all of the possible responses were not represented). Univariate analysis helps the evaluator develop a "feel" for the data. Typically, the data are arranged in either ascending or descending order to facilitate finding "gaps" or missing values. Univariate analysis begins the process of making sense of data collected for a program evaluation.

All too frequently, evaluators who have only a cursory knowledge of analysis think they have analyzed the data when all they have done is to report what data were obtained. We once came across an "evaluation" of a program that consisted of more than thirty pages of data that looked something like that in table 11.1.

The pretest and posttest values were average scores on a five point scale where 1 = poor, 3 = fair, and 5 = great. Respondents had been asked to evaluate training that they had received at a series of workshops held around the state. The data were arranged by date and locality in which the training was provided. While the "evaluator" had listed the questions used in the final evaluation report, there was no information on the reliability or validity of any scale(s) contained on the instrument.

Not only is thirty pages of such data tedious to wade through, it is also difficult to know what to conclude. For instance, are the increases shown in table 11.1 (e.g., Q2 increases from 3.20 to 3.60 under the column headed Parents) statistically significant? If they are not statistically significant, then they are not really increases at all but represent scores that

263

Table 11.1
Evaluation Summary

	Parents		Professional Staff	
	Pretest n = 62	Posttest n = 47	Pretest n = 32	Posttest n = 24
Q1	3.24	4.54	3.50	4.30
Q2	3.20	3.60	3.80	4.50
Q3	3.70	3.90	3.50	4.20
Q4	2.80	3.10	2.00	2.30
Q5	2.50	2.22	2.00	3.30
Q6	2.30	2.80	2.22	2.45
Q7	2.60	4.70	3.40	4.00
Q8	3.40	4.00	4.40	5.00
Q9	2.10	1.75	4.50	2.60

are essentially equivalent. What the "evaluator" did not realize is that it is the *overall* scores and not the item-by-item scores on an instrument that should be used for analysis. It is the *collection of items* that makes an instrument reliable. Any one item may or may not be useful for detecting significant change or improvement. In this instance, the evaluators concluded (I suppose by visual inspection) that the training increased participants' knowledge "in all areas—indicating that the training sessions were effective." This conclusion could very well be unwarranted. The evaluator does not know (nor does the reader of the evaluation report know) if participants' scores were significantly improved. This can only be learned when a statistical test is employed. Further, unless we know more about the instrument, it is entirely possible that it was unreliable. Perhaps it would show improvement even when another more reliable instrument would not. In this instance, how important would the evaluators' findings be? What effect do you think the loss of subjects between the pretest and posttest would have?

Analysis is more than displaying the responses or data that were obtained. Look, for instance, at the example of data display in figure 11.1.

These data look as if they could be test results of some kind. However, until we know more about the data it is extremely difficult to interpret what these numbers may indicate. Could these be the ages of persons in a nursing home? The weights of a class of fifth graders? The I.Q. scores of children enrolled in a remedial math class? Let's assume that they are the results of a final examination in an undergraduate research class. Knowing this much, we now may develop a strategy for trying to

Figure 11.1
Data Display

88	94	66	73	81
77	78	65	97	69
73	90	90	94	82
75	87	79	99	74
86	91	75	85	91

understand the data. We might, for instance, array the data in terms of the highest and lowest scores (figure 11.2).

By simply arraying the data, we can easily identify that the highest score was 99 and that the lowest was 65. Further, if we knew that grades were awarded according to the following scheme,

$$A = 100 - 91$$
$$B = 90 - 81$$
$$C = 80 - 71$$
$$D = 70 - 61$$

then figure 11.3 informs us that there are six A's, eight B's, eight C's, and three D's on this particular test.

Generally, we start analysis by looking at the data one variable at a time (univariate analysis) to see what we have. Often, evaluators use computers to array their data. An ordered array of data showing the number of instances each value occurs is called a **frequency distribution.** Note in the example in table 11.2 that the data have been grouped by response category.

From even a cursory glance, we can determine that very few respondents (about 3 percent) gave the program a poor rating. In fact, almost half of the respondents gave the program a good rating. By combining those who rated the program either "Good" or "Excellent," we could determine that 81 percent of respondents were pleased with the program.

In the next example, table 11.3, you can see how a frequency distribution (univariate analysis) can help you to understand who has been included and who may be missing from your sample. We can see that there are many more older than younger respondents. Note that there are no respondents between the ages of twenty-two and thirty. In fact, the median age for this sample is sixty-one years. If the clients in your program are known to be much younger, a distribution like this may suggest that the sample is biased—that the younger clients' opinions are not reflected to the degree one might expect.

Figure 11.2
An Array of Sources

	Figure 11.3	
99		99
97	"A" Range	97
94		94
94		94
91		91
91		91
90		90
90		90
88	"B" Range	88
87		87
86		86
85		85
82		82
81		81
79		79
78		78
77		77
75	"C" Range	75
75		75
74		74
73		73
73		73
69		69
66	"D" Range	66
65		65

Besides wanting to understand who responded and who didn't (the make-up of your sample), another reason for looking at each variable individually is to determine if any errors were made in preparing or recording the data. This would be immediately obvious, in table 11.3,

Table 11.2
Client Ratings of Quality of Program

("How would you rate the quality of our outpatient program?")

Rating	Frequency	Percent	Cumulative Percent
Excellent	173	33.0	33.0
Good	254	48.4	81.4
Fair	80	15.2	96.6
Poor	18	3.4	100.0
Total	525	100.0	

for instance, if you knew that there were no fifteen-year-olds in the outpatient program. The fifteen-year-old listed there may have been a fifty-one-year-old for whom the digits were transposed. Before further analysis is done with this variable, the correct age should be checked on the original questionnaire.

There are times when an evaluator is limited to univariate analysis. On these occasions, frequency distributions provide arrays for understanding the range of scores and the number of cases or respondents associated with each value. Another advantage of having a computer produce frequency distributions is that the evaluator can request measures of central tendency such as the mean, median, or mode. The **mean** is the arithmetic average of scores. This is useful for understanding the "typical" case or client. However, the mean can easily be distorted when there are a few extreme scores.

Table 11.3
Respondents' Ages

Age	Frequency	Percent	Cumulative Percent
15	1	1.8	1.8
22	2	3.6	5.5
30	1	1.8	7.3
32	1	1.8	9.1
34	2	3.6	12.7
38	1	1.8	14.5
39	1	1.8	16.4
42	1	5.5	18.2
43	1	1.8	20.0
44	3	5.5	25.5
48	2	3.6	29.1
52	3	5.5	34.5
57	2	3.6	38.2
58	4	7.3	45.5
61	3	5.5	50.9
64	2	3.6	54.5
65	5	5.5	63.6
66	2	3.6	67.3
67	2	3.6	70.9
68	2	3.6	74.5
70	5	9.0	83.6
71	2	3.6	87.3
72	3	5.5	92.7
75	3	5.5	98.2
81	1	1.8	100.0

For instance, in table 11.3, the mean is 56.96 years if the fifteen-year-old is a legitimate respondent, but 57.62 if the respondent is coded as a fifty-one-year-old. However, the **median**, as the middle value in a frequency distribution, remains unchanged at sixty-one. The median position is that value half-way between the top and the bottom. Since there are fifty-five respondents in table 11.3, we can locate the median by counting down from the top to the twenty-eighth case or from the bottom up to the twenty-eighty case. The **mode** is the most common category or value. In table 11.3 there are two modes, sixty-five and seventy. The data would be described as being bi-modal.

The mean is easily distorted in the presence of extreme values. In the next example, note that the mean of 28.57 years is not representative of the bulk of the respondents. In fact, only one of them is older than twenty-eight, and that individual is considerably older. When data are obviously skewed in a small sample like that in table 11.4, the median provides a more accurate portrait than the mean.

In addition to the mean, median, and mode, another univariate

Table 11.4
Small Sample Distribution of Ages

Age	Frequency	
17	1	
18	1	
19	1	
20	1	< Median = 20
21	1	
22	1	
83	1	< Mean = 28.57

Table 11.5
Sample of Clients' Ages

Age	Frequency	Percent
20	1	10
27	2	20
28	1	10
30	1	10
33	1	10
36	1	10
39	1	10
41	2	20
Total	10	100%

statistic, the standard deviation, should be included when preparing tables and reporting data. The **standard deviation** is a measure of variability that provides information about how much scores tend to differ from each other and the mean.

In table 11.5, the standard deviation is 7.0, and the mean is 32.2. In normally distributed data, where the mean and median are situated close together on a bell-shaped curve, 68 percent of the observations fall within one standard frequency of the mean—half of these (34%) fall above and half (34%) fall below the mean. Ninety-five percent of the observations fall within two standard deviations of the mean, and 99.7 percent fall within three standard deviations. The standard deviation is small when the deviations from the mean are small and larger when the observed values tend to be far from the mean. Note that table 11.5 also shows the number of cases on which each percentage is based—many journals require this in their tables. Means, medians, and standard deviations may not be interpreted easily if you do not know the theoretical range of possible scores that could be obtained with that instrument (another reason for becoming familiar with the literature before you begin an evaluation).

BIVARIATE ANALYSIS

Once you have edited the data, corrected any mistakes, and learned what you can from the univariate analysis, you are ready to begin looking at variables two at a time. This is called **bivariate analysis** of data. Evaluators look at variables two at a time to test hypotheses or to examine the strength of associations.

Consider, for example, a specially funded program designed to provide information about the transmission of AIDS to a population considered to be at "high risk" for contracting AIDS. The evaluator conducts pretests and posttests using a reliable instrument that measures knowledge about AIDS transmission. The evaluator has a series of pretest and posttest scores that look very much like the data in table 11.6. Looking at these scores as they would be arrayed in a single frequency distribution would not help the evaluator to know if the program participants were actually more knowledgeable after receiving the educational presentation. To test the hypothesis that there was an improvement in knowledge after the presentation, the scores need to be separated into two groups: pretest and posttest. Then the evaluator can attempt to determine if any observed differences in the average scores are statistically significant.

You can tell by looking at table 11.6 that the intervention group improved its average score by 20 points from the time of the pretest to

Table 11.6
Average Scores from an AIDS Education Presentation

	Pretest Score	Posttest Score
Intervention Group (n = 46)	65	85
Control Group (n = 115)	64	70

the posttest. However, the control group (who got no intervention) also showed some improvement. As an evaluator, you want to know whether the intervention group made significantly more improvement than the control group. In order to determine if there are important differences between the groups at posttest, the evaluator will need to conduct a **t-test**, a statistical procedure for comparing differences between two groups. The t-test can be computed manually or on a mainframe or a personal computer using statistical software. For instance, the procedure "t-test" in SPSS produces a summary report with a probability statement regarding the likelihood that the scores obtained from the two groups could have occurred by chance.

Usually, social scientists are interested in finding probabilities of .05 or less. Conducting a t-test and discovering a probability level of less than .05 would indicate that the average posttest scores for the control and intervention groups were not similar—that the intervention group's scores had improved quite a bit more than the control group's scores. In other words, there were real differences between the control and intervention groups at the time of the posttest. Further, it would be unlikely that the differences between the scores would have happened by chance alone. A probability of .04 would mean that differences in the two groups' average scores would have occurred by chance only 4 times out of 100.

Had the evaluator been able to randomly assign subjects to the experimental and control groups, it would not be necessary to conduct a t-test to determine if the two groups were equivalent at the time of the pretest. However, when random assignment is not possible and the evaluator is using a nonequivalent control group design, then a t-test could be used to establish that the groups were similar or equivalent at the beginning of the study.

Note that the t-test can be applied only on quantitative data measured at the **interval level** of measurement. These variables are sometimes described as being continuous—variables such as weight, age, and scores from tests and scales. Intervals of equal length are required (the difference between 173 pounds and 172 pounds is the same as the difference between 101 and 100 pounds).

Different t-tests are available. If you were comparing pretest scores from a compulsive eating inventory administered to patients in one program with the pretest scores obtained from patients in a different hospital, you would use an independent samples version of the t-test. The independent samples version would also be used with the example in table 11.6, when the posttests of the control group were being compared to the posttests of the intervention group (two different groups are being compared). However, if you want to see if the 64 pretest average and the 70 posttest average for the control group is a statistically significant improvement, you need to use the paired samples version of the t-test (because the t-test is being conducted on only one sample where pre- and posttest scores are matched).

Sometimes evaluation designs require more than two groups. For instance, you might have a control group (no intervention), a group receiving intensive intervention, and another group receiving a less intense intervention. (Or, you might compare a control group with groups receiving inpatient and outpatient treatment.) When there are more than two groups, the t-test cannot be used. Instead, a statistical procedure known as **one-way analysis of variance** is used. (The SPSS command is "one way.") This procedure is similar to the t-test, and the computer printout will provide mean scores for each group and a probability statement like the one produced with a t-test.

While the t-test and one-way analysis of variance are versatile tools for the evaluator to use, mention must also be made of **chi-square**. Chi square is another useful statistical procedure to use when doing bivariate analysis and the procedure of choice when the data are not interval but nominal. **Nominal data** are measured by categories—as when we classify people based on descriptive categorization (e.g., Democrat or Republican, Vietnam veteran, American Indian).

Let's assume that you are evaluating a program where numerical scores are not available. However, the staff have a well-established procedure for determining, at the point of closing a case, those clients for whom the intervention was successful and those for whom it was not successful. The new director asks you to draw a random sample of clients in the outpatient program and to determine the proportion who have successful outcomes.

Examining a sample of two hundred cases closed in the last six months, you find the following pattern:

271

Client Outcome	Cases	Percent
Successful	126	63%
Unsuccessful	74	37%
Total	200	100%

In this example, we are looking at only one variable, client outcome, that is measured by the categories of success or lack of success. This dependent variable is measured at the nominal level. As you share this data with the new executive director, she asks if you can determine if the program is more successful with female than with male clients. If we were to test the hypothesis that the staff were more successful with females than with males, chi square would be the appropriate statistic to use. The easiest way to compute this is to enter the data into a computer and use the computer to make statistical computations. In the SPSS program, a simple command like "crosstabs tables = success by sex" will produce a table like 11.7 and the corresponding chi square statistics.

It is difficult to tell by looking at table 11.7 whether there may be a statistically significant difference in the male and female success rates. We cannot conclude that there is a statistical difference in success rates without computing the chi square. In this example, the chi square is very low (less than 1), and the associated probability level is .54, which

Table 11.7
Cross-tabulation of Program Outcomes by Gender

Client Outcome	Female		Male
		I	
		+	
		I	
Successful	75	I	51
	(65%)	I	(60%)
		+	
		I	
Unsuccessful	40	I	34
		I	
	(35%)	I	(40%)
		+	
Total	115	I	85

	Chi square	d.f.	Significance Level
	.37	1	.54

Table 11.8
A t-test for Examining Success by Number of Treatment Episodes

Variable	Number	Mean	F Value	2-Tail Proba- bility	Pooled Variance Estimate t- value	Probability	Separate Variance Estimate t- value	Probability
Group 1 (Failure)	74	4.08						
			7.01	.000	12.0	.000	14.65	.000
Group 2 (Success)	126	12.44						

indicates that there is no statistically significant difference between the success (or failure) rates in this sample of male and female clients (p <.05 would mean there was statistical significance).

Now let's suppose that as you share this information with the executive director she tells you her hypothesis that clients with successful outcomes received more treatment than those who were not judged to be successful. To test this hypothesis you would use a t-test, because the dependent variable of interest is the number of treatment episodes (a variable measured at the interval level).

Table 11.8 shows that, on the average, clients with successful outcomes received 12.4 episodes of treatment, while unsuccessful clients received 4 episodes. We can understand whether the differences between these two groups are statistically significant by looking at the entry under "2-Tail Probability." Since the probability of obtaining the F value that was actually produced is less than .05, we can assume that the variances within each of the groups are not similar. Therefore, we should go to the t-value under the heading of "Separate Variance Estimate." Looking under that column, we find that the probability associated with that t-value would have occurred by chance less than 1 time in 1,000. In other words, the average number of treatment episodes received by the successful clients and the unsuccessful clients is statistically significant (p <.001). (Had the 2-tail probability been larger than .05, we would have used the t-value associated with the "Pooled Variance Estimate.")

If we were interested in going a step farther, we could test the hypothesis that successful women clients received more intervention than successful men. Once again, we would use a "t-test" command that would produce a printout like that in table 11.9.

We can see in table 11.9 that the successful female clients did in fact receive more intervention than the male clients. Successful female clients averaged thirteen treatment episodes compared to slightly over

273

Table 11.9
T-test for Examining Clients' Successful Treatment Episodes by Sex

Variable	Number	Mean	F Value	2-Tail Proba- bility	Pooled Variance Estimate		Separate Variance Estimate	
					t-value	Probability	t-value	Probability
Group 1 (Female)	75	13.2						
			1.37	.24	1.83	.07	1.88	.06
Group 2 (Male)	51	11.3						

eleven for successful male clients. These differences are only marginally significant, because a probability level of .07 exceeds the standard criterion of .05.

MULTIVARIATE ANALYSIS OF DATA

Multivariate analysis of data usually refers to the use of such procedures as multivariate analysis of variance, multiple regression, and discriminant analysis—subjects taught in intermediate level statistics courses. However, we can begin to understand the usefulness of a multivariate perspective by constructing a table that will allow us to examine three variables at once.

Let's assume that you have conducted an evaluation and presented the findings to your executive director. At this point, another question is raised, perhaps because a client complained about services in one of the agency's three satellite offices. The executive director suspects problems with one of the offices, because complaints tend to come primarily from that geographical area and only rarely from the other two sites. She asks you to look at the success rate for men and women clients for each of the agency's three locations. Table 11.10 provides an illustration of a table that presents three variables at one time.

As can be seen in table 11.10, 87 percent of the males receiving an intervention in Area 1 had a successful outcome—the best rate for either sex in any of the three areas. Males fared the poorest in Area 3, where only 41 percent had successful outcomes. Females did almost equally well in areas 1 and 2, and like males, did the poorest in Area 3. Overall, 40 percent of the male clients experienced a successful outcome compared to 60 percent of the females. Not only did the evaluator find that some locations seemed to be more successful with males than with females, it is also apparent that there are fewer successful clients produced at the Area 3 office than in the other two locations. Areas 1 and 2 were successful with a majority of their clients, but Area 3 was not.

Evaluators and researchers must be vigilant in their search for **extraneous variables** (variables which may be overlooked and not included in a study or evaluation but which influence the findings). Table 11.10 demonstrates how an evaluator concerned only with the dependent variable of a program's overall success rate could be missing an opportunity to provide additional and valuable information to the program director. By controlling for the extraneous variables of location and gender, the evaluator provides the program director with a better understanding of how and where the program succeeds. In order to further improve the agency's success rate, the director will need to focus on increasing the number of successes in Area 3. By anticipating that success may differ by location and client gender, the evaluator has improved the usefulness of the evaluation report. Armed with this information, the program director may want to test hypotheses or notions about why males have fewer successes than females or why the success rate is so low in Area 3 (e.g., poor morale, inadequate supervision, staff in need of training).

The evaluator can anticipate extraneous variables by keeping in mind that success with clients is seldom uniformly distributed across all clients. Evaluators need to speculate about the characteristics of clients who would be likely to show the least and the most progress. Programs may be differentially effective depending upon clients' education, financial and social resources, and so on. Besides the clients' characteristics, the evaluator ought to consider any relevant factor which could interact with the intervention or have an influence upon it. By identifying these

Table 11.10
Successful Outcomes by Gender and Location

	Area 1	Area 2	Area 3	Row Total
Male Clients	23	25	37	136
Successes—Male	20	16	15	51
Percent of Male Clients	(87%)	(64%)	(41%)	(40%)
Female Clients	39	45	31	115
Successes—Female	26	31	18	75
Percent of Female Clients	(67%)	(69%)	(58%)	(60%)
Total Clients	62	70	68	200
Successes—Total	46	47	33	126
Overall Success Rate	(74%)	(67%)	(49%)	(63%)

variables and collecting information on them, the evaluator is able to comprehend the extent of their influence and produce an evaluation report containing real analysis.

MYTHS ABOUT STATISTICAL SIGNIFICANCE

There are very few researchers or evaluators who would not love to find "statistically significant" differences when they push the raw data they've been collecting all those many months through their statistical software programs. We've gone to some lengths to explain levels of measurement and the associated statistical procedures so that you will be able to detect any statistically significant differences between or among the groups in your study. However, in the quest to find $p < .05$, we do well to keep in mind that *slight differences may be statistically significant, but not clinically significant.*

For example, imagine a group of thirty clients who are suffering from anxiety problems. They are administered the Clinical Anxiety Scale (see chapter 9) prior to the start of an intervention and then again after six weeks. A paired-samples t-test (because each individual's pretest is compared with his or her posttest) results in the data shown in table 11.11.

The Clinical Anxiety Scale is designed so that a score of 30 is a clinical cutting score (indicative of a problem). From table 11.11 we can observe that at pretest the group as a whole showed a high level of anxiety—well above the cutting score. And, we can see that there is a statistically significant reduction in anxiety. Unfortunately, the data suggest that while a few clients may have shown major improvement, the group as a whole was still experiencing severe levels of anxiety at the point of the posttest. Clinically, if one were to observe this sample of clients in a formal treatment program, they would have many of the same symptoms and problems that they had at the pretest—practically speaking, there was no meaningful improvement. By way of another

Table 11.11
Comparison of Pre- and Posttest Anxiety Scores
(paired samples t-test)

	Mean	Standard Deviation	t-value	df	Probability
Pretest	49.6	10.37			
n = 30			4.94	29	$p < .001$
Posttest	46.8	9.65			

example, Weinrott, Jones, and Howard (1982) reported that youths in one type of group home had a mean GPA of 1.7 and that a comparison group had a mean GPA of 1.4. While the difference between their GPAs was statistically significant, it was educationally negligible.

So, while evaluators must look for statistical significance as a means of determining when a program is effective, they must also ask the important question regarding outcome: Are clients better off because of the intervention? Statistical significance is influenced by the size of the sample. Trivial differences in small groups can become statistically significant if the sample size is increased sufficiently. When we are working with very large samples, there is some risk that we could discover statistically significant relationships that are inconsequential in terms of whether real changes have occurred.

There are several ways to deal with this problem. One approach is to compute a reliable change index (Jacobson et al., 1984; Christensen and Mendoza, 1986; Jacobson and Truax, 1991), which subtracts clients' pretest scores from their posttest scores and divides that value by the standard error of difference between the two test scores. Any reliable change index larger than 1.96 would be unlikely to result (p < .05) without actual change taking place (Jacobson and Truax, 1991).

To compute this criterion for improvement, you need the standard deviation of the control group and pretreatment experimental group, the test-retest reliability of the instrument, the individual pretest (x_1) and posttest (x_2) scores, and this formula (Jacobson and Truax, 1991):

$$RC = \frac{x_2 - x_1}{S_{diff}}$$

Where $S_{diff} = \sqrt{2(S_E)^2}$ and $S_E = $ Std dev $\sqrt{1 - \text{reliablity}}$

Another method for weighing the importance of statistically significant findings is to examine the amount or proportion of variance in the dependent variable that is explained by one or more of the independent variables. This value can then be used to make judgments about substantive improvement or change.

With t-tests, the proportion of variance (PVE) explained can be computed with the following formula:

$$r^2 = \frac{t^2}{t^2 + df}$$

Using the data supplied in table 11.12, take the t-value of 2.64, square it $(2.64^2 = 6.97)$, divide that by 32.22 (6.97 + 25.25), and end up

277

Table 11.12
Satisfaction with Quality of Life, Posttest Scores

| | Cases | Mean | Std Dev | Pooled Variance | | |
				t-value	df	Probability
Treatment Group	18	151	20.8			
Control Group	20	117	53.0	– 2.64	25.25	.01

with .22. If you could be certain that the intervention were exerting an effect, at most, 22 percent of the variance in CAS scores could be accounted for by the intervention (pretest/posttest comparison). The intervention might account for less, but most likely would not be responsible for more than 22 percent. Given a study that you were not able to control perfectly, you cannot usually claim that the intervention caused the change, but using the PVE statistic, you can calculate the maximum possible influence of the intervention *if* it were responsible for the observed changes.

Similar formulas for computing the proportion of variance explained are available for chi square and the test statistic F (see Rubin and Conway, 1985). These statistics are equivalent to a squared Eta, a squared Pearson correlation, a squared Phi coefficient, or a squared multiple correlation coefficient in terms of assessing improvement due to intervention. (Further references that may be helpful to you include Hudson, Thyer and Stocks, 1985; Cohen and Cohen, 1983; and Freidman, 1968.)

UNDERSTANDING TRENDS

Assume that you are evaluating a community's intervention program for persons who have been arrested the first time for driving while under the influence (DUI). After some deliberation, you decide that the best measure of the effectiveness of the intervention is the number of persons who are rearrested for DUI. Accordingly, you begin to gather your data. A pattern is revealed as you examine the data over a five-year period.

In table 11.13, we observe that while the number of DUIs remains about the same over the five-year period, it appears that the intervention is less effective over time. However, a number of alternative explanations are possible. First, the police may have added staff or are making a greater effort to arrest drunken drivers. Second, since there are more cars on the road with mobile phones, it is possible that more citizens are calling the police when they spot an inebriated driver—resulting in more drinking drivers being arrested. Third, judges and magistrates may be less inclined to dismiss charges of DUI. Without a control group, it is difficult to understand the increasing number of those who are rearrested each year for DUI.

Let's add a control group to the example. By examining DUIs and rearrests in another similar sized community, we might be able to better comprehend the trends in our own community (table 11.14).

While it is entirely possible that a greater proportion of DUIs in Community A are being rearrested than when the program first began, data from Community B reflects a similar pattern of a greater percentage of DUI drivers being rearrested. The conclusion that the program is becoming less effective over time does not seem to be warranted. To understand why rearrests are increasing, the evaluator could look at whether the number of police or car phones increased over the five-year period or determine if there were changes in legislation (such as lowering illegal blood alcohol levels from .10 to .08) that would affect the total number of DUI arrests.

In trying to make sense of trends, you must also be alert to seasonal trends or variations. We once examined the productivity of professional staff in a community mental health center after the installation of a new reporting system. We found that while the amount of client counseling showed dramatic improvement almost immediately after the new system began in August, productivity fell during a two-week period at Christmas. (This is understandable because fewer clients had problems during that period and a large percentage of therapists took vacation time and were not available.) After Christmas, productivity climbed some, then fell considerably during a period of extremely bad winter weather. But once again, productivity increased steadily reaching a high for the year during the second week of May.

Table 11.13
DUIs and Rearrests, 1991–1995

	Number of DUIs	Program Recipients Rearrested
1991	385	31 (8%)
1992	380	38 (10%)
1993	377	38 (12%)
1994	390	55 (14%)
1995	372	60 (16%)

Table 11.14
DUI Rearrests during the Years 1991–1995

	Community A			Community B	
Year	Number of DUIs	Rearrested		Number of DUIs	Rearrested
1991	385	31 (8%)		340	48 (14%)
1992	380	38 (10%)		336	47 (14%)
1993	377	45 (12%)		351	53 (15%)
1994	390	55 (14%)		344	59 (17%)
1995	372	60 (16%)		360	70 (19%)

At that point, some staff were ready to give credit for the increased level of productivity to the new reporting system. However, if you look closely at figure 11.4, you may see another explanation. Productivity may tend to be higher in the warm months of spring (March, April, May) than in the middle of summer or winter. What figure 11.4 may represent

Figure 11.4
Individual Counseling Productivity: Advent of Management
Information System

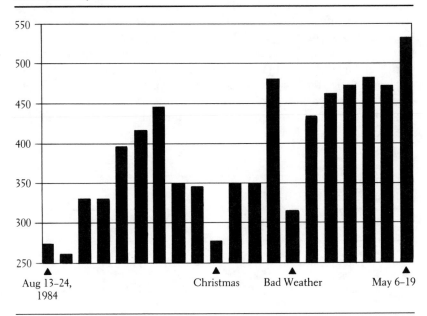

is a seasonal variation in productivity which may have been present under the old reporting system as well. There are not enough data provided to conclude that productivity is higher in May than it was in May of the prior year, for example. Even though there are twenty different measurements of productivity (corresponding to bi-monthly pay periods), the period of time covered is less than a year. We would be in a better position to conclude that productivity had significantly increased if we were able to compare with data from the previous year. If we think about the period of time necessary to observe an intervention or program change as a "window," the larger the window the better chance we have of accurately comprehending the effects of that intervention or program change. It is almost always better to look through a larger window (look at more data) than to assess a potential trend by looking through too small a window (not enough data).

We run the risk of erroneously concluding that we understand a phenomenon or a trend even when we view very little of it. For instance, the data in table 11.15 were obtained from eight different Big Brother/ Big Sister agencies on the percent of persons who followed through with an application after initially making an inquiry about the process (Roaf, Tierney, and Hunte, 1994). What might you conclude if your sample had included only data from Agency D? Agency H?

USING STATISTICS IN REPORTS

Just as it is possible to fail to use statistics when they are needed, it is also possible to inundate the readers of your evaluation report with too much data—too many tables—and to cite the results of too many statistical tests. It is vitally important that you consider the audience who will be reading your evaluation report. You should not write over their heads

Table 11.15
Adults Making Application as a Percent of All Inquiries

Agency A	42.1%
Agency B	53.2%
Agency C	44.2%
Agency D	21.9%
Agency E	54.9%
Agency F	47.3%
Agency G	32.1%
Agency H	72.0%
Average	43.4%

Table 11.16
Marital Status of Respondents

	Number	Percent
Single	8	14.5
Married	28	50.9
Separated/Divorced	10	18.3
Widowed	9	16.3
Total	55	100.0

and present statistical information that they are not likely to understand. With some audiences, you may want to note that statistically significant differences were found and not report the actual t or X^2 values. Usually it is not necessary to show any formulae used in the calculation of statistics (unless you are writing for a group of university professors). Present information that is important for understanding the major findings— not everything contained in the computer printout.

Evaluators can get carried away with all of the information available to them. We saw a good example of this when a student was preparing a table of respondents' characteristics for a study she had completed. She could have simply reported the information on marital status as it is reflected in table 11.16. Instead, she unnecessarily complicated things by adding all the rest of the information obtained from the computer printout. She included such information as the standard deviation (.911), the kurtosis (−.439), the skewness (.518), the variance (.830), the median (2.0), the mean (2.33), the standard error (.124), and so forth. Such information makes very little sense when we are talking about the variable of marital status. (These statistics would make much more sense when variables are not discrete categories but instead are interval level data such as test scores.) Actually, the student could have reported the information without using a table.

There may be times when you will want to provide such information as standard deviations or skewness to your readers, but such technical information is not going to be digested easily by most lay audiences. One way to judge how much statistical detail to provide to your audience is to ask friends or colleagues to read your rough draft and give their opinion. Another way is to look at what information tends to be presented in research reports carried in the journal you read most.

Remembering that evaluation is applied research, evaluators must keep in mind the pragmatic aspects of the findings. Even some findings that are not statistically significant may be important to report—especially those that result in recommendations or suggestions to the management. One way to display data so that it can be easily digested by audiences is with graphics like bar charts and pie charts. A wide range of charts and graphs can be produced by statistical software programs.

Even without a computer, you can design striking charts manually that will help you to clarify numerical data. (See the references at the end of this chapter for suggestions of useful books.)

FINAL THOUGHTS

This chapter has provided an overview of how to start analyzing data. Obviously, there are many more sophisticated statistical procedures than could be presented here. Even if you don't have a computer at your disposal, some statistical procedures are relatively easy to compute manually. And, publications exist to assist you with this. (See, for example, Pilcher, 1990; DiLeonardi and Curtis, 1988; Weinback and Grinnell, 1995; or Craft, 1990.)

Sometimes students say that all they want to know about a program is whether the intervention correlated with successful outcomes. They anticipate that a correlation of .50 or so will convince the readers of their evaluation reports that the intervention was worthwhile. In fact, a **correlation** expresses only the amount or degree of relationship between two variables. For instance, we conducted a study and found a correlation of .51 between students' ages and the number of years of experience they had volunteering in social service agencies. Although .51 is a moderately strong correlation, only 26 percent of the variance in the dependent variable is explained by the independent variable. (The percentage of the variance explained is found by multiplying the correlation by itself.) Seventy-four percent of the interaction between the two variables was not explained.

What level of correlation can you expect in your studies? Nunnally (1978) noted that "correlations as high as .70 are rare, and the average of all correlations reported in the literature probably is less than .40" (p. 143). Rubin and Conway (1985) surveyed social work research literature and found that on the average 13 percent of dependent variable variance was explained; for evaluations of the effectiveness of clinical interventions it was approximately 10 percent.

There will be times when correlations are needed for program evaluations, but not often. Correlations indicate whether two variables are moving in the same direction—if the variables tend to increase or decrease together. They do not establish "proof" that one variable caused another. In the previous example, older students tended to have more

Figure 11.5
Sample Charts Generated by a Computer

Success Rates by Program

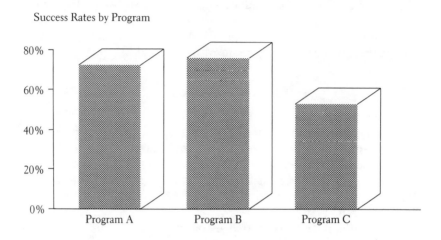

Clientele by Age Category

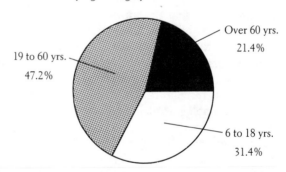

Success Rates by Program

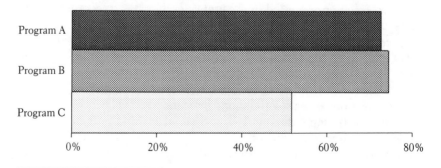

years of experience in social service agencies, but their age did not "cause" them to volunteer. Similarly, volunteer experience did not "cause" the respondents to grow older.

Although we did not want to overlook mentioning correlations (they are useful for helping to gauge the influence of an extraneous variable and for identifying hypotheses to be tested in-depth in subsequent studies), they are not particularly helpful in establishing that one program is better than another. Correlations are easy to generate on the computer and relatively easy to understand, but they are not a powerful enough tool for program evaluation purposes.

While it is more common for students of evaluation to fail to use statistical procedures when they are needed than to overuse them, readers are cautioned against computing a large number of correlations or other statistical tests just to hunt for "statistically significant" findings. If enough statistical tests are computed, some statistically significant differences will be produced.

Suppose you had one dependent variable (e.g., recidivism) and you indiscriminately correlate forty separate socio-demographic variables with this dependent variable. You could expect this "shotgun" approach would yield two statistically significant findings when significance is determined at the .05 level (i.e., .05 multiplied by 40 = 2). Even though these "significant" findings may not have been connected with the initial hypotheses or research questions, it sometimes is difficult to keep this in perspective when a bivariate test turns up something statistically significant. In your excitement over finding something statistically significant, you may forget that its occurrence was a fluke. The problem with conducting numerous bivariate tests is that a few significant results will occur if you conduct enough statistical tests, but such findings are likely to be related more to chance than to anything else. Avoid this problem by not computing correlations on all possible combinations of variables just to find something statistically significant. If you have many socio-demographic variables and you have no idea which of these will make the best predictors, use a more powerful statistical procedure (e.g., multiple regression analysis) to incorporate all of the variables simultaneously. However, even this method is no guarantee that all chance findings will be eliminated.

Finding significant differences just by chance is a **Type I error**. Type I errors lead you to conclude that a relationship exists between two variables (e.g., rejecting a null hypothesis) when there is no real relationship—merely a statistical fluke. Typically, we reduce the probability of making a Type I error by lowering the significance level. When it is terribly important to avoid making a Type I error, the traditional significance level of .05 can be lowered to .01 or less. However, by lowering the risk of a Type I error, the odds of making a Type II error are increased. In **Type II errors**, the null hypothesis is accepted when, in fact, there is a relationship between two variables.

In program evaluation and practice research, a Type II error is less problematic than a Type I because the Type II error claims that no difference exists between two groups (e.g., a treated one and an untreated one) when in reality a reliable difference (i.e., a statistically significant one) does exist. A Type I error is more problematic because it claims effective treatment when in reality the influence of the intervention could be clinically trivial.

Although social scientists seem to be more concerned with the risk of making Type I errors than Type II errors, it is possible to estimate the risk of committing a Type II error by using statistical power analysis. Tables have been prepared (Cohen, 1987) to enable evaluators to estimate the probability of committing a Type II error when using different statistical tests.

Statistical procedures are routinely used and, indeed, are essential for most evaluations based upon quantifiable data. However, the use of statistical procedures does not guarantee that the resulting information will be meaningful. It is quite possible that, because of the laws of probability, a few occurrences of statistical significance will be found when these findings have little value or meaning. Knowing that this is expected to happen when a large number of statistical tests have been produced will make it easier for the evaluator to discard them and to focus on the salient relationships. Don't be afraid to ask for statistical consultation when necessary.

QUESTIONS FOR CLASS DISCUSSION

1. How much change do you and the others in the class have in pockets or purses? List all these amounts on the board. Manually prepare a frequency distribution. What is the mean? Is this nominal or interval data?
2. Using the data obtained in question 1 as the dependent variable, think of independent variables that could be used for bivariate analysis of the data. How might the data be grouped in several of these bivariate analyses? Would a t-test, one-way analysis of variance, or chi square be the appropriate statistical test?
3. A student once conducted an evaluation and in a report began analyzing the data along this line:

Client A showed the most improvement. This is understandable in that he and his spouse seem to have ironed out the domestic difficulties which have plagued them for the past four years. Client B progressed less than other clients. Whether a coincidence or not, this client has not had an intimate relationship in the last five years. Client C made minimal progress, possibly because her boyfriend violated his parole and was returned to prison. Client D made great strides after acknowledging her earlier sexual trauma. Client E made minimal progress, possibly because her marriage of seventeen years broke up during this period. . . .

What is wrong with analyzing data in this manner? If the report consisted of only this type of information, would you conclude that there had been an analysis of the data?

4. Bring in examples of data from the agencies in which you have worked, interning or volunteering. Look for trends in the data. Are there peak periods or times when fewer clients seek services? What other variables are needed to better understand apparent patterns in the data?

5. Discuss knowledge of and experience with statistical software programs available for personal and mainframe computers. Which seem most user-friendly? Which are more powerful?

6. Look through journals, magazines, and newspapers in order to bring in examples of ways that data are summarized and reported in tables, charts, and graphs. Which examples are most easy to read, and which are the most difficult?

MINI-PROJECTS: EXPERIENCING EVALUATION FIRSTHAND

1. Visit the university computer center to learn what statistical software is available for their mainframe and personal computers. Are manuals for these programs in the library? Are consultants available to assist you in working with these programs? Summarize what you learned from this visit in a brief report.

2. Using either real or fictitious data, test a hypothesis using statistical software on a computer. Be sure to state your hypothesis, how your data were obtained (or if they were manufactured), and the statistical procedure used. Submit the corresponding printout, circling the most important items.

3. Find a journal article evaluating an intervention and read it for the statistical procedures used. Write a brief paper summarizing: the

outcome variable(s), the hypotheses tested, the statistical procedures used, and your reaction to the author's use of these tests. Were too many or not enough used? Were they appropriate? Did the report clearly benefit from the use of statistics? What could the author have concluded if no statistics had been used? Were the results clinically as well as statistically significant?

4. Locate a journal article that describes how a t-test was used to examine pretest-posttest differences in a group of clients and to obtain a "statistically significant difference." Calculate the PVE. Does the obtained PVE alter your interpretation of the phrase "statistically significant difference"?

REFERENCES AND RESOURCES

Christensen, L., and Mendoza, J.L. (1986). A method of assessing change in a single subject: An alteration of the RC index. *Behavior Therapy*, 17, 305–308.

Cohen, J. (1987). *Statistical power analysis for the behavioral sciences*. New York: Academic Press.

Cohen, J., and Cohen, P. (1983). *Applied multiple regression/correlation analysis for the behavioral sciences*. 2d ed. Hillsdale, NJ: Lawrence Erlbaum.

Craft, J.L. (1990). *Statistics and data analysis for social workers*. Itasca, IL: Peacock.

DiLeonardi, J.W., and Curtis, P.A. (1988). *What to do when the numbers are in: A user's guide to statistical data analysis in the human services*. Chicago, IL: Nelson–Hall.

Freiman, J.A., Chalmers, T.C., Smith, H., and Kuebler, R.R. (1978). The importance of Beta, the Type II error, and sample size in the design and interpretation of the randomized control trial. *New England Journal of Medicine*, 299, 690–694.

Freidman, H. (1968). Magnitude of experimental effect and a table for its rapid estimation. *Psychological Bulletin*, 70, 245–251.

Hudson, W.W., Thyer, B.A., and Stocks, J.T. (1986). Assessing the importance of experimental outcomes. *Journal of Social Service Research*, 8 (4), 87–98.

Jacobson, N.S., and Truax, P. (1991) Clinical significance: A statistical approach to defining meaningful change in psychotherapy research. *Journal of Consulting and Clinical Psychology*, 59, 12–19.

Jacobson, N.S., Follette, W.C., and Revenstorf, D. (1984). Psychotherapy outcome research: Methods for reporting variability and evaluating clinical significance. *Behavior Therapy*, 15, 336–352.

Kraemer, H.C., and Thiemann, S. (1987). *How many subjects? Statistical power analysis*. Beverly Hills, CA: Sage.

Mattaini, M.A. (1993). *More than a thousand words: Graphics for clinical practice*. Washington, DC: NASW Press.

Nunnally, J.C. (1978). *Psychometric theory*. New York: McGraw-Hill.

Pilcher, D.M. (1990). *Data analysis for the helping professions*. Beverly Hills, CA: Sage.

Roaf, P.A., Tierney, J.P., and Hunte, D.E.I. (1994). *Big brothers/big sisters: A study of volunteer recruitment and screening*. Philadelphia, PA: Public/ Private Ventures.

Royse, D. (1995). *Research methods for social workers, 2d ed.* Chicago, IL: Nelson-Hall.

Rubin, A., and Conway, P.G. (1985). Standards for determining the magnitude of relationships in social work research. *Social Work Research and Abstracts*, 21 (1), 34–39.

Thyer, B.A. (1987). Statistics and research. *Social Work*, 32(6), 552.

Weinbach, R.W. (1989). When is statistical significance meaningful? A practice perspective. *Journal of Sociology and Social Welfare*, 16 (1), 31–37.

Weinbach, R.W., and Grinnell, R.M. (1995). *Statistics for social workers*. White Plains, NY: Longman.

Weinrott, M.R., Jones, R.R., and Howard, J.R. (1982). Cost-effectiveness of teaching family programs for delinquents: Results of a national evaluation. *Evaluation Review*, 6 (2), 173–201.

TWELVE

Writing the Evaluation Report

Many evaluators dread writing the report summarizing their evaluation efforts. This may stem from not knowing what to report, where to begin, how much detail to give, or which style to use. However, if the outline in this chapter is followed, the final report should be complete and cover all major bases. The outline is one that professionals in the field can use when writing reports for their peers or such groups as boards of directors as well as one that graduate and undergraduate students can use when preparing evaluation reports. While some minor modification may be needed, the same basic structure is used whether one is writing a thesis, an evaluation report, or an article for a professional journal, or applying to a funding source for a grant.

MAJOR CONTENT AREAS

While there is merit in trying to find an evaluation report to use as a guide for writing your report, you could spend a considerable amount of time searching for a "good" one to use for a model. Even if you locate a report that you think might serve as a model, there is always the possibility that the report could be of questionable value. A "defective" model might be worse than not having one at all.

Evaluators vary enormously in their competence, and the quality

291

BOX 12.1
Major Content Areas for Evaluation Reports

1. Introduction
   a. Description of the problem
   b. Statement of the problem or questions to be explored
   c. Significance of the problem and rationale for studying it
2. Literature Review
   a. Theoretical and historical perspectives
   b. Identified gaps in the literature
   c. Reiteration of purpose of the evaluation
3. Methodology
   a. Evaluation design and data collection procedures
   b. Sampling design
   c. Description of subjects
   d. Description of instrumentation
   e. Procedures for analyzing the data
4. Results (Findings)
   a. Factual information presented (including tables, charts)
   b. Statistical and practical significance
5. Discussion
   a. Brief summary of the findings
   b. Explanation of any unexpected findings
   c. Application to practice
   d. Weaknesses or limitations of the evaluation
6. References
7. Appendices

of evaluation reports you find in social service agencies will reflect this. Sometimes these reports are useful examplars of how *not* to evaluate programs. For these and other reasons, your time would be more profitably spent going to the library and locating several journal articles reporting evaluations in a relevant area. But even these can serve only as rough guides. Journals differ. Some journals require hefty bibliographies and a great amount of statistical or technical detail, and others don't. Journals vary a great deal by the audience for whom they are written (e.g., scholars or practitioners). For those who are bewildered by the proper components to include in an evaluation report, the outline of key components in Box 12.1 is explained in greater detail.

Introduction

The purpose of the introduction is to describe why an evaluation was conducted. This is done by placing the program within some context or frame of reference. For instance, Stout and Rivara (1989) reviewed the evidence supporting sex education in the schools and start off with the following:

> The United States has the highest teen-age fertility rate of any developed nation, with more than 1 million teen-age pregnancies occurring in the United States each year, or about 3,000 per day.[1] . . . In a 1982 national survey of urban areas, it was revealed that 75 percent of school districts offer sex education, although it was reported elsewhere that less than 10 percent of students are exposed to comprehensive, quality programs. Most of these programs are short, with 75 percent lasting for less than 20 hours.[3,4] (P. 375)

A similar article by different authors demonstrates again how a program designed to address a social problem is placed in a perspective in the introduction:

> Annually, in the United States, approximately 700,000 unmarried females aged nineteen years or younger become pregnant. Of these pregnancies, 85 percent are unintended.[1] The negative health and social outcomes of unintended, premarital, adolescent pregnancy and subsequent premarital childbirth and child-rearing present to the medical and public health communities a challenge of the greatest magnitude.[2] Over the past decade, numerous federal, state, and local efforts have been implemented to reduce the occurrence of unintended adolescent pregnancy. To date, however, there have been few reports of success in obtaining the outcome objective—significant reduction in unintended pregnancy among unmarried adolescents.[3-5] (Vincent, Clearie, and Schluchter, 1987, p. 3382)

From these brief excerpts the reader becomes aware of the extent of teen-age pregnancies as a social problem and begins to see the need for programs designed to reduce teen pregnancies.

The introduction ought to state the questions that were the catalyst for the evaluation. If the questions cannot be clearly stated, then it follows that the evaluation not only will be confusing to read, but may also not provide the type or kind of information needed by the decision makers.

In the fourth paragraph of the Stout and Rivara (1989) article, the reader learns what questions particularly concern the authors:

> The effort to implement these programs in communities raises several questions: Specifically, what evidence exists that sex education has any

effect on gain in knowledge and change in attitudes with regard to the material it presents? What effect do these programs have on sexual activity and contraceptive behavior? How are the ultimate target areas of adolescent pregnancy, abortion, and birth rates affected by these interventions? (P. 375)

While Stout and Rivara sought the answers to specific questions, some authors prefer to describe the purpose of the evaluation in a less direct manner. Sometimes the hypotheses or questions that directed the study are a little more veiled, but nonetheless serve to guide the evaluator's efforts. This can be seen in the following example:

> The current study was designed to rate the satisfaction of patients, their relatives, and clinicians with psychiatric evaluations and treatment plans, and to assess the degree to which initial satisfaction correlated with patient treatment compliance and clinical improvement. (Bulow et al., 1987p. 290)

An example of stated hypotheses developed for an evaluation of a prepaid mental health plan for business can be found in Carpenter, Boyenga, and Schaible (1985):

1. The enrollee population under the prepaid plan will show a greater awareness of the community mental health center and its services than will persons in the service area not under the prepaid plan.
2. The enrolled population will express a more positive attitude toward the mental health center and the possibility of using its services than will persons in the community who are not covered by the prepaid plan. (P. 96)

Although examples of both specific and general questions to be explored can be easily found in the literature, we strongly believe beginning evaluators are better off investigating a small list of specific questions. Generally, the evaluation comes about because the people who fund or sponsor it have specific questions or hypotheses that they want answered or investigated. As a rule, it is easier to find the answers to specific questions than it is to more general questions.

An evaluation is kept focused by the questions that are asked. If the questions are too general, it is easy for the evaluator to lose sight of the purpose of a program evaluation and to become concerned with trivial matters. Unless the study or research is exploratory, there ought to be specific questions or hypotheses that need to be examined. Constantly keep in mind that the purpose of the program evaluation is to provide useful information to program managers about how to improve their programs.

After the evaluator has: (1) described the problem or program being studied and (2) listed the specific questions to be explored, it is time to: (3) discuss the rationale for the study. In developing a rationale, sometimes it is necessary to inform the reader how the present evaluation is different from previous evaluations. In the next example ("A Preventive Intervention Program for the Newly Separated: Final Evaluations"), the authors establish that marital disruption is a stressful life event that has led agencies to develop preventive programs for persons experiencing marital disruption. The authors go on to state why they used thirty-month and four-year interviews in their evaluation of the program:

> The purpose of this report is to present the results of two final evaluations of such a preventive intervention program. Prior evaluations have examined the program six months after its inauguration and again eighteen months after its inauguration. (Bloom et al., 1985, p. 10)

It is always a good practice to state the rationale for the evaluation. Note how Velasquez and Lyle (1985) handle this in comparing the results of day treatment versus residential treatment for juvenile offenders:

> This article presents a case study of one public social service department's attempt to obtain and present program evaluation findings that would assist a county board of commissioners to determine whether day treatment provides a means for treating adjudicated juvenile delinquents and status offenders who might otherwise be placed in residential treatment settings. . . .
> A primary reason for the interest taken in this project by the county board was the method of funding. Unlike residential treatment, for which federal fiscal participation is available, the costs of the day treatment approach would be borne entirely by the county. Thus it was important that the study address the cost differences between the two service approaches. At the same time, it was necessary to avoid encouraging decision makers to fund such an approach solely on the basis of expected or actual cost savings. The therapeutic merit of both methods of treatment could not be ignored. (P. 146)

Review of the Literature

Once the parameters of the social problem or concern have been described and the purpose and rationale of the evaluation stated, the evaluator is ready to begin reviewing the pertinent literature. The purpose of the literature review is to summarize for the reader the major findings of other researchers and evaluators that are relevant to the evaluated program.

A well-developed literature review helps explain the underpinning of the intervention by identifying major theoretical explanations of the social problem or phenomenon that prompted a human service program. Human service programs are always based upon readily identifiable assumptions that often can be easily traced to theoretical explanations of the phenomenon. For example, Majchrzak (1986), in reporting the results of a program designed to lower rates of unauthorized absenteeism (UA) among the Marines, has identified three models of absenteeism behavior:

> One type follows a "decision model" whereby UA is the result of a deliberate economic analysis with personal preferences weighed against sanctions, a second type follows a "pain avoidance model" in which UA is an impulsive act by those unable to cope with the military, and a third type follows an "adjustment model" in which UA is used as a means of resolving a problem not handled appropriately by the situation. (P. 254)

In order to further understand how these theoretical models may provide insight into the Marines' actual absenteeism behavior, interviews were conducted with a small group of Marines, and, later, a survey was conducted of all field battalion and company commanders stationed in the United States. These data were examined with battalion-level UA rates. Majchrzak (1986) then found that UA was strongly related to leaders' actions in the unit, although the data were not causal or specific enough to provide useful guidance to field commanders. However, from these efforts, "a program of effective leader actions was developed from previous literature and the tentative conclusions drawn to date in the research. This program was then experimentally implemented to determine its causal impact on UA" (p. 255).

The theoretical models upon which an intervention is based are important. Drug prevention programs might be based on a temperance model, a disease model, or developmental, sociocultural, or life-style risk-reduction models. We know that there are a lot of reasons why youth experiment with drugs. Some of these reasons have to do with self-definition, autonomy, social modeling, risk taking, peer pressure, and value formation (Braverman and Campbell, 1989). If the intervention is based upon a model or theoretical approach that has been discredited or for which there is little empirical support, this information needs to be communicated to the reader. Knowing that an intervention being evaluated is based upon an approach that is outdated or has weak grounding in research may give rise to questions about the program that might not have arisen otherwise.

Students often observe how difficult it is to identify the theoretical bases of interventions. Indeed, it may be easier to create a "new" treatment approach than to elaborate upon how one is supposed to work. Berrick and Gilbert (1991), for instance, have noted that there are an estimated four hunded to five hundred curricula for sexual abuse prevention training programs. However, in a content analysis of forty-one of these programs, "empowerment" was the guiding conceptual framwork 61 percent of the time. Two percent were guided by developmental theory and 2 percent by learning theory. The authors go on to say:

> The remainder were not explicitly identified with a particular framework, but among the programs designed for preadolescent children, 86 percent of the materials mentioned "body ownership," and they all taught assertiveness skills, which are basic elements of the empowerment model. (P. 31).

Can you imagine the choice available to you as an administrator trying to decide which program to purchase or implement? Would it matter to you if the intervention was built around a special edition of a *Spiderman* comic book in which Spiderman discloses his own sexual victimization as a child? Is that medium better for reaching young children than theatrical productions, or puppets, or films?

The literature review ought to help you to understand how well the program works in terms of the amount of "success" experienced in other locations or agencies and problems encountered during the evaluation, as well as potential instruments or aspects of methodology that might be useful. For instance, suppose you are asked to evaluate a program that provides intervention for persons arrested for Driving Under the Influence (DUI). You and the program sponsor agree that subsequent DUI arrests will be the dependent variable. How long a period of time after the intervention has ceased should be allowed to elapse before you can conclude that the program was successful? Six months after the first arrest? Twelve or eighteen months after the first arrest? By reviewing the literature, you would find an article in which Maisto, Sobell, Zelhart, Connors, and Cooper (1979) reported that the average period of time between first and second arrests for driving under the influence of alcohol, based on state driver's license records, was 23.5 months. Without reviewing the literature, overly optimistic results of the program's effectiveness would be obtained if too short a follow-up interval was designed.

Gaps in the literature. It is not uncommon for new or innovative programs to be launched that do not build upon prior evaluative or research studies. Evaluators of trailblazing programs will not have an abundance of literature to draw upon to help with understanding the significance of the impact made by the new intervention. For example, assume that virtually no evaluative studies have been conducted on programs designed to teach safety in a sheltered workshop to persons with mental retardation. You came to this conclusion after spending several weekends in the library. You read every listing under the broad topic of mental retardation and still come up empty-handed. What do you do?

In a situation like this, the evaluator tries to conceptualize an analogous problem for which there may be literature. For example, one of our graduate students was unable to find literature on the teaching of safe work practices in a sheltered workshop. However, she was able to find literature on a comparable problem—getting young children to use their safety belts. Research on efforts to promote the use of safety belts is an area where there is considerably more literature (see, for example, Sowers-Hoag, Thyer, and Bailey, 1987), and it approximates the kind of problems one might experience in teaching safety issues to persons with mental retardation. One could also look at the research on safety belt promotion with adults (see, for example, Cope, Moy, and Grossnickle, 1988).

Another way of providing a context for understanding the teaching of safe work habits would be to look at efforts to reduce hazards within a specific industry. Fox, Hopkins, and Anger (1987), for instance, conducted research on the use of a token economy to help reduce lost-time injuries in two dangerous open-pit mines. Employees earned stamps for being in work groups that experienced no lost-time injuries, for not causing injuries, and for making safety suggestions.

Each of these examples was found by searching abstracts under the descriptor "safety." However, relevant literature may also have been found by searching under different topics. Perhaps the teaching of job initiative to severely mentally retarded sheltered workers (McCuller, Salzberg, and Lingnugaris/Kraft, 1987) would be seen as a problem similar to teaching this group about safety procedures. Sometimes it is possible to find other relevant articles serendipitously. You can help serendipity (accidental discoveries) happen by browsing through journals likely to carry research related to the problem of interest, and by telling your friends about projects you are working on and asking them for any leads they may have on relevant literature.

Questions that students sometimes ask are: "How much literature should be reviewed?" and "How do I know when I have reviewed enough literature?" These are difficult questions to answer because the amount of literature on one topic may be quite voluminous and on another rather scanty. Suggested guidelines are:

1. Make sure that the major (sometimes the first or classical) studies in the field are included in the literature review. You'll tend to see these studies cited time and time again. They establish the first efforts to explore or evaluate the problem. Subsequent studies have built upon what was learned in those early studies. Sometimes our perspectives aren't nearly broad enough. We may think that our new program is the first of its kind when actually there have been many prior and similar programs. Did you know, for instance, that sex education programs in public schools date back to the beginning of the century?

2. Include current studies of the problem in the literature review. (Besides searching *Psychological Abstracts* and *Social Work Abstracts* for recent studies, the *Social Sciences Citation Index* can help you locate other journal articles on the same topic. Once you have found one or more major studies, use them as referents in the *Social Sciences Citation Index*. Articles that have cited the major study (referent) in their bibliographies are listed each year. Articles that list the referent study in their bibliographies are highly likely to be on the same topic and, therefore, to be of interest to you.

3. Assume that there is some relevant literature to be found. Often, students assure me that they cannot find any literature on their topic—having spent a total of three hours in the library. Depending upon the importance of the evaluation you are doing, you may have to spend twelve, sixteen, or thirty-six hours in the library to find useful literature. Like most other things, the more hours you spend searching, the more likely you are to find what you are seeking. But it is more important to "work smart" than to merely put in hours. One student bitterly complained to me that she spent over eight hours reading through the *New York Times* on microfilm to find an exact reference she needed. It did not occur to her to ask the reference librarian for assistance. Had she done so, she would have discovered that a *New York Times Index* is produced each year. Using this reference, she could have found her citation in five minutes or less.

Don't be afraid to use computer searches to help you locate useful articles. While it may seem strange at first, you'll learn quickly how to operate the system, and you will be amazed at the ease with which potentially valuable references on your topic are found. And if you search all the right places for literature and still come up emptyhanded, brainstorm other topics or subject headings that may provide productive material. Discuss with friends or colleagues what kinds of problems or programs would be analogous, and then look for examples of these in the literature. Double your efforts.

As a rough guide, if you have followed all of these suggestions and still have found only three or four relevant studies, then you know that there isn't a wealth of literature to draw upon. This is confirmed when, after much searching, you locate one more piece of relevant literature and on examining its bibliography, discover that it does not introduce you to any new studies. When do you have "enough" literature? Whenever you believe that you have a good understanding of the literature on the program or problem—from the earliest study to those appearing in the current year.

After you have reviewed the literature in your evaluation report (and there is no reason to go into great detail about all the findings in each and every study), restate for the reader the purpose of your evaluation. Depending upon the amount of the literature reviewed, it may be necessary to again indicate its uniqueness or similarity to prior efforts.

Methodology

The purpose of the methodology section of your report is to explain how you conducted your evaluation. You should give sufficient details to allow another investigator or evaluator to replicate the study. Commonly, subsections and subheadings are used to differentiate the various components of the methodology.

The first information often presented under the Methodology usually pertains to the subjects. Your readers will want to know how many there were, how they were selected, and something about their characteristics—such as the male/female composition, average age, and other demographic information. Here is a example from a study of homeless adults contacted at a drop-in center and soup kitchen (Magine et al., 1990):

> Of the 74 homeless individuals, 67 (90%) were men; 52 (70%) were white, 21 (28%) were black, one was Hispanic. The average age of the sample was 36 (SD = 9.7, range 20 to 58). Twenty-four subjects (32%) were between 20 and 30 yr., 27 subjects (36%) were between 31 and 40 yr., 15 subjects (20%) were between 41 and 50 yr., eight (11%) were 50 yr. Seventy-one sujects (96%) had either never married or were separated or divorced. The average subject had completed 10.4 yr. of education (SD = 3.0, range 1 to 16 yr.). Ten subjects (14%) reported some education beyond high school; two had completed college. Mean monthly income reported was $251 (mdn = 163, SD = 244). Nine subjects (12%) reported having absolutely no income; 15 (20%) reported monthly incomes of $600 or more.

Although in explaining the purpose of your evaluation you may have already mentioned the evaluation design used, it is appropriate to go into more depth in the procedure subsection of the methodology. You may want to discuss how the random assignment or recruitment process was conducted. See, for example, how this was treated in a cost-effectiveness evaluation of alcoholism treatment (McCrady et al., 1986):

> Informed consent was obtained and baseline data collected during the initial hospitalization. Subjects were randomly assigned on a 2:1 basis to either Partial Hospital Treatment (PHT; n = 114) or Extended Inpatient Treatment (EIP; n = 60). The number of subjects assigned to the two conditions was unequal because the hospital needed to have inpatient beds available; the 2:1 ratio did not jeopardize the power to detect significant results in the study. Patients assigned to the PHT were detoxified on an inpatient basis and then commuted from home, attending treatment 6½ hours per day, Monday through Friday. (P. 709)

Here is an example describing the methodology from an evaluation of a shoplifting diversion program (Royse and Buck, 1991):

> Information on re-arrests was obtained from computer searches of arrest data maintained by the County Attorney. Since this information resides in the public domain, there was no need for release of information or consent forms. Of the 246 participants who had completed the diversion program between its beginning (May 1, 1986) through May 31, 1988, a sample of 99 was randomly chosen. Any re-arrests for shoplifting from the time of the initial arrest through the end of May, 1990, were recorded. Those completing the diversion program were compared with three other groups of shoplifters: those who entered the program but who did not complete it (n = 42); those who were not admitted into the program, largely because they failed to keep appointments to arrange for diversion or because they elected to go to a hearing on the charge (n = 24); and a random sample (n = 87) of persons arrested for shoplifting in the two years prior to the start of the diversion program (May 1, 1984, through April 30, 1986).

The reader of the evaluation report not only needs to understand what evaluation design was used and how the data were collected, but also needs to be informed of the instruments employed in the evaluation. See how we (Royse and Toler, 1988) handled this in the next example:

> Beginning in June, 1986, both new and long-term patients at the outpatient dialysis center were asked to complete the Symptom Checklist 90-Revised. ... The Symptom Checklist 90-Revised (Derogatis, 1983) is a 90-item self-report instrument measuring psychological stress with nine symptom scales and three global indices. The SCL-90-R uses a 5-point response scale ranging from "not at all" (0) to "extremely" (4). The reliabil-

301

ity and validity of the SCL-90-R have been well documented. Test-retest and internal consistency coefficients have been reported to range from .77 to .90 on the nine dimensions (Derogratis, 1983). The SCL-90-R has been used in a broad variety of clinical and medical contexts and received positive independent evaluations. (P. 828)

The last topic to be covered in the methodology section is how the data are to be analyzed. Data analysis should be planned at the time that the evaluation design is being considered. This is done so that evaluation does not produce data which cannot be analyzed as desired. (More rigorous analyses usually need interval level data.) This is the way Saunders and Parker (1989) discussed how their data were analyzed in an article on examining treatment follow-through of men who batter:

> Multiple regression analyses predicting dropout during assessment, during treatment, or at any point were conducted. Referral source was added hierarchically to the equation after all the other independent variables to determine its additive effect and to uncover possible suppression in its relationship with attrition. Finally, interaction terms that combined referral source and each independent variable (each standardized before multiplying) were constructed and tested for their unique contributions to attrition. (P. 23)

Reports of practice research should also describe the measures used to inform clients of anticipated risks and benefits of the intervention and how their consent was obtained.

When you believe that you have provided enough information for the reader of your evaluation report to replicate your study (assuming that someone would desire to do so), then you are finished with this section and ready to move on to the next.

Results (Findings)

The Results section of your evaluation report contains what you have learned from collecting and analyzing your data. You provide the answers to the questions that were previously asked or information about the hypotheses that were tested. Just the facts are presented in this section—statistically significant differences, results of pre- and posttesting, and so on. The implications of the findings (what the findings may mean practically and pragmatically) are dealt with in the Discussion section of your report.

The mass of data accumulated over a year or eighteen months or so of evaluating a program can present something of a problem to those

302

writing evaluation reports, because they can be struck by a compulsion to "tell all." Wanting the sponsor to feel that the contract amount was truly earned, evaluators may compile such an awesome assemblage of tables, charts, and dry, boring paragraphs that only the boldest of academics would attempt to wade through that portion of the report.

Chelimsky (1987) acknowledged this problem: "To its author all of the evaluation's findings seem important. It is painfully difficult to trim surgically what is not relevant, to condense, to rank, to decide not only which finding is most important, but which is most important that is also manipulable by policy" (p. 15). Cronbach et al. (1980) referred to the problem of evaluators wanting to document everything as "self-defeating thoroughness."

Decide which of your findings are the most important or have the greatest implications for social work practice. Don't fall into the trap of trying to report every statistically significant correlation.

Keep in mind that the most helpful of evaluation findings will contain standards for comparison. These may come from other studies found in the literature, in your control group, in other agencies in the area, and so on. Those who read the evaluation report will be able to interpret your findings with much more ease if they can contrast the success of the program you have evaluated with similar data from other programs. Thirty-five percent recidivism is a "good" rate compared to a similar program experiencing a 65 percent re-offense rate.

If you have a lot of data, you probably will want to make use of tables, because they allow you to present a great deal of information in a small amount of space. Refer to the *Publication Manual* of the American Psychological Association (1994) for information and examples as to how tables should be prepared.

It's good form to show the number of persons in each group as well as the mean and standard deviation of scores. When percentages are used, always show the number of persons on which the percentages are based. Refer also to the APA manual for ways to present the results of your statistical tests (e.g., t-tests, one way analysis of variance). In addition to the probabilities obtained, you should include the t or F value and the degrees of freedom. To make sure that you are not ascribing greater importance than you should to a statistically significant finding, Thyer (1991) recommends reporting the PVE, the proportion of variance explained in the dependent variable by the independent variable(s).

It is unrealistic to expect that busy people will take the time to read tens of pages of detailed tables or reproductions of computer printouts. It is the evaluator's responsibility to write for the audience who will be reading the evaluation report and to select the most important findings to highlight for that audience. Most evaluation reports are too technical if they contain more than six tables. If the program being evaluated was complex and there are numerous important findings, the evaluator may want to prepare a technical report in addition to a smaller evaluation summary designed to be given to the group of decision makers and other interested members of the public. Because it is easy to produce too many crosstabulations and statistical tests, it is tempting to force into the Results section much more of this information than most readers care to consume.

Discussion

In the Discussion section, clearly explain which of the hypotheses were supported and which were not. This is where you interpret your findings for the reader. If there were research questions instead of hypotheses, state what was actually found relative to the purpose of the evaluation. The focus in this section is on the implications the findings suggest for other professionals and those who run similar programs.

If your findings run counter to what was predicted or expected, provide explanations or discuss alternative theories to account for why the results turned out the way they did. Perhaps there was some source of bias that was not immediately obvious at the time the study was planned. Or, maybe the study was not implemented exactly as it had been proposed. For example, in an article entitled, "How Helpful Are Helplines? A Survey of Callers," Gingerich, Gurney, and Wirtz (1988) report in the Results section that more than half of the callers contacted one to two weeks after their initial call to a helpline rated their problems less severe at the time of the follow-up phone call. After the findings have been presented, the authors begin the Discussion section by writing:

> The findings of the present study must be interpreted with considerable caution, because the sample of respondents was not taken randomly. Clearly, selection factors may have influenced the counselors' decision to participate in the study, whom they chose to ask to participate, the callers who consented, and the callers who actually completed the follow-up interview. ... The callers who were asked to participate in the study were probably considered by their counselors to be under less emotional stress ... and possibly more positive toward the helpline than were other callers. (Pp. 638–639)

The authors go on to say that it would be tempting to conclude that the helpline produced the change in the clients' problems but that the study could not rule out several competing explanations. Explanations such as sampling biases are limitations. Every study or evaluation has some limitations, and it is the evaluator's responsibility to point out the major ones. McCrady et al. (1986) reported the following limitations:

> One limitation of the study is that 32 percent of the initial subjects did not participate in the extended follow-ups. Because there was no differential dropout rate from the two experimental groups, comparisons between the groups are appropriate, but the dropouts might affect the overall levels of treatment outcome across groups. (P. 712)

Wing and Gay (1991) reviewed a study challenging the belief that Alcoholics Anonymous (AA) was an effective form of treatment. Look at the limitation they found: the study's author created AA groups instead of sending patients to already existing AA groups. Further, there was no anonymity, freedom to select membership, or sponsorship. Patients were required to attend, had to sign in, and did not have sponsors. Could that help explain why the initial study concluded AA was ineffective?

Also, quite appropriate in the Discussion section is a comparison to any similar (or dissimilar) findings contained in studies mentioned in the literature review section. However, there is no need to be repetitive. Don't force data from other studies into your Results section and then introduce it again in the Discussion section. If you have a control group, or even if you don't, there may be no need to refer to the success of other programs in the Results section. Save it for the Discussion section where it will have more punch. When your findings are contrasted with those studies identified earlier in your evaluation, the reader is able to place your results within a context that is easily understood. Again, borrowing from McCrady et al. (1986), we can see how this might appear in brief form:

> Our findings, as well as two recent studies (LaPorte, McLellan, Erdlen, and Parente, 1981; Sobell, Sobell, and Maisto, 1984), have found no differences in outcomes between subjects who were easily followed and those who were not, and few differences between subjects who continued or discontinued in research follow-ups. (P. 712)

Some professional journals may require a separate section they call "Conclusion." Whether you use a separate Conclusion section or place your concluding thoughts in the Discussion section is a matter of individual taste or a journal's style. It is important, however, that you have conclusions. Did the program perform as it was designed? Should the program be continued? Are clients being helped? The answers to such

305

questions as these make the evaluation relevant and interesting to those who will be reading your evaluation report.

When discussing the benefits of a new program or intervention, you may become too exuberant and make claims that go beyond your findings. It is helpful to remember that evaluations rely upon convenience samples of clients from a single agency and that it is rarely possible to generalize to the larger population of all clients with the same problem. For example, a stress reduction program that worked for long distance bus drivers in Alaska may not reduce stress in a sample of bus drivers in New York City. You are allowed to speculate, however. It is reasonable to assume that the stress reduction program designed for Alaskan bus drivers *may* work for bus drivers in other *rural* areas.

References

If you cite studies in your evaluation report (and you probably should if you have done even a cursory review of the literature), then you owe it to your readers to provide a bibliography or a listing of these references. We find the APA style (the one used in this book) to be convenient and it is widely used in professional journals. You insert the last name of the author and the year of the publication in the correct place in your report and then list the full citation at the end of the document. The APA style does not use footnotes at the bottom of the page, and there is no danger of getting your notes in the wrong sequence or out of order, since the references are arranged alphabetically.

Appendices

Appendices are usually found in long evaluation reports and typically include such items as a copy of instruments that were employed during the course of the evaluation, a sample copy of the instructions that were read or given to the subjects, cover letters that went out to participants, and perhaps bulky tables that you feel are important to include but too lengthy to place in the Results section. It is not always necessary to have an Appendix. For instance, if the data from your evaluation came from the health department, no mailings were done, and no questionnaires were given to respondents, then you may have no need for an Appendix at the end of your report. If you are writing a report of your evaluation for a journal article, it is usually necessary to limit the manuscript to sixteen to twenty pages, and an Appendix is not wanted. Anyone wanting additional technical information or copies of instruments is expected to contact the author.

MISTAKES TO AVOID

Over the years we have read a number of papers written by students in which they have reported an evaluation, or proposed an evaluation design for a specific program, supplied "dummy" data, and then discussed the findings. It is always interesting to see the diversity of the products created by students having access to the same lectures and texts. Occasionally, a student will make a major mistake for which we have no explanations. (A student once wrote an evaluation report where pre- and posttest scores were averaged together.) More often, students' mistakes come from going beyond their limited data (ignoring the fact that their samples were not random or representative), from not sufficiently defining their concepts, from using inadequate instruments, from not recognizing major sources of bias or limitations, or from failing to conduct any analysis except the univariate. These are all problems that you should recognize by now. However, just to make sure that your evaluation report doesn't contain any "fatal flaws," we have assembled several examples of problems that we tend to find from time to time. As you come across evaluation reports in your practice or in the literature and begin to read them more critically, keep your eyes open for these mistakes.

Misunderstanding the Purpose of the Literature Review

One student who was assigned to critique an evaluation report wrote, "Although I did not verify the articles reported in the literature review section, I assume that they, as conscientious authors, left no stone unturned." The purpose of the literature review is to familiarize the reader with what is known about the problem under investigation and the intervention that has been applied. The literature review should provide the reader with enough information to understand the intervention, the theoretical model on which it was based, the ways these interventions have been evaluated in the past, and with what results. Your reaction may be that the literature review is too skimpy (important literature may have been missed) or that it seems appropriate. Normally, it is not your job to verify the existence of articles cited in the literature. (Unless, of course, you suspect that someone is making them up.)

Too Small a Sample

An example of a program that is likely to impact only a small number of clients is an intensive in-home family intervention program. Such programs are designed so that each caseworker has responsibility for

307

two to four families at a time. If only one or two caseworkers are employed in a program like this and if the evaluation period runs for one year, the population of clients served by this program is modest at best.

A problem with attrition is always a potential threat with very small samples. If your sample is twelve clients, the loss of data at a follow-up one or two years later is a real possibility. Some families move out of the area, families break up, children run away from home, and family members may be arrested or sent to prison, may become hospitalized, or may even die. Even when families are located, they may not always agree to participate in the evaluation. You could lose one or two clients, maybe even three, from such a small sample and still not be in a bad shape to conclude something about the intervention if it were clearly effective or clearly ineffective. Say, for instance, that ten of twelve clients improved. However, imagine a scenario where five clients improved and four did not, and three clients can't be located for the follow-up. Do you conclude that the program worked more times than not? How confortable would you be in recommending that this program be expanded when there is the possibility that seven of twelve clients were *not* helped by the intervention?

In such a program as this, it may be unrealistic to expect to conduct a rigorous evaluation too early when the number of "graduates" is very small. It would be better to do a formative evaluation at the end of the first year and a more thorough one at the end of year two or at a time when a larger number of families have been served.

In an intensive program like family preservation, another threat to the internal validity of the study would be the likelihood that these families were specially selected and not randomly assigned. Because only a small number of families can be served by this program, there is a greater probability that families who are believed to have the best chance of succeeding would be hand-picked.

A small sample may also create problems when the evaluator assumes that clients entering a program at one time of the year (e.g., during the summer months) are representative of clients entering the program at other times during the year. If you think that the clientele varies by season or other predictable cycle (for example, requests for services at the end of the month might be different from those at the beginning of the month), your sample should not be restricted to clients entering or served during part of that cycle or season. This would result in an unrepresentative cross-section of the total clients served by the program.

Insufficient Information about Instruments

Students often think that a "good" evaluation is guaranteed if they are able to locate an already prepared instrument in the literature. The fact that an instrument has been photocopied or appears in print does not necessarily make it one that ought to be used in your evaluative study.

Occasionally, a student makes a statement in a paper to the effect that "two instruments were used to assess learning outcomes" but does not discuss who developed the instruments or for what purpose, whether the instruments are reliable, or if any studies have been done to show that they have validity. Neither is it sufficient to write, "This instrument has been researched for validity and reliability and proven to have both." The evaluator should provide sufficient information to enable the reader to determine for him- or herself that the instrument is sound. An informed reader of an evaluation report will want to know about the instruments used. How many items did the instrument contain? How was it administered? How has the instrument been used in other studies?

Another mistake to avoid is taking selected items from an already prepared scale or instrument and combining these with several new items. The resulting scale or questionnaire may not have as much reliability and/or validity as the old scale or instrument. Any adjustment, revision, or substitution made to an already prepared scale has the potential for affecting its psychometric properties. The more extensive these changes, the greater the likelihood that the instrument's reliability and validity have been changed in some way. You will not know whether the change is for better or worse unless additional psychometric studies are conducted with the revised instrument. So, if you find a good instrument that you want to use, try not to modify it unless it is absolutely necessary to make changes to fit a different population or age group.

Failure to Use a Comparison Group

Social work students seem to particularly dislike the concept of control groups. We suspect this is because they believe that there is something unethical about their use. What they often do not realize is that control groups can be constructed without denying clients services. In many instances, it is impossible to make sense of evaluative data without a control group. Two brief examples will demonstrate this.

A former student asked us to help interpret some data he had prepared in conjunction with evaluating an inpatient mental health facility for emotionally disturbed adolescents. He was able to show that 75 percent did not return to the facility. We asked him if he knew what recidivism rates were reported in similar facilities in the area or in the literature, but he knew of none. We asked if there could be legitimate reasons why some of the adolescents might not return to the facility. In fact, there were some very good reasons why adolescents might not return to the same facility. They were not eligible to return if they had committed a felony, been arrested and sent to a detention facility, or moved out of state, or if their eighteenth birthday was within three months. These and other reasons could easily explain why a large proportion of the adolescents did not return to the facility—and none of the reasons had anything to do with the effectiveness of the treatment they received.

Another student was doing a survey of social workers' attitudes about panhandlers. He spent quite a bit of time writing and refining a questionnaire. He collected his data, wrote his report, and just before the semester was over, came to talk to me about his project. He realized, too late to do anything about it, that while he knew what social workers' attitudes were, he couldn't conclude anything because he had no control group. He didn't know whether social workers were more empathic than other professionals or lay citizens toward panhandlers. If he had used a control group of non-social workers, the data from the social workers would have been more meaningful.

Presenting Individual Scores

It is the evaluator's job to condense, summarize, and otherwise make sense of all the data that have been collected. It is *not* necessary to inform the reader of an evaluation report of the pretest and posttest scores of every participant in the study. Instead, show the average pretest score for the control and intervention groups and the average posttest score. You may want to talk about the highest and lowest scores, or standard deviations, but very seldom would it ever be necessary to document each and every score. Generally, when this occurs in an evaluation report, we presume the author did not know how to go about analyzing the data and is trying to make up for this by presenting the reader with bulk rather than a perceptive grasp of the data.

Lack of Specificity

It seems that some writers of evaluation reports believe that others have the ability to read their minds. We make this assumption when we read a statement like the following: "Due to the controversial nature of the topic, every precaution was taken to ensure the anonymity of the persons taking part in the study." A reader with some understanding of these processes would want to know exactly what precautions were taken. Perhaps the writer meant that no names, addresses, or phone numbers were gathered. However, if Social Security numbers were used in order to match subjects at pretest and posttest, does this protect anonymity? Did the evaluator create a coding system to protect anonymity? Does protection of anonymity mean that the names were cut off or marked out by a student assistant before the questionnaires were given to the researcher? These questions would not have been raised if the author had been more specific.

Overgeneralizing

To understand this mistake, imagine an evaluation of an AIDS educational program for elementary school students. A study was completed of 250 fifth and sixth graders in one rural school district. Assume that the students are more knowledgeable about AIDS after the educational intervention than they were at the beginning. The evaluator concludes that the program is a success, and "the findings indicate that social workers across the United States should encourage school administrators to adopt comparable AIDS educational programs and expand these programs to all grades in their elementary schools."

The problem with this statement is, first of all, that since the population of students involved in this study came from only one rural school district, the author is overgeneralizing. There is no way of knowing, for instance, if the results would have been the same if students came from urban or suburban areas or even from different rural areas. Are students living in rural Montana different from those living in rural Mississippi or rural Vermont? Since the evaluation was limited to students in only one small school district, that is the only geographical area for which the intervention is known to have worked. It may be that the unique blend of socio-demographic characteristics found in the population receiving the intervention makes it quite unlike other populations of "typical" fifth and sixth graders.

Since no statement was made about there being a control group, there is always the possibility that the increase in knowledge about AIDS came from greater coverage of this topic on television or other media. Perhaps it came about because a respected person in the community died of AIDS and this became a popular topic of conversation—with a result that parents and other adults requested and distributed, on their own, informational brochures about AIDS to the fifth and sixth graders. Maturation is another threat to the internal validity of this study. As they grow older, fifth and sixth graders may become more interested in

311

sex and related matters and begin a process of self-education about AIDS. This becomes more of a problem the longer the time interval between pretest and posttest.

Even if the program were a success with fifth and sixth graders, there is no evidence that the same program would work with younger children (second, third, or fourth graders). So, a statement that the program ought to be expanded to all grades is unfounded. It is a belief or value statement, not a finding of the evaluation. The statement that social workers should encourage school administrators across the country to implement such a program is based on the assumption that other school districts are doing nothing and that their children are ignorant of AIDS. Even without this intervention, children in other school districts may be more informed than the children in the rural school district receiving the intervention. Unless there is data for support, it is presumptuous to assume that all children across the United States need such an intervention. A sampling of students from around the state or from other school districts would help to establish that other fifth and sixth graders also need the intervention. This sample could also serve as a comparison or control group against which the "success" of the students receiving the educational intervention could be gauged.

Lack of Consistency

Periodically, we come across a report or a manuscript in which the following mistake has been made: analysis is conducted with variables without *a priori* foundation in the literature review. This problem seems to occur most often when evaluators or investigators try to find something statistically significant to report. Evaluators may be tempted to test for differences by gender, race, income, educational level, and so on until they find what is regarded as something of importance. However, if differences by sex, race, and so forth were not important enough to be included in the literature review or in the hypotheses, then the examination of these differences in the Results section is not logical. The converse is also true—the evaluation would be incomplete if the literature review and hypotheses were concerned with differences by sex, race, and so on, but the analysis failed to report these comparisons.

CHECKLIST FOR WRITING AND ASSESSING EVALUATION REPORTS

Using the topics that have been covered in this chapter, we can construct a simplified checklist for insuring that all the essential elements are contained within an evaluation report. (This checklist can also be used to help you evaluate reports you may be reading.)

1. **Introduction**
   Does the Introduction provide a clear notion of:
   ☐ a. the problem?
   ☐ b. the program?
   ☐ c. the purpose of the evaluation?
   ☐ d. the rationale for the evaluation?

2. **Literature Review**
   Does the Literature Review provide:
   ☐ a. a relevant context for understanding prior programs and evaluation efforts of these programs?
   ☐ b. a thorough survey of historical and current literature?

3. **Methodology**
   Does the Methodology section describe:
   ☐ a. an evaluation design?
   ☐ b. sampling procedures?
   ☐ c. subjects?
   ☐ d. procedures for data collection?
   ☐ e. instruments used?

4. **Results**
   Does the Results section contain:
   ☐ a. findings relative to the stated problem(s) or purpose of the evaluation questions?
   ☐ b. appropriate statistical tests?

5. **Discussion**
   Does the Discussion section address:
   ☐ a. practical implications?
   ☐ b. generalization of the data?
   ☐ c. limitations of the study?

Be concerned with reasonableness in all areas. Do the hypotheses or questions raised seem reasonable? Do they appear to follow what is known about the problem and gaps in the literature? If control groups are used, do they seem to be appropriate groups for comparison? Is the sample large enough for the conclusions that are drawn? Do the findings logically follow from the procedures that were used?

Are there any major sources of bias or limitations that have not been recognized?

Reasonableness also applies to the length of the evaluation report. If you write a report that is too long, few people will read it. If the report is too short, important details may be omitted. Our advice is to write for *your audience*. If you think none of them will read an eighty page report, then condense. Journal articles typically run sixteen to twenty pages and manage to crowd an awful lot of information into that format. Instead of guessing what your audience will digest, pilot test a draft copy on someone representative of your audience who would be cooperative enough to give you needed feedback. Schalock and Thornton (1988) suggested a "test" where a program description or evaluation report would be considered against whether it would make sense to a skeptical, willing, careful, but generally reasonable audience.

Although we have dealt with the evaluation report section by section, realize that the report should make a harmonious whole. The initial question should lead to the literature being reviewed, which should be followed by a discussion of the ways the problem has been studied in the past. These methods have a direct bearing on the procedures used in the study and the way the data are analyzed. And, the conclusions should relate to the initial question(s) being asked.

Finally, when writing your report, don't forget to proofread it closely. In fact, you should probably read and revise the manuscript three or four different times to make sure it communicates as clearly as possible. Doing your writing on a computer or word processor simplifies things and is much less cumbersome than using a typewriter. You'll be amazed at how quickly you'll learn to turn out professional looking reports.

QUESTIONS FOR CLASS DISCUSSION

1. Which parts of the evaluation report appear to be the most difficult and the easiest to write? Give reasons for your beliefs.
2. Discuss the kinds of mistakes that are easily made when writing.
3. How is writing a term paper different from writing an evaluation report? In what ways are they similar?

MINI-PROJECTS: EXPERIENCING RESEARCH FIRSTHAND

1. Show all that you have learned about program evaluation by drafting a small evaluation report of a fictitious program. This time,

however, build in all manner of problems (e.g., threats to the internal validity). Exchange your "evaluation" with someone else in your class. Then compare notes regarding the number of problems that were detected and what could have been done to strengthen the "evaluation."

2. Locate an actual program evaluation from an agency (or find a journal article reporting on one). Critique the report or article using the guidelines suggested in this chapter. Write a brief paper summarizing your points.

REFERENCES AND RESOURCES

American Psychological Association. (1994). *Publication manual*, 4th ed. Washington, DC: APA.

Beebe, L. (1993). *Professional writing for the human services*. Washington, DC: NASW Press.

Berrick, J.D., and Gilbert, N. (1991). *With the best of intentions: The child sexual abuse prevention movement*. New York: Guilford Press.

Bloom, B.L., Hodges, W.F., Kern, M.B., and McFaddin, S.C. (1985). A preventive intervention program for the newly separated: Final evaluations. *American Journal of Orthopsychiatry*, 55 (1), 9–26.

Braverman, M.T., and Campbell, D.T. (1989). Facilitating the development of health promotion programs: Recommendations for researchers and funders. *Evaluating Health Promotion Programs*. New Directions for Program Evaluation, no. 43. San Francisco, CA: Jossey–Bass.

Bulow, B.V., Sweeney, J.A., Shear, M.K., Friedman, R., and Plowe, C. (1987). Family satisfaction with psychiatric evaluations. *Health and Social Work*, 12 (4), 290–295.

Carpenter, R.A., Boyenga, K.W., and Schaible, T.D. (1985). Evaluation of a prepaid mental health plan for business. *Community Mental Health Journal*, 21 (2), 94–108.

Chelimsky, E. (1987). What have we learned about the politics of program evaluation? *Evaluation Practice*, 8 (1), 5–21.

Cope, J.G., Moy, S.S., and Grossnickle, W.F. (1988). The behavioral impact of an advertising campaign to promote safety belt use. *Journal of Applied Behavior Analysis*, 21, 277–280.

Cronbach, L.J., Ambron, S.R., Dornbusch, S.M., Hess, R.D., Hornik, R.C., Phillips, D.C., Walker, D.F., and Weiner, S.S. (1980). *Toward reform of program evaluation*. San Francisco, CA: Jossey–Bass.

Dhooper, S.S. (1983). Coronary heart disease and family functioning. *Journal of Social Service Research*, 7 (2), 19–38.

Fox, D.K., Hopkins, B.L., and Anger, W.K. (1987). The long-term effects of a token economy on safety performance in open-pit mining. *Journal of Applied Behavior Analysis*, 20, 215–224.

Garfield, S.L. (1984). The evaluation of research: An editorial perspective. In A.S. Bellack and M. Hersen (eds.), *Research methods in clinical psychology*. New York: Pergamon Press.

Gingerich, W.J., Gurney, R.J., and Wirtz, T.S. (1988). How helpful are helplines? A survey of callers. *Social Casework*, 69 (10), 634–639.

Hendricks, M., and Papagiannia, M. (1990). Do's and don'ts for offering effective recommendations. *Evaluation Practice*, 11 (2), 121–125.

Henson, K.T. (1995). *The art of writing for publication*. Needham Heights, MA: Allyn and Bacon.

Holfer, R. (1994). A good story, well told: Rules for evaluating human services programs. *Social Work*, 39(2), 233–236.

Magine, S.J., and Royse, D., Wiehe, V.R., and Nietzel, M.T. (1990). Homelessness among adults raised as foster children: A survey of drop-in centers. *Psychological Reports*, 67, 739–745.

Maisto, S.A., Sobell, L.C., Zelhart, P.F., Connors, G.F., and Cooper, T. (1979). Driving records of persons convicted of driving under the influence of alcohol. *Journal of Studies on Alcohol*, 40, 70–77.

Majchrzak, A. (1986). Keeping the marines in the field: Results of a field experiment. *Evaluation and Program Planning*, 9 (3), 253–265.

McCrady, B., Longabaugh, R., Fink, E., Stout, R., Beattie, M., and Ruggieri-Authelet, A. (1986). Cost-effectiveness of alcoholism treatment in partial hospital versus inpatient settings after brief inpatient treatment: 12-month outcomes. *Journal of Consulting and Clinical Psychology*, 54 (5), 708–713.

McCuller, G.L., Salzberg, C.L., and Lignugaris/Kraft, B. (1987). Producing generalized job initiative in severely mentally retarded sheltered workers. *Journal of Applied Behavior Analysis*, 20, 413–420.

Moxley, J.M. (1992). *Writing and publishing for academic authors*. New York: University Press of America.

Royse, D., and Buck, S. (1991). Evaluating a diversion program for first-time shoplifters. *Journal of Offender Rehabilitation*, 17 (1/2), 147–158.

Royse, D., and Toler, J. (1988). Dialysis patients and patterns of symptom report on the Symptom Checklist-90-R. *Psychological Reports*, 62, 827–831.

Saunders, D.G., and Parker, J.G. (1989). Legal sanctions and treatment follow-through among men who batter: A multivariate analysis. *Social Work Research and Abstracts*, 25 (3), 21–29.

Schalock, R.L., and Thornton, C.V.D. (1988). *Program evaluation: A field guide for administrators*. New York: Plenum Press.

Simon, R.J., and Fyfe, J.J. (1994). *Editors as gatekeepers: Who, what, why and how gets published in the social sciences*. Lanham, MD: Rowman & Littlefield.

Sowers-Hoag, K.M., Thyer, B.A., and Bailey, J.S. (1987). Promoting automobile safety belt use by young children. *Journal of Applied Behavior Analysis*, 20, 133–138.

Stout, J.W., and Rivara, F.P. (1989). Schools and sex education: Does it work? *Pediatrics*, 83 (3), 375–379.

Thyer, B. (1991). Guidelines for evaluating outcome studies on social work practice. *Research on Social Work Practice*, 1 (1), 76–91.

Thyer, B. (1994). *Successful publishing in scholarly journals*. Thousand Oaks, CA: Sage.

Velasquez, J.S., and Lyle, C.G. (1985). Day versus residential treatment for juvenile offenders: The impact of program evaluation. *Child Welfare*, 64 (2), 145–156.

Vincent, M.L., Clearie, A.F., and Schluchter, M.D. (1987). Reducing adolescent pregnancy through school and community-based education. *Journal of the American Medical Association*, 257 (24), 3382–3386.

Wing, D.M., and Gay, G. (1991). A critical literature review of alcoholism treatment cost-benefit/effectiveness. *Journal of Nursing Quality Assurance*, 5 (4), 28-40.

INDEX